LIVING STONES YEARBOOK 2013

LIVING STONES
YEARBOOK
2013

Christianity in the Middle East:
Theology, History, Politics, and Dialogue

LIVING STONES OF THE HOLY LAND TRUST
Registered charity no. 1081204

© Living Stones of the Holy Land Trust 2013

All rights reserved. No part of this publication may be reproduced or utilised in any form or by any means electronic or mechanical, including photocopying, recording or by any information storage and retrieval system, without permission in writing from the publisher.

Living Stones Yearbook 2013
Christianity in the Middle East: Theology, History, Politics, and Dialogue
First published 2013 by
Living Stones of the Holy Land Trust
(Regd. Charity no. 1081204)
www.livingstonesonline.org.uk

ISBN 978 0 9552088 2 9

Managing Editor
Leonard Harrow

Editors
Mary Grey
Duncan Macpherson
Anthony O'Mahony
Colin South

Produced by Melisende UK Ltd
Printed and bound in England by 4edge Ltd

CONTENTS

INTRODUCTION	ix
CONTRIBUTORS	xiv
THE BIBLICAL NARRATIVE: CANONICAL 'ANCIENT ISRAEL' *Michael Prior*	1
GENOCIDE, ETHNOCIDE, AND THE SITUATION OF MIDDLE EAST CHRISTIANS TODAY *Terry Tastard*	20
CHRISTIANITY AND THE ISRAELI-PALESTINIAN CONFLICT *Rosemary Radford Ruether*	35
HEALTH CARE IN THE OTTOMAN HOLY LAND AND MOUNT LEBANON PRIOR TO WESTERN PROTESTANT MEDICAL MISSIONARY ENTERPRISE *Ramsay F Bisharah*	51
CHRISTIAN SYRIA *Ignace Dick*	70
CAN WE RE-IMAGINE ISLAM AS SOLELY WITH A MECCAN IDENTITY, AS SET OUT IN THE WRITINGS OF KENNETH CRAGG? *David Derrick*	84
DIALOGUE: WHAT IS THE POINT OF IT? *Hugh Boulter*	108
MARY KAHIL: A LIFE GIVEN FOR MUSLIMS *Sr Agnes Wilkins OSB*	123
SHENOUDA III AND THE COPTIC ORTHODOX CHURCH IN MODERN EGYPT: SOME REFLECTIONS *Anthony O'Mahony*	142
RUSSIAN ORTHODOXY AND ISLAM—ETHICS AND SPIRITUALITY IN EDUCATION *Basil Cousins*	162

LIVING STONES OF THE HOLY LAND TRUST

'An ecumenical trust seeking to promote contacts between Christian communities in Britain and those in the Holy Land and neighbouring countries.'

Our SPIRITUAL PATRONS include

In the Middle East:

Archbishop Elias Chacour, Melkite Archbishop of Galilee
Bishop Suheil Dawani, Anglican Bishop in Jerusalem
HB Patriarch Gregorius III, Melkite Patriarch of Antioch
Bishop Giantos-Boulos Marcuzzo, Latin Patriarchal Vicar for Israel
Patriarch Emeritus Michel Sabbah, formerly Latin Patriarch of Jerusalem
HB Patriarch Fouad Twal, Latin Patriarch of Jerusalem
Archbishop Theodosios of Sebastia, Greek Orthodox Patriarchate of Jerusalem
(Nizar Hanna)

Elsewhere:

Archbishop Yegishe Gizirian, Armenian Church
Rt Revd and Rt Hon The Lord Hope of Thornes, formerly Archbishop of York
Cardinal Cormac Murphy O'Connor, formerly Archbishop of Westminster
Archbishop Vincent Nichols, Archbishop of Westminster
Canon Paul Oestreicher, Anglican and Society of Friends
Revd Kathleen Richardson, Baroness Richardson of Calow, former President of Methodist Conference and Moderator of the Free Church Federal Council
Bishop Desmond Tutu, former Archbishop of Cape Town
The Most Reverend Kallistos, Metropolitan of Diokleia (Timothy Ware)

COMMUNICATIONS

www.livingstonesonline.org.uk

Communications with the Chair or Editor can be made through:
chair@livingstonesonline.org.uk
or editor@livingstonesonline.org.uk

All enquiries regarding subscriptions to the Honorary Treasurer:
treasurer@livingstonesonline.org.uk

NOTE

It is appreciated that articles derive from authors in a range of disciplines and demonstrate a variety in approach. The spelling of some specialised terms, local place-names and proper names in particular may vary considerably according to the contributor and discipline. These variations, however, should cause no problems to readers.

Submissions for inclusion in the *Yearbook* are welcome and papers for consideration should be sent to editor@livingstonesonline.org.uk. Notes for submission of papers and house style are available upon request from the editor.

INTRODUCTION

The second volume of the *Living Stones of the Holy Land Yearbook* appears at a time of great tension and conflict in many countries of the Middle East. The war in Syria has raged for three years with little sign of a peaceful end. In Egypt the conflict between the Muslim Brotherhood and the army is as yet unresolved, while Coptic Christians continue to suffer enormous damage to Churches and related Christian buildings. Because much international attention focuses on Syria, far less interest has been shown recently toward the on-going Occupation of the West Bank and Gaza in Palestine, and the worsening suffering of Arab Christians and Muslims. This is despite the beginning of peace talks initiated by John Kerry, US Secretary of State. These conflict situations have influenced the choice of articles in this volume. So we begin with four contributions that focus on the Living Stones of Palestine/Israel.

A strong theme running through this volume is one of memorial. So it is very appropriate to begin with an unpublished contribution from the late founding member of Living Stones, Revd Dr Michael Prior, whose tenth anniversary we will mark next year, 2014. This article, 'The Biblical Narrative: Canonical "Ancient Israel"' was written in February 2004, five months before his fatal accident, and it represents the final stage in the development of his critique of Zionist ideology.

This focus on remembering is picked up in a later article in this volume by Anthony O'Mahony, 'Shenouda III and the Coptic Orthodox Church in Modern Egypt'. The much-loved Pope Shenouda II died on 17 March 2012 after being in position for 40 years. As this article relates, he will be remembered by history as a significant figure in the history of Coptic Christianity but also as an important figure for the wider Eastern Christian tradition.

Following Michael Prior is an article by Fr Terry Tastard, a priest of the Diocese of Westminster and a member of Living Stones Theology Group. His article, 'Genocide, Ethnocide, and the situation of Middle East Christians today' challenges the Nazi campaign to exterminate the Jewish people as a whole as paradigmatic for genocide. Seeking a broader understanding of genocide, he proposes another way of understanding the plight of Middle East Christians, emerging from the very processes that produced the concept of genocide. Referring to the ideas of the Polish priest, Raphael Lemkin, he suggests that the cultural aspect of extermination, central to Lemkin's thinking offers a critical tool, namely the concept of *Ethnocide*, which could be used to denote the concept of erasing the identity and thus the survival of a national, ethnic or religious group. It can be applied where the violence inflicted on a minority does not amount to genocide but where the long-term survival of the group is at stake. Three test case studies are offered—Turkey, Israel and Egypt. A key difference applied to the Middle East is that genocide *leads to extinction; ethnocide encourages emigration.*

The third article on this theme is by Professor Rosemary Radford Ruether who has long campaigned and written on justice for Palestine.

Her article, 'Christianity and the Israeli-Palestinian Conflict' offers seven perspectives on the conflict, including Christian Zionism, its history in Britain and in the United States with a critique from evangelical traditions; pro-Israel and increasingly critical views of Israel in mainstream Protestant Churches; the developing views of the Vatican; Orthodox traditions, with particular attention to the views of the Orthodox in the Arab world and the Palestinians. The Jerusalem Sabeel Document, 'Principles for a Just Peace in Palestine-Israel' (2004) articulates a Palestinian Christian vision for a just peace, further expanded and reaffirmed in the *Kairos Palestine* document issued by Palestinian Christian leaders in December, 2009.[1]

The next contribution is by Dr Ramsay F Bisharah. This offers insight into the traditional multidisciplinary medical care practices prevalent in the late eighteenth and early nineteenth century in the

---

1 The UK response to this document, Kairos UK, was promulgated in August 2013, at the Greenbelt Christian Festival.

Introduction

Ottoman provinces of the Levant, notably the Holy Land and Mount Lebanon. He describes the often inadequate health care system in the region prior to a combination of Ottoman government attempts at relevant reforms and the sudden impact of modern Western health care resulting from an influx of Western medical missionaries from Britain, continental Europe and America.

Given the tragic conflict in Syria, Living Stones cannot fail to focus attention on this troubled country. As the outcome of the war is yet unknown what is offered here is a background paper to a history of the Churches in Syria before March 2011 by Fr Ignace Dick, 'Christian Syria', translated from the French by V Chamberlain. His article commences with Syria's importance in the early Christian communities in Damascus and Antioch, with the country's contribution to the Church through theologians, martyrs, writers and early monasticism; he also describes the tensions of the Christological controversies. After the Arabic conquest Christians were still the majority—though Arabic became the common language. As we are taken through the various conquests of Syria we are shown the resilience of Christianity in adapting to new and often deteriorating circumstances—benefitting from the well-established educational system. The present situation is a compromise between secularism and Islamic *shari'a*. Given the current conflict and the plight of 2 million refugees, one of Fr Dick's final sentences 'Christians feel completely at home in Syria' strikes a tragic note.

A second major strand in this Volume is that of dialogue between Christians and Muslims, both here in Britain and in the Middle East. The first article on this theme by David Derrick, an Anglican priest and former head teacher.

This article 'Can we re-imagine Islam as solely with a Meccan identity, as set out in the writings of Kenneth Cragg?' fits also with the genre of memorial. The Rt Revd (Albert) Kenneth Cragg, who died in November 2012, was the foremost Anglican scholar of Christian-Muslim relations.

This article not only offers some of the richness of Kenneth Cragg's scholarship, but illustrates the creative engagement between Christian and Muslim scholars around key issues—including their critique of Cragg's position. The focus here is the distinctions between the Meccan and the Medinan surahs in the Qur'an. Cragg questions whether the original intention was to give a theology of unity based on the Meccan surahs, or to give a political Islamic authority based on the Medinan surahs. A pivotal point is whether to regard the Qu'ran as history or theology. Another key issue is the role Muhammad in the transmission and reception of the messages of the text of the Qur'an. Exploring similarities between Mohammad and the biblical prophets he finds that while biblical biographies of the prophets enhance understanding of the 'inner psyche of prophetic experience', the Qur'an is subtly different: there is no biographical prelude for the reader to locate the incidence of Muhammad's self-awareness. Yet he notes that, 'A habit of meditation intensified around his fortieth year.'

Cragg's own experience and 'vision' of Islam is unique. Nevertheless, there are also difficulties with his interpretation of Muhammad's use of power, particularly when considering Cragg's own disdain of power leading to Cragg's 'sense of antithesis between the ministries of Muhammad and Jesus'.

The paper's underlying question, this sense of 'yes-and-no', when contrasting Mecca and Medina, is answered by re-imagining an Islam which has a solely Meccan identity. Bishop Kenneth Cragg asserts also that this is a Christian mission and a human duty.

The second dialogue article is by Dr Hugh Boulter. The original version of this paper was presented to the Living Stones Theology Group in September 2012, now expanded partly to take comments into consideration concerning the nature of dialogue itself and the implications for a theology of change. The author enlarges his own British-based research with comments from other members of the group from a Middle-Eastern perspective and context. He suggests dialogue is a dynamic process which helps us to engage with religious issues in a constantly changing context and generating new understanding. He also explores the central role of the Holy Spirit in guiding the whole process.

The third Christian-Muslim dialogue article, 'Mary Kahil: a life given for Muslims' is written by Sister Agnes Wilkins OSB from Stanbrook Abbey, Yorkshire. The unique feature of this contribution is the focus not only on the life of Cairo-based Mary Kahlil, and her commitment to Christian- Muslim relations, but the nature of her relationship with Louis Massignon, the French celebrated Islamic scholar. Together they founded a movement which was a very

Introduction

Christian way of relating to Muslims, not by trying to convert them, but by praying for them, loving them, and being 'substitutes' for them before God. This *Badaliya,* as it came to be called, is still a Christian spiritual movement today. The article tells of the degree of sacrifice this demanded in Mary Kahlil's life and her influence on Massignon, though mostly from a distance.

The final article of the 2013 Volume, 'Russian Orthodoxy and Islam—ethics and spirituality in education' is by Basil Cousins, an independent scholar. This is of great interest to all who are concerned about faith development in contemporary Russia emerging from Tsarist and then Communist strictures. It is inspired by two nineteenth-century reformers in faith education, one Christian Orthodox—Nikolai Il'Minskii—and the other Muslim—Ismail Gasprinskii. The author's concern is to show how contemporary developments have been influenced by their pioneering work.

The editors hope that readers will find these contributions helpful in understanding some contemporary situation in conflicted Middle Eastern contexts.

The Editors

CONTRIBUTORS

Ramsay F Bisharah PhD, was born in Jerusalem, Palestine on 22 December 1937. He attended St George's School in Jerusalem and in 1948 upon leaving Palestine as a refugee, he followed up his schooling at the English Quaker Boarding School, Brummana High School, Brummana, Mount Lebanon. He received his PhD from the University of Iowa in 1970 in Infectious/Tropical Diseases, Preventive Medicine and International Health Administration. He worked at NASA on Apollo 14, 15 and 16 Missions. He also received a Commonwealth Fund Fellowship for post-doctorate work in infectious/tropical diseases at AUB Medical Centre, Beirut, Lebanon. His study on Ludwig Schneller, *The Life and Work of Father Johann Ludwig Schneller* was published in 2009 (Melisende, London). He is now an independent researcher into the medical missionaries of nineteenth-century Ottoman Holy Land and Mount Lebanon.

Hugh Boulter's first degree was in Modern History from Oxford. He is a founder member of and former Chair of the Oxford Diocesan (Anglican) Committee for Inter-faith Concerns and a former Chair of Biblelands (now Embrace the Middle East), the ecumenical charity which supports Christian led projects in the Middle East. His doctoral thesis from Bristol University (2003) is entitled *The Spirit in Islam: A Study in Christian-Muslim Dialogue and Theology of Religions.*

Basil Cousins, an independent scholar, undertook research for his thesis on the Russian Orthodox scholar-missionary and educationalist Nikolai Il'Minskii in the nineteenth century at Heythrop College, the University of London, 2003. His publications include, 'Spreading the

Gospel to the Frontiers of the Empire: Nikolay Il'minsky, the Russian Orthodox Church and Islam in the nineteenth century', in: *Journal of Eastern Christian Studies*, Vol. 63, no. 1-2, 2011, and 'The Orthodox Church, Islam and Christianity Christian-Muslim Relations in Russia', in *Christian Responses to Islam: Muslim-Christian Relations in the Modern World*, A O'Mahony and Emma Loosley (eds), (Manchester University Press, 2008).

David Derrick is an Anglican priest and former head teacher who has lived and worked in London's inner boroughs since 1967. His recent research at Heythrop College centred on the work of Kenneth Cragg.

Fr. Ignace Dick of the Melkite Greek Catholic Patriarchate in Damascus is a well-known figure in the Middle East and especially Syria. He has an established reputation as an important scholar of Arabic Christian literature. He has been responsible for a number of important critical editions; with books on the modern history of Christianity in the Middle East and the Melkite Church, and on Christianity in present-day Syria.

Anthony O'Mahony is Reader in Theology and the History of Christianity, Director, Centre for Eastern Christianity, Heythrop College, University of London. He has published widely on the modern history of Christianity in the Middle East and its contemporary context including (co-ed), *Christian Responses to Islam: A Global Account of Muslim-Christian Relations* (Manchester University Press, 2008); (co-ed) *Eastern Christianity in the modern Middle East* (Routledge, 2010); *Christianity and Jerusalem: Studies in Theology and Politics in the Modern Holy Land* (2010); (co-ed) with John Flannery, *The Catholic Church in the contemporary Middle East: Studies for The Synod of the Middle East* (Melisende, 2010).

Fr Michael Prior CM. The late Fr Prior was Head of the Department of Theology and Religious Studies and Professor of Bible and Theology at St Mary's University College, Twickenham; see also pp. 1-2.

Rosemary Radford Ruether is the Carpenter Professor Emeritus of Feminist Theology at the Graduate Theological Union in Berkeley, California. She is presently teaching as a research scholar at the Claremont Graduate University and Claremont School of Theology in Claremont, California. She is author of thirty-five books and twelve book collections. Two such books are *Faith and Fratricide: The Theological Roots of Anti-Semitism* (reprint: WIPF and Stock Publishers, Eugene, Oregon, 1996) and, with Herman J Ruether, *The Wrath of Jonah: The Crisis of Religious Nationalism in the Israeli-Palestinian Conflict* (Fortress Press, Minneapolis, MN, 2002, 2nd edition).

Fr Terry Tastard is a priest of the Diocese of Westminster. His PhD thesis in history was on the English Christian response to the Holocaust. He is the author of two books, *The Spark in the Soul: Spirituality and Social Justice*, and *Ronald Knox and English Catholicism*.

Agnes Wilkins, OSB, is a nun of Stanbrook Abbey who has been interested in the Christian dialogue with Islam for several years. For example 'Straight Writing on Crooked Lines', in *Touched by God: Ten Monastic Journeys,* edited by Laurentia Johns OSB (Continuum, London, 2008). She has published widely on the Christian monastic encounter with Islam : 'Thomas Merton's Encounter with Islam', in *Catholics in Interreligious Dialogue: Monasticism, Theology and Spirituality*, edited by A O'Mahony and Peter Bowe OSB, Gracewing, 2006; 'Louis Massignon, Thomas Merton and Mary Kahil', in *Society for Syro-Mesopotamian Studies*, [Special issue on 'The Life and Thought of Louis Massignon'], Vol. 20, 2008; 'Monasticism and Martyrdom in Algeria', in *The Downside Review* [Special issue on 'Catholic Encounters with Islam'], Vol. 126, no. 444, 2008.

THE BIBLICAL NARRATIVE: CANONICAL 'ANCIENT ISRAEL'
Michael Prior

INTRODUCTION BY DUNCAN MACPHERSON

Next year will be the tenth anniversary of the death of Michael Prior, a founding member and for a long time the chair and the larger than life inspiration of Living Stones. Michael was a Vincentian priest and a scripture scholar who became dedicated to the proposition that scholarship could also be politically committed, an approach reflected in his Jesus the Liberator: Nazareth Liberation Theology (Luke 4.16-30) *(1995).*

Michael's interest in issues of justice and peace in the Holy Land began in the seminary during the Six-Day War of June 1967 and he recalled believing that he 'was observing a classic David versus Goliath conflict, with diminutive, innocent Israel repulsing its rapacious Arab predators.' However, during his first study visit to the Holy Land in 1972 he sensed something wrong in what he regarded as the 'obvious Apartheid of Israeli-Arab society'. Ten years later, on a student study tour, he was further radicalised when he witnessed at first hand curfews and house demolitions and meeting young men who had been tortured and held without trial. Even then however he had no doubts about the legitimacy of the Jewish State or of validity of the security argument for the Israeli occupation of land seized after the 1967 war. It was only during the course of a sabbatical year in 1983-84 that he began to raise questions about the role of the Biblical narrative of promise and possession of land in the expansionist activity that he witnessed.

He became convinced that much Western Biblical scholarship encouraged active or passive collusion in the oppression of the

> Palestinian people, and his The Bible and Colonialism: a moral critique *(1997) examined the way in which the Biblical narrative of Exodus and the Conquest had been used to justify colonialism, not only in Palestine, but in Latin America and South Africa.*
>
> His *Zionism and the State of Israel: a moral inquiry (1999) represented a move to offering a radical moral critique of Zionism, underlining its secular roots and the relatively recent character of support for Zionism by religious Jewry. He now argued that the problem was not the occupation of 1967 but the 'original sin' of 1948 and that the expulsion of the Palestinians had been planned by the founding fathers of Zionism long before the Nazi Holocaust or the war in 1948. The unpublished article which follows was written in February 2004, just five months before his fatal accident, and it represents the final stage in the development of his critique of Zionist ideology. It also represents a challenge to all those whose acceptance of divine authorship of the Bible leaves them with an interpretation of the Old Testament that characterises Yahweh, in Michael's words, as 'the great ethnic cleanser'.*
>
> *Michael considered several possible ways of rehabilitating morally unacceptable parts of the Old Testament but found them all, to some degree, unsatisfactory. His untimely death left others to discover a credible response to his challenge.*

The injustice done by Zionists to the indigenous population of Palestine has, until recently, been passed over in much Western discourse. Indeed, in some religious circles the Zionist enterprise is even clothed in the garment of piety. This is obviously the case in the Christian Zionist constituency, but adulation for the Zionist project is apparent also in the mainstream. People involved in Jewish-Christian dialogue, in particular, deploy a unique vocabulary of favour, not least 'The Miracle of Israel's Rebirth'.[1] Characteristically, also, they repeat the whole range

---

1 'The living reality of the State of Israel should evoke the respect and admiration of the Christian theologian. How could the renewal of the land be anything to the theologian but a wonder of love and vitality, and the reborn state be anything but a sign of God's concern for his people? (Monsignor John Oesterreicher, in Fisher, Rudin and Tanenbaum 1986: p. 35), and Christians should 'rejoice in the

The Biblical Narrative: Canonical 'Ancient Israel'

of the canonical Zionist narrative. Herzl the Zionist visionary, we learn, pursued his 'messianic pilgrimage' with a zeal 'infused with a compelling humanitarianism combined with traces of Jewish mysticism'. And now that Herzl has died, the 'mystery' and 'majesty' of Zionism appears in its glory from his tomb (Drinan 1977: 32, 39); the Zionists never intended any disadvantage to the Palestinians; the Arabs 'emigrated' from Israel in 1947 and 1948, despite 'the objective evidence that Israelis in many instances urged Arab residents to remain'; etc. Typically there is no mention of the destruction of the Palestinian villages, and no reference to natural justice or the imperatives of international law—even from Jesuit Father Robert F Drinan, former Dean of Boston College Law School, who was a member of the US House of Representatives (Democrat-Massachusetts) for a ten-year period (Drinan 1977). I have shown elsewhere how the Jewish-Christian dialogue as we know it is altogether subservient to the programme of Political Zionism (Prior 2003a).

Western support for the Zionist enterprise is particularly striking from a moral perspective. Whereas elsewhere the perpetrators of colonial plunder are objects of opprobrium, the Zionist conquest is widely judged to be a just and appropriate accomplishment, with even unique religious significance. How was this possible? The answer lies in the Bible, and its religious authority.

Colonisers invariably seek out some ideological principle to justify their actions, and when these involve dubious deeds of exploitation the search is all the more intense. Awaiting the turn of the tide on the Thames as he embarked on another colonial expedition, Joseph Conrad's Marlow, musing on the whole enterprise of imperial conquest, noted that 'the conquest of the earth is not a pretty thing when you look into it too much'. Indeed, it was 'just robbery with violence, aggravated murder on a great scale, and men going at it blind - as is very proper for those who tackle a darkness'. Conquerors needed only brute force, and a justifying ideology. 'What redeems it is the idea only. An idea at the back of it ... and an unselfish belief in the idea—something you can set up, and bow down before, and offer a sacrifice to ... ' (*Heart of Darkness*, pp. 31-32).

A perusal of the emerging nationalisms which burgeoned throughout Europe in the second half of the nineteenth century

---

return of the Jewish people to a small sliver of their ancient homeland—if not from compassion and a sense of justice at least from a sense of guilt and repentance' (Father Edward Flannery, in Fisher, Rudin and Tanenbaum 1986: p. 76).

quickly reveals the attempt to root each one in a glorious past of heroes and even demigods. In addition to fabricating continuity with whatever glories one could detect in the nation's real history, the domain of folklore was mined assiduously in the attempt to link up the ordinariness of contemporary life with a putatively eminent national past. National groups invariably constructed a foundational nationalist narrative consisting of not only historical memories, but of *myths of origins*. Where possible and desirable, religion was mobilised to sacralise national sentiment. In the case of Zionism, however, there was a problem, in addition to the fact that its ideologues were stridently anti-religious. Judaism's holiest collection of books, the Talmud, which was accorded precedence over even the Torah, since its deliberations constituted the ultimate source on all matters of Jewish comportment *(Halakha)*, was next to useless. In fact, it was worse than useless.

Although the Talmud had been central to Jewish identity since medieval times, it did not offer anything like the support necessary to advance the Zionist project. It had no glorious story of a nation, few heroic figures, and little narrative of a glorious past. And, most critically, it did not promote any particular relationship to an ancient homeland, nor advance the sentiment of longing to return. It could scarcely promote the ideal of Political Zionism, since it had no 'geography which arouses longing in the reader or a sense of connection to an ancient home' (Halbertal 1997: 131). Rather than lamenting exile, and longing for return home, the perspective of the Talmud accepted the exile as determined by God, and any attempt to end it before the coming of the Messiah would be an abomination. Instead, the Talmud concentrated on living out the details of the Jewish law in any and every experience of daily life, wherever a Jew found her/himself. Rather than reflecting sentiments of longing and return, its overall thrust was antipathetic to Political Zionism.

The Bible, on the other hand, provided many of the ingredients of a 'master narrative', in particular, those relating to the promised land, exile from, and return to it, elements that easily fed into the Zionist project of establishing a state for Jews in the ancient homeland of Palestine. In the Biblical narrative there was a first 'exile' in Egypt, a second in Babylon, from each of which there was a homecoming. Now, close on 2000 years after the Romans 'exiled Jews in their entirety from Palestine'—which they did not, of course—Zionism would gather them in. The Bible's 'exile-return' motif, then, provided the necessary 'foundation myth' or 'master commemorative narrative' for Zionism. To this day, as David Gunn has shown, quotations from the Bible are presented on the top of pages on the website of the Israeli Ministry of Foreign Affairs, like religious proof-texts, lending (divine) authority to the achievements of Zionism.[2] That the Bible read in its totality implies that exile invariably follows settlement because of the injustice of the leaders—'Exile is potentially only an injustice away' (Gunn 2003: 260)—however, is conveniently ignored.

The link between the Bible and Zionism is firmly established in the popular mind also.[3] Zionism's claims to exclusive Jewish title to the 'land of Israel' *(Eretz Yisrael)* are constantly predicated on the basis of the Bible, particularly of the narratives of the promise of land to Abraham and his descendants (Genesis 12-50), the preparation for entry into the land (Exodus, Leviticus, Numbers and Deuteronomy) and the execution of the promise in the narrative of Joshua's conquest (Joshua). Even for secular or atheist nationalists, uninterested in it as the repository of a theological claim, the Biblical narrative can be invoked to function as the 'historical account' of Jews' title to the land. Thus, for Ben-Gurion, Israel's first Prime Minister, the Bible was the 'Jews' sacrosanct title-deed to Palestine... with a genealogy of 3,500 years.'[4] Although it was a secular ideology and enterprise from the beginning, and was bitterly opposed by the Jewish religious establishment, when it suited their purposes the proponents of Zionism—including Herzl himself—however non-religious, atheistic or agnostic, could look to the Bible for support. Such is the case, even though the predominantly secular

---

2 'Facts About Israel (1996)', at www.mfa.gov.il/mfa/go.asp?MFAH00080.
3 The Google search engine has some 44,800 entries for the combination "Bible" + "Zionism" (accessed on 3 February 2004), many, of course, representing the view that there is no essential connection between the two.
4 Ben-Gurion 1954: p. 100. Ben-Gurion regularly convened the 'Prime Minister's Bible Study Circle', which included President Zalman Shazar. His lecture, 'The Bible and the Jewish People' (Nahalal, 20 July 1964) makes abundant use of Biblical texts, especially those dealing with the promise of restoration. While he alludes to the Hebrew prophets and their concern for justice, Ben-Gurion does not deal with the injunctions to disinherit the Canaanites, the Joshua legend, nor with the Biblical traditions that reflect racist, ethnicist, xenophobic and militaristic tendencies. His sole, oblique reference to the indigenous Palestinians, is that while the whole world regarded Israel with respect and admiration, 'Our Arab neighbours have as yet not made peace with our existence, and their leaders are declaring their desire to destroy us' (Ben-Gurion 1972: 294). See also Dayan 1978.

Zionist movement was a rebellion against, and a conscious repudiation of classical Judaism and its theological tenets. For many political Zionists, religion was irrational, non-empirical, imperialistic, and an altogether repressive and regressive force, from which no anthropological validity, social bonding, psychological insight, or existential illumination could be expected. Indeed, for many of its supporters one's way to salvation was to escape from the prison of the sacred.

Nevertheless, according to the late Chief Rabbi of the British Commonwealth, Lord Sir Immanuel Jakobivits,

> The origins of the Zionist idea are of course entirely religious. The slogan, 'The Bible is our mandate' is a credo hardly less insistently pleaded by many secularists than by religious believers as the principal basis of our legal and historical claim to the Land of Israel ... Modern Political Zionism itself could never have struck root if it had not planted its seeds in soil ploughed up and fertilised by the millennial conditioning of religious memories, hopes, prayers and visions of our eventual return to Zion... No rabbinical authority disputes that our claim to a Divine mandate (and we have no other which cannot be invalidated) extends over the entire Holy Land within its historic borders and that halachically we have no right to surrender this claim (Jakobivits 1982: 19-20).

His successor, current Chief Rabbi Jonathan Sacks, considers that the State of Israel is for many religious Jews 'the most powerful collective expression' of Jewry, and 'the most significant development in Jewish life since the Holocaust'.[5] In the course of his speech at the Service for Israel's Fiftieth Anniversary, Sacks portrayed the birth of the state as a coming to the promised land in line with the Biblical stories of Abraham and Sarah, Moses and the Exodus, Ezra and Nehemiah. His speech reflected also the core elements of the 'canonical' Zionist reading of Jewish history.[6] Within a few generations of Chief Rabbis, then, Political Zionism had been metamorphosed from being an

---

5 *The Daily Telegraph*, 31 December 1993, p. 21.
6 Speech at the Service for Israel's Fiftieth Anniversary in the Presence of HRH The Prince of Wales, at St John's Wood Synagogue, London, 29 April 1998.

anathema, and a repudiation of Judaism and the Scriptures, to becoming a core ingredient of Jewish religious life: it had moved from the secular to the sacred.

The role of the Biblical narrative within the Zionist ideology increased significantly in the wake of the 1967 War and the rise of *Gush Emunim*. The Biblical paradigm was the backdrop for the Zionist self-portrayal as the (sole) 'descendants of the Biblical children of Israel', while the natives [Arabs] were 'Canaanites'. This introduced into the secular discourse a religious authority justifying the new conquest of the land and the maltreatment of its population. Measured against the divine right of the colonisers, appeal to the human rights of the local population, considered to be 'interlopers', 'sojourners' and obstacles to the divine plan, carried no conviction.

More recently, the otherwise forward-looking and ecumenically eirenic statement *Dabru Emet* ('Speak the Truth'), signed by 150 prominent Jews in the USA (12 September 2000, and by more since), promotes exclusively Jewish claims to Palestine, clothing the Zionist enterprise in the garment of piety, even though its determination to create a state for Jews would require the 'ethnic-cleansing' of the indigenous Arab population. Acceptance of these claims and its contemporary implications is a requirement of the conventional Jewish-Christian dialogue:

> Christians can respect the claim of the Jewish people upon the land of Israel. The most important event for Jews since the Holocaust has been the reestablishment of a Jewish state in the Promised Land. As members of a Biblically-based religion, Christians appreciate that Israel was promised—and given—to Jews as the physical centre of the covenant between them and God. Many Christians support the State of Israel for reasons far more profound than mere politics. As Jews, we applaud this support.

Virtually everything, then, rests on the authority of the Bible. While other factors, such as 'endemic', 'irridentist' antisemitism in nineteenth-century Europe, the barbarism of the *Shoah* in the twentieth, etc., could be invoked as justifications for establishing a state, they might not be considered adequate to warrant ethnically cleansing Palestine of its indigenous non-Jewish population. The Zionist conquest would need an even bigger 'idea' to redeem it, and the Bible was to hand (see Prior 1999b).

Whatever pangs of conscience one might have in the modern period about the expulsion of a million Palestinian Arabs, and the destruction of their villages to ensure they would not return—if one could bring oneself to acknowledge that such was the reality, and indeed the intention of Zionism—the Bible could be appealed to to salve it. It could provide the most authoritative legitimisation for the Zionist conquest, claiming that it was merely restoring the land to the Jews in accordance with the clear intentions of God as recorded in its narrative. The divine provenance of the Bible and the authority that springs from such origins would supply the moral authority that was otherwise lacking. Thus, the normal rules of morality could be suspended, and ethnic cleansing could be applauded, even by the religious spirit.

THE MORAL CHALLENGE TO THE BIBLICAL NARRATIVE

The land traditions of the Bible, however, pose fundamental moral questions, at two levels. At the level of content, the divine promise of land in the Biblical narrative is integrally linked with the *mandate*—not merely the permission—to exterminate the indigenous peoples of Canaan. Even the Exodus narrative is problematic on moral grounds. While it portrays Yahweh as having compassion on the misery of his people, and as willing to deliver them from the Egyptians, and bring them to a land flowing with milk and honey (Exodus 3.7-8), that was only part of the picture. Although the reading of Exodus 3, both in the Christian liturgy and in the classical texts of liberation theologies, halts abruptly in the middle of v. 8 at the description of the land as one 'flowing with milk and honey', the Biblical text itself continues, 'to the country of the Canaanites, the Hittites, the Amorites, the Perizzites, the Hivites, and the Jebusites'. Manifestly, the promised land, flowing with milk and honey, had no lack of indigenous peoples, and, according to the narrative, would soon flow with their blood.[7] At the level of the use to which these morally problematic texts have been put—what

---

7 For an exposition of the offending Biblical texts and a fuller commentary on them, see my 'Moral Critique' (Prior 1997).

scholars call the Reception History of the text—there is a further moral problem. These Biblical land traditions have been deployed in favour of various colonial enterprises, including Zionism. Far from being charters for liberation, then, they have been deployed as instruments of oppression (see Prior 1997).

Altogether, then, in the light of the double problematic of the land traditions of the Bible—their projection of genocide as being divinely *mandated*, and their deleterious use in favour of oppressive colonialism—perhaps every copy of the Bible should contain a health warning: 'Reading this Book may Damage Somebody Else's Health'. It is possible, of course, to insist that the relevant land traditions are historical in the sense that they approximate to what actually happened—and many evangelical do so. To do so, however, leaves one with a god who is a xenophobic nationalist and a militaristic ethnic-cleanser. Reliance on the authority of the gift of land from such a god, then, should be problematic for any reader who might presume that the divinity would entertain the values of the Fourth Geneva Convention and the Universal Declaration of Human Rights, at least. On moral grounds, therefore, one is forced to question whether the *Torah* in fact provides divine legitimacy for the occupation of other people's land, and the virtual annihilation of the indigenous peoples.

By modern standards of international law and human rights the land narratives of Exodus-Joshua *mandate* 'war-crimes' and 'crimes against humanity'. To dismiss their contemporary moral implications by pleading that such texts ought not to be judged by the standards obtaining today is not sufficient. Nor is it acceptable either to seek refuge in the claim that the problem lies with the predispositions of the modern reader, rather than with the text itself. One must acknowledge that much of the *Torah*, and the Book of Deuteronomy in particular, contains menacing ideologies, and racist, xenophobic and militaristic tendencies. Manifestly, the Book of Joshua is a morally scandalous component in a collection of religious writings. The implications of the existence of such dubious moral dispositions and actions, presented as *mandated* by the divinity, within a book which is canonised as Sacred Scripture invites the most serious investigation.

The Challenge to the Historicity of the Land Traditions of the Bible

Much of Biblical studies, as Keith Whitelam has demonstrated (1996), has been propelled by the search for 'Ancient Israel' as the taproot of Western civilisation, and the antecedent of Christianity. What might otherwise be considered reasonably to be a highly problematic moral precedent—the Biblical narrative's presentation of the genocide attendant upon the establishment of Biblical Israel—required no apologia. God, according to the Biblical narrative, had ordained it so, and the times were 'primitive'. Moreover, with the nineteenth-century European assurance of people that human culture was evolving in an inexorable rise from savagery to civilisation—reaching its evolutionary zenith in the form of Western Christendom, preferably of the Reformed type, and best of all American—divine breaches of modern Human Rights protocols could be easily tolerated. Thus, even William Foxwell Albright, the doyen of Biblical archaeologists, had no qualms about the plunder attendant upon Joshua's enterprise, which he understood in a largely historically reliable way.[8] An analogous indulgence obtains in the modern period also in the benign Western assessment of the Zionist enterprise, which cleanses the land of its indigenous defilers, and so Albright himself also judged that through Zionism Jews would bring to the Near East all the benefits of European civilisation (1942: 12-13).

Even for people not revolted at the portrayal of God as the Great Ethnic Cleanser two lines of thought converge to challenge a naïve reading of the land traditions. Rather than reading ancient texts from within the context of contemporary categories of race, ethnicity, nation, etc., the first task of the Biblical scholar is to establish the literary forms of the texts one is studying. In simple terms, does every occurrence of verbs in the past tense imply that the narrative is essentially history, as we broadly understand that term as giving insight into the period described in the narrative? And, is every use of the future tense in the

---

[8] 'From the impartial standpoint of a philosopher of history, it often seems necessary that a people of markedly inferior type should vanish before a people of superior potentialities, since there is a point beyond which racial mixture cannot go without disaster ...Thus the Canaanites, with their orgiastic nature worship, their cult of fertility in the form of serpent symbols and sensuous nudity, and their gross mythology, were replaced by Israel, with its pastoral simplicity and purity of life, its lofty monotheism, and its severe code of ethics' (Albright 1957, pp. 280-81).

The Biblical Narrative: Canonical 'Ancient Israel'

Biblical narrative indicative of prophetic texts which will be fulfilled in a literalist way in our present, or in some future? Christian Zionists, and many evangelical Christians, would answer both questions affirmatively. As well as presenting moral problems, such predispositions in reading the Biblical text conflict with general principles of literary criticism, and ignore critical evidence. Space allows only an indication of current developments in Biblical scholarship.[9]

Recent Biblical scholarship, aided by increasing archaeological evidence, makes it impossible to evaluate the Biblical narratives of land as pointers to what actually happened in the period portrayed in the text. In the wake of the seminal works of Thomas L Thompson (1974) and John Van Seters (1975) it is now part of the scholarly consensus that the patriarchal narratives of Genesis do not record events of an alleged patriarchal period, but are retrojections into a past about which the writers knew little, reflecting the author's intentions at the later period of composition, perhaps that of the attempt to reconstitute national and religious identity in the wake of the Babylonian exile, or even later (see further Prior 1997: 216-23). In such circumstances it is naïve to cleave to the view that God made the promise of progeny and land to Abraham after the fashion indicated in Genesis 15.

Neither do the Exodus-Settlement accounts present empirical facts of history. The archaeology of Palestine shows a picture quite different from that of the religiously motivated writings of the Bible. The evidence from archaeology and extra-Biblical literature, supplemented by insights from the independent methodologies of geography, sociology, anthropology, historical linguistics, Egyptology, Assyriology, etc., points in a direction altogether different from that implied by Joshua 1-12. This extra-Biblical material suggests a sequence of periods marked by a gradual and peaceful coalescence of disparate peoples into a group of highland dwellers whose achievement of a new sense of unity culminated only with the entry of the Assyrian administration. The Iron Age I settlements on the central hills of Palestine, from which the later kingdom of Israel developed, reflect continuity with Canaanite culture, and repudiate any ethnic distinction between 'Canaanites'

---

9 For further discussion on reinterpreting the Biblical evidence, and on the relevant literary and historical questions concerning the Patriarchal Narratives, the Pentateuchal Narratives, and the Israelite Conquest-Settlement Narratives, see Prior 1997: pp. 216-52. See also my comments on 'Towards a Moral Reading of the Bible' in Prior 1997, pp. 253-86.

and 'Israelites' (see further Prior 1997: 228-47; 1999a: 159-83). The Biblical narrative, then, unless read in a naïve, literalist fashion, offers little succour to ethnic-cleansers.

But even if the Patriarchal narratives of Genesis and the narratives of Exodus-Leviticus-Numbers-Deuteronomy-Joshua portrayed the past approximately as it happened one would still have to contend with their ethical stance in portraying Yahweh as the great ethnic-cleanser. Were these narratives acknowledged to belong to the genre of legend rather than history, or to be confined to the realm of mere rhetorical discussion of ancient literature in its various genres, few would object. But when they have vital significance for people's lives even in one's own generation problems arise. As we have seen, much of the legitimacy associated with the establishment of the State of Israel, and the esteem it enjoys in religious circles, derives its major moral legitimisation from a particular reading of the 'Hebrew Bible'. And the matter is not merely rhetorical.

Important conclusions follow from the claim of exclusive Israelite/Jewish rights to Palestine. 'Jews' hailing from any part of the globe, who themselves were never displaced from Palestine, have the 'right of return'. Without the Bible, such a claim to legitimacy would have no currency in the wider world wherein, for one, a communal right of return operates only when a defined community has been subjected to recent expulsion—a *sine qua non* for orderly international behaviour. From a moral perspective there is a more problematic implication. The Jewish 'right of return' easily translates into the 'right to expel' the indigenous population, an aspiration which, as we have seen, was at the core of the Zionist enterprise from the beginning. And, since Jews have sole tenure, a claim deriving from a naïve reading of the Biblical narrative, the recently expelled Palestinian Arabs have no right of return (see Prior 2001).

Conclusion
Facing Hard Truths

Any discussion of the enterprise of Political Zionism and its climax in the creation of the State of Israel must come to terms with a number of embarrassing truths, the denial of which only adds to self-delusion and self-righteousness. There is a fundamental moral problem at the core of the Zionist programme which no amount of special pleading, or pretence to innocence, can side-step. This relates to the Zionist determination to establish a state for Jews at the expense of the indigenous Arabs. Theodor Herzl knew what was needed to establish such a state in a land already inhabited. Moreover, there is a 'mountain' of evidence in the Zionist archives tracing the consistency of this line of thinking within the Jewish leadership in Palestine. It demonstrates that the expulsion of the indigenous Arabs was foreseen as necessary, was systematically planned—not least through establishing three successive 'Population Transfer Committees'—and was executed at the first opportunity, in 1948. The damage done to the indigenous population in 1948, then, was neither accidental nor due to the unique pressures of war, but was at the heart of the Zionist enterprise from the beginning. To accord legitimacy to such activity is highly problematic. To criticise the Zionist ethnic cleansing of Palestine in 1948 on the basis that it did not complete the job—the current position of Benny Morris—is even worse.

The espousal of Zionism by a majority of Jews world-wide marks the nadir of Jewish morality, and the degree to which a thoroughly Zionised Judaism debases Jewish-Christian dialogue, and even Christianity itself is a matter of grave concern. In that scenario, the planned and systematically executed dislocation of the indigenous population of Palestine, far from incurring the wrath of post-colonial liberalism, becomes an object of honour, and even of religious significance. It is in the unique case of Zionism that ethnic cleansing is applauded by the religious spirit. It would be a pity if mutually respectful Jewish-Christian relations demanded the suspension of the normal rules of a universalist morality.

We have seen that the core ingredients of the 'canonical' Zionist narrative, in its secular, in its religious, and in its Biblical categories are strained under the weight of ongoing modern scholarship from disparate disciplines. Rather than being generated by religious idealism, the Zionist aspiration was prompted by a host of nationalist movements within the turbulent politics of post-French Revolution, nineteenth-century Europe (Prior 1999a: 51-66). Political Zionism was rejected by both Orthodox and Reform wings of Judaism from the start: it was heretical, in the case of the former, and contrary to the mission of Judaism for the latter. Only gradually, but dramatically in the wake of the 1967 Israeli-Arab War, 'Religious Jewry' (with notable exceptions) rowed in with the achievement of secular Zionism, and in some circles 'sacralised' it (Prior 1999a: 67-102).

With respect to the history of ancient Jewry, the authoritative studies of such as Betsy Halpern-Amaru, John Barclay, Isaiah Gafni, *et alii*, undermine the 'Myth of the Ubiquitous and Perennial Jewish Longing for Palestine'. Rather than reflecting historical realities that myth has been imposed by Zionists, with no regard for the diversity of Jewish history and experience (see Prior 1999a: 212-18). In addition to suffering in various places at different times, Jews in several countries acquired positions for themselves which they have found eminently satisfying. Indeed, the majority of international Jewry chooses to live other than in Israel.

The claim in our own age that the Biblical narrative, however repulsive its deployment as part of the ideological support for colonialism in the past, legitimises the 'ethnic cleansing' of the Palestinian Arabs should not remain unchallenged within the Biblical academy. Biblical scholars, at least, might be expected to protest against outrages perpetrated in the name of fidelity to the Biblical covenant. Biblical research should be conducted with an 'ethics of accountability', i.e., with a concern for exposing 'the ethical consequences of the Biblical text and its meanings', especially when these have promoted various forms of oppression, not least through 'colonial dehumanisation', and for making their findings known to a wider public (Schüssler Fiorenza 1999: 28-29). Biblical exegesis, in addition to probing into the circumstances of the composition of the Biblical narratives, should concern itself also with the real conditions of people's lives, and not satisfy itself with comfortable survival in an academic or religious ghetto, stimulating only its own 'in-house' constituency.

It is a particularly important task to identify the different literary forms of the Bible, and to distinguish between tracts that are historical, mythological, legendary, etc. In the attempts to reconstruct the conditions of 'Early Israel' it would be unwise to neglect the late and theologically-oriented accounts we find in the Bible. Nor should the Biblical narrative determine ethnic identities that obtained hundreds of years earlier. It appears now that the 'Israel' of the period of the Biblical narrative represented a multiplicity of ethnic identities, reflecting the variety of provenances in the Late Bronze-Iron Age transition, and that brought about by three waves of systematic, imperial population transfer and admixture (Assyrian, Babylonian and Persian). The predication of Israelite *ethnic distinctiveness* prior to the Persian period is illusory, and the unity of the Biblical *benei Israel* (children of Israel) is a predilection of the Biblical authors, rather than the reality reflecting a commonality of ethnic identity or communal experience.

The needs of the much later final redactors of the Biblical narrative dominated their ideological stance, which we may wish to call religious or pastoral, and issued in an ideal model for the future which they justified on the basis of its retrojection into the past of Israelite origins, the details of which only the surviving conflicting folkloric traditions provided. If we excuse the Biblical writers for their misrepresentation of the past on the basis of their exhortatory motives for their own circumstances, we ought not to be equally indulgent with theologians and Church-Synagogue people for whom the evidence of what happened in the past is more reliable. The legendary account of Joshua 1-12 offers no legitimizing paradigm for land plunder in the name of God, or by anyone arrogating to himself His authority. Indeed, the extra-Biblical evidence promotes a respect for the evolution of human culture, rather than for a process that can deal with change only by way of violent destruction.

Much of my Biblical research on the hermeneutical and moral problems of the employment of the Hebrew Bible in favour of Zionism, counters the 'canonical' Zionist narrative that the Bible provides the legitimisation for the State of Israel. It exposes the pretence that Zionism was a religious enterprise by pointing to its secular, and mostly anti-religious origins. Its findings contradict the core ingredients of the established Zionist historical narrative and render it unsustainable academically. Since the hegemonic Zionist narrative provides the lens through which most of the Western world view the recent history of the region, any undermining of its truth-claims has significant implications. Such findings are not matters on which there are inevitably merely different opinions and viewpoints. Many of them belong to the realm of historical fact, attested to by a mountain of archival and other documentary evidence, much of it in Zionist sources, the ongoing publication of samples of which is an irritant to those hitherto embracing the conventional Zionist fabrication of the recent past. Exposing the untruths of fabricated nationalist ideologies is a step in the direction of establishing dialogue on a foundation of truths, however unpalatable.

While generations of religious people have derived both profit and pleasure from the retelling of the Biblical stories, the victims of the colonialist plunder are likely to be less sanguine in their attitude to the texts, and would welcome any attempt to distinguish between the apparent ethnocentricity of the God of Genesis to 2 Kings, and the paranaetic and political intentions of authors writing much later. A major epistemological question arises. Do texts which belong to the genre of folkloric epic or legend, rather than of a history which describes what actually happened, confer legitimacy on the 'Israelite' possession of the land, and on subsequent forms of colonialism which looked to the Biblical paradigm, understood as factual history, for legitimization later? Does a judgement which is based on the premise that the genre of the justifying text is history in that sense not dissolve when it is realized that the text belongs to the genre of *myths of origin*, which are encountered in virtually every society, and which were deployed in the service of particular ideologies?

REFERENCES

Abu Lughod, Ibrahim (ed.). 1987 (second ed.). *The Transformation of Palestine. Essays on the Origin and Development of the Arab-Israeli Conflict*. Northwestern University Press, Evanston.

Albright, William Foxwell. 1942. 'Why the Near East needs the Jews', *New Palestine* 32: pp. 12-13.

Albright, William Foxwell. 1957. *From the Stone Age to Christianity: Monotheism and the Historical Process*. Doubleday, New York.

Aruri, Naseer (ed.), *Palestinian Refugees and their Right of Return*, Pluto Press, London and Sterling VA.

Barclay, John M.G. 1996. *Jews in the Mediterranean Diaspora from Alexander to Trajan (323 BCE-117 CE)*. T&T Clark, Edinburgh.

Ben-Gurion, David. 1954. *The Rebirth and Destiny of Israel*. Philosophical Library, New York.

Ben-Gurion, David. 1971-72. *Zichronot* (Memoirs), Vol. 1-4, 'Am 'Oved, Tel Aviv.

Childers, Erskine B. 1987. 'The Wordless Wish: From Citizens to Refugees', in Abu-Lughod 1987: pp. 165-202.

Conrad, Joseph. 1989. *Heart of Darkness*. Penguin, London.

Dayan, Moshe. 1978. *Living with the Bible*. Jewish Publication Society, Philadelphia/William Morrow, New York.

Drinan, Robert F. 1977. *Honor the Promise: America's Commitment to Israel.* Doubleday, Cape Town, NY.

Ernst, Morris L. 1964. *So Far so Good.* Harper, New York.

Fisher, Eugene J, A James Rudin and Marc H Tanenbaum. 1986. *Twenty Years of Jewish-Catholic Relations.* Paulist, Maywah, N J.

Flapan, Simha. 1979. *Zionism and the Palestinians 1917-1947.* Croom Helm, London.

Flapan, Simha. 1987. *The Birth of Israel: Myths and Realities.* Croom Helm, London and Sydney.

Gafni, Isaiah M. 1997. *Land, Center and Diaspora. Jewish Constructs in Late Antiquity.* Sheffield Academic Press, Sheffield.

Gunn, David M. 2003. '"Next Year in Jerusalem": Bible, Identity, and Myth on the Web', in Thompson 2003: pp. 258-71.

Halbertal, Moshe. 1997. *People of the Book: Canon, Meaning, and Authority.* Harvard University Press, Cambridge, MA, and London.

Halpern-Amaru, Betsy. 1994. *Rewriting the Bible: Land and Covenant in Post-Biblical Jewish Literature,* Trinity Press, Valley Forge.

Herzl, Theodor. 1896. *Der Judenstaat. Versuch einer Modernen Lösung der Judenfrage.* Leipzig und Wien: M. Breitenstein's Verlags-Buchhandlung, *The Jewish State. An Attempt at a Modern Solution of the Jewish Question,* the seventh edition, revised with a foreword by Israel Cohen. Henry Pordes, London, 1993.

Herzl, Theodor. 1960. *The Complete Diaries of Theodore Herzl.* 5 vols (ed.) Raphael Patai, trans. by Harry Zohn. Herzl Press, New York.

Herzl, Theodor. 1983-96. Vol. I (1983) *Briefe und Autobiographische Notizen. 1886-1895.* Vol II (1983) *Zionistiches Tagebuch 1895-1899.* Vol. III (1985) *Zionistiches Tagebuch 1899-1904* (Vols I-III, ed. by Johannes Wachten *et al.*). Vol. IV (1900) *Briefe 1895-1898.* Vol V (1993) *Briefe 1898-1900.* Vol. VI (1993) *Briefe Ende August 1900-ende Dezember 1902.* Vol. VII (1996) *Briefe 1903-1904* (Vols IV-VII, ed. by Barbara Schäfer *et al.*) Propylaen Verlag, Berlin.

Herzl, Theodor. 2000 (third printing). *Altneuland. Old New Land,* translated from the German by Lotta Levensohn, republished by Markus Wiener Publishers, Princeton.

Hitchens, Christopher. 1988. 'Broadcasts', in Said and Hitchens (eds) 1988: pp. 73-83.

Jakobivits, Immanuel (Chief Rabbi). 1982. *The Attitude to Zionism of Britain's Chief Rabbis as Reflected in their Writings.* The Jewish Historical Society of England, London: Lecture delivered to The Jewish Historical Society of England in London, 9 May 1979

Khalidi, Walid. 2002. 'The Resolutions of the Thirty-Fourth World Zionist Congress, 17-21 June 2002', *Journal of Palestine Studies* 32 (Issue 125, Autumn): pp. 59-77.

Kidron, Peretz. 1988. 'Truth Whereby Nations Live', in Said and Hitchens 1988: 85-96.

Kimmerling, Baruch. 1983. *Zionism and Territory. The Socio-Territorial Dimensions of Zionist Politics.* Berkeley, University of California, Institute of International Studies (Research Series, No. 51).

Lemche, Niels Peter. 2000. 'Ideology and the History of Ancient Israel', *Scandinavian Journal of the Old Testament* 14 (no. 2): pp. 165-93.

Masalha, Nur. 1992. *Expulsion of the Palestinians: the Concept of 'Transfer' in Zionist Political Thought, 1882-1948.* Washington, D.C.: Institute for Palestine Studies.

Masalha, Nur. 1997. *A Land without a People. Israel, Transfer and the Palestinians 1949-96.* Faber and Faber, London.

Masalha, Nur. 2000. *Imperial Israel and the Palestinians: The Politics of Expansion, 1967-2000.* Pluto, London.

Masalha, Nur. 2003. *The Politics of Denial: Israel and the Palestinian Refugee Problem.* Pluto Press, London and Stirling VA.

Morris, Benny. 1987. *The Birth of the Palestinian Refugee Problem, 1947-1949.* Cambridge University Press, Cambridge.

Morris, Benny. 1990. *1948 and After: Israel and the Palestinians.* Oxford University Press, Oxford.

Morris, Benny. 1993. *Israel's Border Wars.* Oxford University Press, Oxford.

Morris, Benny. 1995. 'Falsifying the Record. A Fresh Look at Zionist Documentation of 1948', in *Journal of Palestine Studies* 24: pp. 44-62.

Morris, Benny. 1999. *Righteous Victims. A History of the Zionist-Arab Conflict 1881-1999.* Alfred A. Knopf, New York.

Pappé, Ilan. 1988. *Britain and the Arab-Israeli Conflict 1948-1951.* Macmillan, London.

Pappé, Ilan. 1992. *The Making of the Arab-Israeli Conflict, 1948-1951.* I B Tauris, London and New York.

Pappé, Ilan. 2002. The Post-Zionist Discourse in Israel: 1990-2001', *Holy Land Studies. A Multidisciplinary Journal* 1: pp. 9-35.

Prior, Michael. 1997. *The Bible and Colonialism. A Moral Critique.* Sheffield Academic Press, Sheffield.

Prior, Michael. 1998. 'The Moral Problem of the Land Traditions of the Bible', in Prior, Michael (ed.). *Western Scholarship and the History of Palestine*, Melisende, London, pp. 141-81.

Prior, Michael. 1999a. *Zionism and the State of Israel: A Moral Inquiry.* Routledge, London and New York.

The Biblical Narrative: Canonical 'Ancient Israel'

Prior, Michael. 1999b. 'The Bible and the Redeeming Idea of Colonialism'. *Studies in World Christianity* 5: pp. 129-55.

Prior, Michael. 2000. 'Zionist Ethnic Cleansing: the Fulfilment of Biblical Prophecy?' *Epworth Review* 27: pp. 49-60.

Prior, Michael. 2001. 'The Right to Expel: the Bible and Ethnic Cleansing', in Aruri 2001: pp. 9-35.

Prior, Michael. 2002. 'Ethnic Cleansing and the Bible: A Moral Critique', *Holy Land Studies. A Multidisciplinary Journal* 1: pp. 37-59.

Prior, Michael. 2003a. 'Speaking Truth in the Jewish-Christian Dialogue', in *A Faithful Presence. Essays for Kenneth Cragg*, ed. David Thomas and Clare Amos, Melisende, London, pp. 329-49.

Prior, Michael. 2003b. 'A Moral Reading of the Bible in Jerusalem', in Thompson 2003: pp. 16-45.

Said, Edward W and Christopher Hitchens (eds). 1988. *Blaming the Victims. Spurious Scholarship and the Palestinian Question*. Verso, London/ New York.

Schüssler Fiorenza, Elizabeth. 1999. *Rhetoric and Ethic. The Politics of Biblical Studies*. Fortress, Minneapolis.

Segev, Tom. 1986. *The First Israelis*. The Free Press, New York/Collier Macmillan, London.

Segev, Tom. 1993. *The Seventh Million. The Israelis and the Holocaust*. (trans. by Haim Watzan). Hill and Wang, New York.

Shahak, Israel. 1975 (2nd ed.). *Report: Arab Villages destroyed in Israel*. Shahak, Jerusalem.

Shapira, Anita. 1992. *Land and Power. The Zionist Resort to Force*. Oxford University Press, Oxford.

Shlaim, Avi. 1988. *Collusion across the Jordan. King Abdullah, the Zionist Movement, and the Partition of Palestine*. Columbia University Press, New York.

Thompson, Thomas L. 1974. *The Historicity of the Pentateuchal Narratives: The Quest for the Historical Abraham*. de Gruyter, Berlin/New York.

Thompson, Thomas L. (with the collaboration of Salma Khadra Jayyusi, eds). 2003. *Jerusalem in Ancient History and Tradition*. T & T Clark International, London.

Van Seters, John. 1975. *Abraham in History and Tradition*. Yale University Press, New Haven/London.

Weizmann, Chaim. 1949. *Trial and Error: The Autobiography of Chaim Weizmann*. Harper and Row, New York.

Whitelam, Keith W. 1996. *The Invention of Ancient Israel: The Silencing of Palestinian History*. Routledge, London and New York.

GENOCIDE, ETHNOCIDE, AND THE SITUATION OF MIDDLE EAST CHRISTIANS TODAY
Terry Tastard

The understanding of genocide has come to be seen in terms of what happened at the Holocaust. The Nazi campaign to exterminate the Jewish people is widely viewed as paradigmatic for genocide as a whole. Flowing from this development, other forms of persecution are not seen as leading to the potential extinction of large, clearly defined groups of people. Yet it can be shown that the campaign to define genocide as a crime under international law did look at genocide in broader terms before opting for a narrower definition. If we can recover this broader understanding of how a people can be brought to extinction, we might find that it provides an alternative approach to alterity and persecution. This in turn could shed light on the situation of Christians in the Middle East today.

THE HOLOCAUST AS GENOCIDE PARADIGM

The Holocaust occupies a special place in historical memory. What horrifies is not only the sheer scale of the killing—the scholarly consensus is that around 5 million Jews died—but also its systematically planned nature. This was not an evil act conceived in the heat of the moment, but a campaign of mass murder that required careful forethought, justifying propaganda, allocation of resources and finally an attempt at concealment. However, two problems arise if we see the Holocaust as the paradigm of genocide.

First, the Holocaust was an example of state violence. The machinery of the Nazi administration was directed towards this end. This remains the case regardless of where one stands on the issue of whether the genocide was consciously planned from the centre of

Nazi power ('intentionalist'), or emerged instead in an *ad hoc* way as the various levels of power sought to read the changing mood of Nazi leadership ('functionalist').

Second, the Holocaust was seen by its perpetrators as an act of racial cleansing inspired by the eugenics movement. It would not be going too far to say it was regarded as scientifically justified.

State Violence

A great deal of Holocaust historical research has gone into trying to establish who took crucial decisions. The research has been handicapped by Hitler's preference for subordinates who would read his mind and then act on their own initiative. He himself said, 'Where would I be if I could not find people to whom I can entrust work which I myself cannot direct, tough people of whom I know they take the steps I would take myself.'[1] There was considerable devolution of actual decision-making. The turning-point was Germany's initial success in its invasion of the Soviet Union in June 1941. Before then plans had been drawn up in Berlin to decimate and expel Slav and Jewish populations from occupied land, to allow Aryan resettlement. The invasion of the Soviet Union had been accompanied by *Einsatzgruppen* under Himmler who had the task of killing anyone behind the advancing front line who was deemed a threat to German hegemony. This included Communists, saboteurs and intelligentsia generally, but by far the largest number killed were Jews, shot by killing squads. Heydrich and others realised that this had inbuilt limitations and would only work in a war situation. On 31 July 1941, Heydrich was authorised 'to co-ordinate the activities of all the agencies of the German government ... and subsequently to submit "the overall plan" for the "final solution to the Jewish question".'[2] The process of planning the Final Solution began to filter through all levels of government. The Wannsee Conference of January 1942 which brought together the leading civil servants of important ministries with military planners, simply finalised this process—the conference lasted only 90 minutes. The machinery of state had swung behind the

---

1 Quoted in Christopher Browning, *The Origins of the Final Solution*, p. 243.
2 Christopher Browning, 'Wannsee Conference', *Encyclopedia of the Holocaust*, Vol. 4, p. 1591. Browning notes (p. 1592) that 8 of the 15 participants had PhD degrees.

genocide. It involved the military (not just the SS), the police, economic planners, transport authorities, and collaborating governments in occupied nations. The result was assembly line methodology, harnessed at the behest of the state to facilitate ethnic murder.[3]

This central, directing role of the state makes it difficult to compare the Holocaust with subsequent genocides. Certainly the Serbian assault on Bosnia-Herzegovina involved government complicity, but without establishing complete control over contested territory. As regards earlier genocides, the destruction of Armenians at the hands of the emerging Turkish state is widely held to be a genocidal action (a definition fiercely resisted by successive Turkish administrations). There are also partial parallels in some colonial campaigns such as the German campaign against the Herero in South West Africa. But the thoroughgoing nature of state support for the Holocaust together with the use of technology marks it off and makes comparisons difficult. The Holocaust was the product of a centralised state working through its institutions and reaching a high degree of consensus among those who operated the levers of power.

Racial and scientific justification

The racial nature of the Holocaust, and its accompanying scientific justification, also distinguish it from other genocides. The social Darwinist model was hugely influential in Germany in the inter-war period. There was a growing belief that the sciences could diagnose and treat both individuals and societies, and that a combination of eugenics and mass medicine could gradually eliminate the social causes of illness and deviance. There was a peculiarly German dynamic at work in this concern with national health. The influence of Darwinism in late nineteenth- and early twentieth-century Germany had popularised concepts of biological unity. The biological cell, the individual, the family and the community were seen as an interacting organic unity.[4] Around 1900 there had been huge sales of biological popularisations by Ernst Haeckel, which sought to show how Darwinism could provide

---

3   This has led some commentators to see the Holocaust as a product of modernity or as a crisis of modernity.
4   See Paul Weindling, *Health, Race and German Politics*, p. 30.

an objective basis for a national spirit. In the 1920s popular interest was maintained by mass education campaigns such as a health week, radio talks and the commissioning of films, some of them specifically eugenicist in approach.[5] Once the Nazis took power, films were used ruthlessly to condition the public to accept killing via euthanasia of the disabled and those with learning difficulties. The films presented the case for elimination by claiming scientific objectivity to stop such people from breeding. One film commentary on a psychiatric asylum said:

> All living things on this earth are engaged in a permanent struggle with the forces of nature ... only the strong will prevail in the end ... In the last few decades, mankind has sinned terribly against the law of natural selection. We haven't just maintained life unworthy of life, we have even allowed it to multiply.[6]

Anti-Semitism played a relatively minor role in early concepts of race hygiene, but by the mid-1920s the right-wing faction of the racial hygiene movement merged with National Socialism. By the time the Nazis came to power in 1933, thoughts of selecting and eliminating the unfit in society moved to the centre of agenda. The Nazi state presented itself as the biological will of the German people and stressed that the rebirth of the German people was linked to biological law.[7] In the words of Detlev Peukert, this 'eugenic, racial-hygiene variant of racism' provided the 'key component parts of the machinery of mass murder', especially by removing the ethical status of those affected.[8] When this was combined with long-standing anti-Semitism and a debased anthropology, the result was a vastly expanded and legitimised category of those to be eliminated for a perceived social good. Ideas of the nation as one organic whole were linked to the belief in human inequality and a desire to cleanse the gene pool of the German nation. The murder of the handicapped served as a model for the final solution and also allowed a progressive desensitisation of the nation and acceptance of what was being done. Hitler viewed the Jews as the embodiment of weakness and

---

5 Weindling, pp. 46-47 and 412-413.
6 Quoted in Burleigh, *Death and Deliverance*, p. 189.
7 Daniel Gasman, *Scientific Origins of National Socialism*, p. 172.
8 Detlev Peukert, 'The Genesis of the "Final Solution" from the Spirit of Science' in David Crew (ed.), *Nazism and German Society*, p. 290.

degeneracy, and made this prejudice a central component of Nazism. The initial successes of Hitler's armies in 1941 seemed to open the way to social engineering on a vast scale, with the Jews eliminated. His obsession with the issue chimed in with the spirit of the times. It fed the fear of those who viewed the German nation as a biological organism threatened with a kind of collective illness embodied in the physically, mentally or racially unfit. Hence the allegedly scientific justification for state intervention to purify the *Volk*. This was not science but scientism, a faux science. The Jews are not a race, but a people, and their diversity is striking. There is no Jewish gene. Nor, of course, was there any reason why they should be targeted and vilified.

On the one hand, the horror of the Holocaust makes it the epitome of genocide. Other situations of mass ethnic murder are measured against the Holocaust to see if they qualify as genocide. On the other hand, there is a tendency to see the Holocaust as unique, a special case. This paradox may mean that other situations of violent assault on particular peoples are depreciated in comparison with the Holocaust, the quintessential act of genocide. These other attacks on population groups may involve lesser numbers, may lack state involvement on a vast scale, or the racial element is missing.

Samantha Power, a Pulitzer prize winning chronicler of the American response to contemporary genocide has written: 'Perversely, America's public awareness of the Holocaust often seemed to set the bar for concern so high that we were able to tell ourselves that contemporary genocides were not measuring up.'[9] The result, she argued, has been a lack of American engagement with these more recent genocides. The American historian Peter Novick came to a similar conclusion. The Holocaust, he said, did not yield lessons, because 'making it the benchmark of oppression and atrocity works in precisely the opposite direction, trivializing crimes of lesser magnitude.' He believes that the talk of uniqueness and incomparability surrounding the Holocaust has promoted the evasion of moral and historical responsibility for subsequent acts of racial violence.[10]

To this we can add that there is a considerable body of literature mostly arguing for the uniqueness of the Holocaust.[11]

---

9 Samantha Power, *'A Problem from Hell'*, pp. 503-4.
10 Peter Novick, *The Holocaust and Collective Memory*, p. 14 and 15.
11 See, for example, S. T. Katz, *The Holocaust in Historical Context*, Vol. 1. For a survey of the debate, A S Rosenbaum (ed.), *Is the Holocaust Unique?*

Genocide, Ethnocide, and the Situation of Middle East Christians Today

To the extent that the above assessment is correct, the concept of genocide would not be applicable to the situation of Middle East Christians today. It is not a new Holocaust. More generally, it is not a situation of programmed mass murder. However, there is another way of understanding the plight of Middle East Christians, and it comes from the very processes that produced the concept of genocide.

THE DEFINITION OF GENOCIDE IN INTERNATIONAL LAW

The definition of genocide in international law came from the work of the Polish jurist Raphael Lemkin (1900-1959). He created the neologism from the Greek *genos*, people, and the suffix *–cide* as in homicide, suicide etc, with the first mention of *genocide* coming in his 1944 book *Axis Rule in Occupied Europe*. His humanitarian concern long predated the Nazi invasion of Poland. As a 21-year-old student at the University of Lvov he became interested in the annihilation of approximately one million Armenians by the Ottoman Empire during the First World War. He asked a law professor why a Turk responsible for many massacres had not been arrested after taking refuge in Germany and was surprised to learn that state sovereignty did not allow this. There was no international law to enable such an arrest.[12] Lemkin resolved to draft a law that would criminalize massacres of population groups and allow cross-border prosecution; and in 1933, by now a lecturer in comparative law and court prosecutor in Warsaw, he unsuccessfully proposed such a law to an international conference on criminal law in Madrid. He was sent by the Polish government in exile to the United States in 1941. In 1946 he served as an adviser to the United States government at the International Military Tribunal in Nuremberg. Through his lobbying at the IMT all twenty-four defendants were charged with conducting 'deliberate and systematic genocide, viz, the extermination of national and racial groups'. But to his disappointment the eventual convictions were on grounds of war crimes and crimes against humanity; there was no mention of genocide. Thereafter he

---

12 On the IMT, see Power, *'A Problem from Hell'*, pp. 49-50; on the Armenian genocide, pp. 15-21. Power says that Lemkin as a child 'had been oddly consumed by the subject of atrocity' (20). The Turk in question was the former interior minister Talaat Pasha; he was assassinated by Soghomon Tehlirian in March 1921 in Berlin. It was the reporting of this incident that drew the initial attention of Lemkin.

was a tireless lobbyist in the United Nations for genocide to be made a crime under international law. He worked virtually on his own.[13]

Lemkin shared Herder's belief that each group has something unique to contribute in the symphony of nations. In an unpublished autobiography he wrote:

> It became clear to me that the diversity of nations, religious groups and races is essential because every one of these groups has a mission to fulfil and a contribution to make in terms of culture. To destroy these groups is to oppose the will of the Creator and to disturb the spiritual harmony of mankind.[14]

To this whiff of German Romanticism he wedded the power of the law, to ensure that the variety of humanity was not stifled by mass murder.

Lemkin's concern clearly embraced both the specific reality of the Holocaust and the wider issues of how a people or a group could be extinguished. The issue was extinction of whole groups, which he saw could take a variety of forms. In his first draft of the convention on genocide submitted to the UN General Assembly, Lemkin had argued that genocide had two aspects, the biological and the cultural. The biological meant mass killings and prevention of births. The cultural aspect of genocide was caused by transfer of children from one group to another, by the destruction of a nation's intelligentsia, by the prohibition of the use of a national language, by the burning of books and the destruction of historical or religious monuments or their diversion to alien use.[15] Genocide, then, in his mind, has both biological and cultural aspects. Whether the biological aspect is always necessary for it to be genocide is not clear from his writings.[16] The

---

13 He first concentrated on the Latin American nations, who often worked as a bloc, and constituted 20 of the 51 members in 1946. After a breakthrough with them he recruited the support of the Indian government, then of the New York and Washington press. After that, he was supported by Jewish groups and by Christian groups in the United States.
14 Lemkin, *Totally Unofficial*, (unpub. autobiography) quoted in S L Jacobs, 'Genesis of the Concept of Genocide'.
15 Cooper, *Raphael Lemkin and the Struggle for the Genocide Convention*, p. 91.
16 Power says 'A group did not have to be physically exterminated to suffer genocide' (p. 43). But compare Dirk Moses, who concludes that according to Lemkin 'Genocide

definition eventually adopted by the United Nations on 9 December 1948 defined genocide in terms of extinction alone; the Americans, the British and the South Africans were all well aware that a wider definition on the lines proposed by Lemkin could leave them open to the charge of genocide. Lemkin conceded this excising of cultural genocide with great reluctance, 'despite the fact that he still attached the utmost importance to the issue.'[17]

The cultural aspect of extinction raises the possibility of understanding a group's plight in other ways than genocide. Is there room for understanding pathological persecution that threatens a group's survival even if it does not include mass homicide? I would suggest that the cultural aspect of extermination which was central to Lemkin's thinking offers us a critical tool in assessing the plight of Middle East Christians today. Before settling on the term *Genocide* he saw another word possibility, namely *Ethnocide*, and we could use this to denote the concept of erasing the identity and thus the survival of a national, ethnic or religious group.[18] The concept of ethnocide has several advantages. It can be applied where the violence inflicted on a minority does not amount to genocide, i.e. to attempted biological extinction, but where, nonetheless, the long-term survival of the group is at stake. In the situation of the Middle East, it is helpful in applying both to Israel and to Muslim-majority societies. Finally, it draws attention to the long-term effects of cultural attrition. As an exercise in the viability of the term it will be briefly applied to Turkey, Israel and Egypt, as test cases.

THE SITUATION OF MIDDLE EAST CHRISTIANS IN TERMS OF ETHNOCIDE: THREE STUDY CASES

A clear example from the edge of the region would be **Turkey**. The pressure on the Greek Orthodox community over the last 90 years has been unrelenting. To take just one category, Lemkin highlighted the alienation or destruction of religious property. One of the clearest examples here would be the closure of the Orthodox seminary and

---

possesses an irreducible biological core' ('The Holocaust and Genocide', p. 539).
17 Cooper, *Raphael Lemkin and the Struggle for the Genocide Convention*, p. 158-159.
18 Jacobs, 'Genesis of the Concept of Genocide', p. 100.

high school on the island of Halki in 1971 because of government regulations; despite a recent promise from the Turkish PM, nothing has happened to allow its re-opening. (This also impacts on another category by Lemkin, the suffocation of a group's intelligentsia or leadership, which is further endangered by the Turkish insistence that the Ecumenical Patriarch be chosen from those who are already Turkish citizens.) Patriarchate-owned properties have shrunk by almost 80 percent, from 8,000 in 1936 to 1,700 at present; 1,100 of the remaining 1,700 are not legally recognized and are especially vulnerable to seizure.[19] A vicious circle sets in: the government decrees that the Christian community in a place is too small to maintain the property, and takes it over for religious use. This in turn puts pressure on the remaining Christians. In the east of the country, the situation of the Syrian Orthodox community has also been precarious, with attempts in 2009 to seize the lands of the historic Mor Gabriel monastery near Kartmin. Catholics too have suffered. Despite a personal request from Pope Benedict XVI the Turkish government has decided that the only church in Tarsus, the city of St Paul's birth, will remain a government museum. It was confiscated by the Turkish government in 1943. In all some 200 properties, including orphanages and hospitals, were confiscated from the Catholic Church in the Ataturk era, and attempts at restitution are complicated by the fact that the Catholic Church has not been allowed legal status in Turkey. Although the reduction in the Christian population is due primarily to the Armenian massacres and the consequences of the disastrous Greek invasion in 1922, since then restrictions on the life of the Christian community have led to its near-extinction. In short, ethnocide in Turkey has been successful.

The claim that the Christian Arabs in **Israel** are flourishing—in effect, that there is no ethnocide—was recently made by the Israeli Ambassador to the United States. In an article appearing in the *Wall Street Journal* he contrasted the plight of Christians in Arab lands with their situation in Israel. He made the astonishing claim that 'Since Israel's founding in 1948, its Christian communities ... have expanded more than 1,000%.'[20] Presumably this is meant metaphorically, since if it were literally true Israel today would be a majority Christian country.

---

19 http://www.orthodoxytoday.org/articles5HelsinkiGreece.php.
20 Michael Oren, 'Israel and the Plight of Mideast Christians', *Wall Street Journal*, 9 March 2012 (online).

Genocide, Ethnocide, and the Situation of Middle East Christians Today

- In 1931, the Christian population of Mandatory Palestine was around 90,000;
- in 1961, the Christian population of Israel was estimated at 56,000;
- by 1987, some 95,000 (using the same borders at the 1961 figure).
- 1994 estimates give 114,000 Palestinian Christians in Israel;
- 2008: according to Wikipedia the overall Christian population in Israel is 153,000, i.e. all Christians, not Arabs alone, but the vast majority would be Arab.[21]

The figures reveal both attrition and survival. The drop between 1931 and 1961 shows that Palestinian Christians in Israel suffered along with other Palestinians in the war of 1948, when over 700,000 Palestinians became refugees, 50,000 of them Christians, more than one-third of all Christians within what had been British Mandatory Palestine.[22] In addition to those driven into exile there has been internal exile. For example, Arabs from villages around Nazareth took refuge in Nazareth itself, from which some of them could watch as Jewish settlers took over their homes and villages.[23] A comprehensive listing of Palestinian villages in Israel depopulated after 1948 lists 28 churches in the index; in many villages the church or mosque, tumbling into ruin, is the only substantial evidence of its previous inhabitants.[24]

On the other hand, the population figures also show recovery, despite high emigration rates enabled by the high standards of Christian education. We also know that there are flourishing Christian Arab institutions such as schools, colleges and community centres. Undoubtedly the ability of the churches to call international attention to prejudicial activities has helped protect the Christian population. The Christian Arabs of Israel have also been able to raise up their own

---

21 Colbi, *Christianity in the Holy Land*, pp. 111 and 188; Horner, *Guide to Christian Churches in the Middle East*, p. 107; Sabella, 'Socio-Demographic Characteristics ...', p. 33. The most recent figure given, from Sabella, presumably includes annexed East Jerusalem and surrounding territory, as it is based on Israeli official statistics.
22 O'Mahony, 'Church, State and the Christian Communities and the Holy Places of Palestine', p. 27.
23 Details in Ilan Pappé, *The Ethnic Cleansing of Palestine*, p. 153.
24 Walid Khalidi (ed.), *All That Remains*, p. 621.

leadership which has taken a prominent role in defending the rights of Arab people generally in Israel. This leadership is also able to dialogue with and speak for the Christian people of the Palestinian Authority. Arab-Israeli cultural institutions receive government funding, even if at a much reduced level compared with Jewish sectors.[25] The *Nakba* is in the past and this is not ethnocide.

However, there is more to be said. It is impossible to quantify the stifling effect of living as a second class citizen. Arab Christians in Israel share in the general situation of Israeli Arabs, what Ilan Pappé has called 'the illusion of inclusion'. The mechanisms are many and subtle. For example, 'only people who have served in the army are eligible for state benefits such as loans, mortgages and reduced university fees. There is also a close link between industry and security in the Jewish state, and many employers insist that potential employees have done army service, which means that significant sections (almost 70 per cent) of industry are closed to Palestinian citizens [i.e. of Israel]'.[26] A recently passed law says that a Palestinian Israeli marrying a Palestinian from the Territories must move there and cannot stay in Israel. There is the issue of building permits in Jerusalem, and the squeezing of the Arab population there. In addition there is a range of pressures that the Israeli government can bring on churches: taxation policy, visas, and the granting of diplomatic status to hierarchs—essential for passing checkpoints. The Christian presence is not being strangled, but it is tolerated rather than being completely free.

In **Egypt** Coptic Christianity is as Egyptian as the pyramids but faces increasing pressure from Islamism. A turning point in the recent era came when President Sadat, in the mid-1970s, turned to Islam to strengthen his position at a time of unrest and protest against his regime. At this time Islamic societies took hold of student unions and harassed Copt and moderate students on campuses. According to a recent history of Coptic Christianity, 'Mass media and pulpits became filled by Islamist voices espousing conspiracy theories about the Coptic Church.'[27] One of the effects of this was difficulty in obtaining permits

---

25 While Arab Israelis constitute 20 percent of the population, they receive, it is reported, only 3 percent of the funding of the Ministry of Culture and Sport: see http://www.ynetnews.com/articles/0,7340,L-4238139,00.html.
26 Ilan Pappé, *The Forgotten Palestinians*, pp. 63-66, quoting from p. 65.
27 Magdi Guirguis and Nelly van Doorn-Harder, *The Emergence of the Modern Coptic Papacy*, Vol. 3, p. 161. The rest of the information given here comes from pp. 163-

to build or repair churches, and this at a time when migration from the countryside to the cities had created urban communities where Christians badly needed new churches. Since then the building of churches—often illegal—or the expansion of monasteries has frequently led to clashes. Vigorous Coptic leadership, especially by the late Pope Shenouda, has resisted pressure on Coptic Christianity which would have marginalised it in national life. Shenouda himself was sent into external exile 1981-1985 by Sadat. But it is significant how often attacks on, or destruction of, Coptic religious sites take place. Three examples across the decades:

> 6 Nov 1972: Chapel built without permission at Khanqa near Cairo burnt by Islamist protestors. Christian homes and shops are destroyed in subsequent violence.
> 6 Jan 1980: On the eve of the Coptic Christmas, bombs explode in seven churches in Alexandria.
> 1 Jan 2011: A suicide bomber kills over 20 and wounds dozens at the al-Qiddisayn church in Alexandria.

In between these incidents were many more, and more have occurred since. A common thread was the slowness of the police and authorities to intervene and the reluctance to prosecute the perpetrators. It has also to be said that latterly there were Muslim protestors to join Copts in demonstrating against such acts of violence. However, the attacks on churches and monasteries are a classic pattern of ethnocide as defined by Lemkin. In the same category come other reports of abduction of women and forced conversions to Islam. Unlike Turkey, the pressure in Egypt comes not from centralised government policy but from Islamist pressure which likes to paint Coptic Christianity as an alien presence. Increasingly, violence against Copts has been triggered by 'rumors or inflammatory sermons', arousing ordinary people against their neighbours. The size of the Coptic population—around 10 percent—and the strength of its leadership means that it will not fade away. It is also defended by a moderate component within Egyptian Islam, and the even smaller secularist tendency. However, there is clearly a strong ethnocidal dynamic at work that would paint Coptic Christianity in terms of alterity, and would limit its ability to grow and

---

171, quoting later from p. 170.

thrive by denying it places of worship, threatening its freedom to gather and worship and by denying it opportunities to enrich its cultural life.

Conclusion

The concept of genocide sets the bar very high when it comes to proving the death of a people. The example of the Holocaust sometimes makes it harder to establish that a particular campaign of massacre is genocidal. That the concept is necessary, indeed essential in today's world is beyond dispute. However, there is also a need for an understanding of how a people can be harried towards extinction without genocide as such. Raphal Lemkin, the deviser of international law against genocide, saw such a need but was unable to formulate it properly before his early death. He was working towards an understanding of ethnocide, the march towards extinction of a people by the suffocation of their identity. The situation of Middle East Christians today illuminates what ethnocide could be like.

In closing, four differences between genocide and a putative concept of ethnocide need to be noted.

First, genocide nearly always needs central direction. The government or controlling forces in a society decide on extermination of a people and move towards this as a conscious decision. This can be case in ethnocide, as argued above with regard to Turkey, but it need not be so.

Secondly, it follows that genocide is intentional. Ethnocide, on the other hand can arise out of the dynamics of a particular society. It can result from communal tensions adroitly exploited, as in Egypt.

Thirdly, genocide can be prosecuted in a court of law. Individual acts of ethnocide might be punishable in local courts, but it is hard to conceive of an overarching international law, and indeed such a law might be too diffuse in its effects. Ethnocide can only be condemned in the court of world opinion.

Finally, in genocide the ultimate outcome is extinction. In ethnocide the outcome can be can be marginalisation as a people finds itself denied identity in the life of a nation. Accompanying this would be a perpetual state of unease, or anxiety, as the victims of ethnocide worried about the erosion of their place in the world. In the long term this must raise questions about their ultimate survival in their present setting. Genocide leads to extinction; ethnocide encourages emigration.

Bibliography

Christopher Browning, *The Origins of the Final Solution*, University of Nebraska Press, Lincoln, Nebraska and Jerusalem, and Yad Vashem, 2004.

Michael Burleigh, *Death and Deliverance: 'Euthanasia' in Germany c. 1900-1945*, CUP, Cambridge, 1994.

Saul Colbi, *Christianity in the Holy Land: Past and Present*, Am Hassefer, Tel Aviv, 1969.

David Crew, 'The Genesis of the "Final Solution" from the Spirit of Science' in David Crew, ed., *Nazism and German Society*, Routledge, London, 1994.

John Cooper, *Raphael Lemkin and the Struggle for the Genocide Convention*, Palgrave Macmillan, Basingstoke, 2008.

Daniel Gasman, *The Scientific Origins of National Socialism: Social Darwinism in Ernst Haeckel and the German Monist League*, Macdonald, London, 1971.

Magdi Guirguis and Nelly van Doorn-Harder, *The Emergence of the Modern Coptic Presidency*, Vol. 3, American University in Cairo Press, Cairo, 2011.

Norman Horner, *A Guide to Christian Churches in the Middle East*, Mission Focus, Elkhart, Indiana, 1989.

Steven L Jacobs, 'Genesis of the Concept of Genocide according to its Author from the Original Sources', *Human Rights Review* 2.1 (2002), pp. 98-103.

Steven Katz, *The Holocaust in Historical Context* Vol. 1, OUP, Oxford, 1994.

Walid Khalidi (ed.), *All That Remains: The Palestinian Villages Occupied and Depopulated by Israel in 1948*, Institute for Palestinian Studies, Washington DC, 1992.

Raphael Lemkin, *Axis Rule in Occupied Europe: Laws of Occupation, Analysis of Government, Proposals of Redress*, Carnegie Endowment, Washington DC, 1944.

A Dirk Moses, 'The Holocaust and Genocide' in Dan Stone (ed.) *The Historiography of the Holocaust*, Palgrave Macmillan, Basingstoke, 2004.

Peter Novick, *The Holocaust and Collective Memory: The American Experience*, Bloomsbury, London, 1999.

Anthony O'Mahony, 'Church, State and the Christian Communities of the Holy Places of Palestine' in Michael Prior and William Taylor, eds, *Christians in the Holy Land*, World of Islam Festival Trust, London, 1994.

Ilan Pappé, *The Ethnic Cleansing of Palestine*, Oneworld, Oxford, 2006.

Ilan Pappé, *The Forgotten Palestinians: A History of the Palestinians in Israel*, New Haven and London, Yale, 2011.

Samantha Power, *'A Problem from Hell': America and the Age of Genocide*, New Republic/Basic Books, New York, 2002.

A S Rosenbaum, *Is the Holocaust Unique?*, Westview Press, Boulder, CO, 2001 (3rd edn, 2008).

Bernard Sabella, 'Socio-Demographic Characteristics: Reality, Problems and Aspirations within Israel' in Michael Prior and William Taylor, eds, *Christians in the Holy Land*, World of Islam Festival Trust, London, 1994.

Paul Weindling, *Health, Race and German Politics between National Unification and Nazism, 1870-1945*, CUP, Cambridge, 1989.

CHRISTIANITY AND THE ISRAELI-PALESTINIAN CONFLICT
Rosemary Radford Ruether

Christianity comprises more than two billion people worldwide, divided between three historical groups of church families: Orthodox and Oriental Catholics (c. 218 million), Roman Catholics (1 billion) and Protestants, including Anglicans and Independents, (c. 800 million). Orthodox and Oriental Catholics are divided among a number of national and historical churches, while Protestants are fractured into hundreds of small and large church bodies. Increasingly there are deep ideological/theological divisions within and between these church bodies. Thus it is hardly to be expected that Christians would have a single perspective on the Israeli-Palestinian conflict.

This essay will discuss seven groupings of perspectives on this conflict. This will include Christian Zionism, its history in Britain and in the United States and its contemporary politics; critics of Christian Zionism from evangelical traditions; pro-Israel and increasingly critical views of Israel in mainstream Protestant churches; the developing views of the Vatican; Orthodox traditions, with particular attention to the views of the Orthodox in the Arab world and Palestinian Christians, both Palestinian intellectuals of Christian background; and Palestinian Christian theologians and church leaders.

CLASSICAL CHRISTIANITY

Classical Christianity embraced theoretically a religiously exclusivist universalism, while in practice various Christendoms, Christian ruled-empires or nations, were embraced. Christians in the first millennium believed that Israel as an elect nation had been superseded by the universal church, the 'New Israel' or elect people of God drawn from all nations. The promised land was the whole creation transformed into a redeemed and spiritualized 'new heaven and earth.' Palestine was venerated as the 'Holy Land' of Jesus' life, death resurrection and hence as a place of pilgrimage.

The Jews were seen as under divine reprobation for having failed to accept Jesus as their Messiah, condemned to wander the earth under the dominance of adversarial peoples. They were to be kept from political power and cultural dominance as an expression of God's wrath. Yet Christianity also taught that redemption was incomplete until the Jews converted to Christianity. This, it was believed, would happen 'in the last days' when Elijah returns, in preparation for the return of Christ, the Last Judgment and transformation of the world into the millennial Kingdom of God. In this classical Christian view there was no place for a nationalist restoration of the Jews to their ancient homeland.

Christian Zionism

This view began to be modified in the sixteenth and seventeenth centuries, particularly among English Calvinists. Protestants rejected allegorical for a literal, historical interpretation of the Bible. The promised land was seen as the actual land of Palestine, and the Jews the historical descendents of the elect people of Hebrew Scripture. At the same time the break up of Western Christendom into rival nations created a new nationalism in which the English, French and Spanish claimed to be the 'new Israel' as nations, rather than as an expression of a universal church. English Protestants particularly created a parallelism between the Jews as the original elect nation and themselves as new elect nation.

In this light the Biblical traditions of the fulfilment of God's promises of redemption were reinterpreted. Instead of nationalist Jewish hopes of redemption being superseded by the universal hopes of Christianity, it was believed that the fulfilment of national Jewish hopes must come first, to be then completed by those of Christianity. This meant that the Jews must first be restored to their ancient land, re-establish their rule over it and rebuild the temple. Only then would Christ return, and the final redemptive acts of history unfold, the resurrection of dead, the Last Judgment and millennial reign of the saints on earth. Some Christian Zionists assumed the Jews would be converted to Christianity before returning to Palestine, while for others this would happen only at the return of Christ.

Belief in the restoration of the Jews to Palestine was common among British evangelicals in the seventeenth century, particularly during the English Civil War, when millennialist thought abounded. One politician, Sir Henry Finch, called for the British government to aid the Jews to return to Palestine. Such ideas faded in the eighteenth century, but were revived in the early nineteenth century as Christian evangelicals sought to counteract Enlightenment rationalism.

The major formulator of a Christian Zionist premillennial dispensationalist theology was John Nelson Darby (1800-1882), founder of the Plymouth Brethren.

For Darby there are two separate covenants, one between God and Israel and the second between God and the Church. The first covenant has not been superceded, but was suspended while the Church carried out the conversion of the gentiles. But in the last days of world history, the covenant of God with the Jews will reassume its priority. The Jews then must return to Palestine, reassert their control of the whole of the promised land and rebuild the temple. In the final apocalyptic crisis, there will be a showdown with the evil powers of the world. Born again Christians will be 'raptured' into the heavens, while the battle of Armageddon is fought between the army of Christ and that of Satan. Once these evil powers are defeated, true Christians, which include 144,000 converted Jews, will descend from heaven and reign over a renovated earth. The return of the Jews to Palestine is the signal that these final events of world history are beginning to unfold.

Darby made six missionary journeys to the United States between 1840 and 1880 and promulgated these views among American evangelicals. The Scofield Reference Bible, the most popular Bible in the United States, disseminated these views through its notations, and evangelists, such as Dwight Moody, made it key to his understanding of the Bible. William Blackstone, author of the popular apocalyptic book, *Jesus is Coming* (1878) recruited 413 leading Americans to petition President Harrison to support a restored Jewish state in Palestine (Blackstone Memorial, 1891). Such efforts were indignantly rejected by

American Reform Jews at the time, as an effort to divert Jews fleeing from Russian pogroms from immigration to the United States.

In the nineteenth and twentieth centuries Christian Zionism came to play an influential role in the imperial designs of the British and then of the Americans. In 1839 evangelical social reformer, Lord Shaftesbury, called for the British government to aid the return of the Jews to Palestine. He also got Parliament to facilitate the founding of an Anglican Bishopric of Jerusalem, appointing a British Jewish convert, the Reverend Dr. Michael Solomon Alexander, as its first incumbent. Shaftesbury saw this as the means for spreading Christianity among the Jews, to prepare the way for the return of Christ.

In the Balfour Declaration (1917) in which the British announced their support for 'the establishment in Palestine of a national home for the Jewish people', and in the founding of the British Mandate for Palestine (1922), British leaders, Lord Balfour, Herbert Samuel, High Commissioner for Palestine, and Prime Minister Lloyd George, mingled what they saw of the advantages to the consolidation of British imperialism of supporting a British-dependent Jewish presence in Palestine with echoes of their Christian beliefs in a unique relationship between Jewish and British national election.

In the United States, a widely disseminated Christian Zionist premillennialist dispensationalism became muted in the first half of the twentieth century as evangelicals retreated from political involvement in the face of a regnant liberalism and secularism. But the establishment of the State of Israel in 1948 brought new faith that the prophesied events of the end of history were about to unfold. The greatly expanded power of Israel with the 1967 war confirmed these beliefs. In the 1970s a newly politicized Christian right movement began to see the possibilities of an alliance with a neo-conservativism, in reaction against the New Left of the 1960s, with its promotion of feminism, gay rights and criticism of American militarism and imperialism.

As liberal Christians became more critical of Israel, American Jewish establishment leaders began to explore an alliance with a newly empowered Christian right. This alliance between the Christian right, neo-conservatives and the American and Israeli Jewish leaders blossomed during the Reagan years. In retreat during the presidencies of George Bush Sr and William Clinton, it exploded into new dominance in American politics during the presidency of George

W Bush. This shift also reflects the increased militancy of Jewish fundamentalist settlers and the dominance of the Likud party over the Labor party in Israel.

This alliance between neo-conservatives, such as Donald Rumsfeld, Dick Cheney, Paul Wolfowitz and Richard Perle, Christian premillennialists, such as Jerry Falwell, Pat Robertson and Ed McAteer, and Jewish establishment leaders with ties to pro-Israel lobbying groups, such as AIPAC (American-Israel Political Affairs Committee) and MEMRU (Middle East Media Research Institute) represents a strange marriage of convenience. Beliefs that America must become a Christian nation and that the Jews in Israel are part of an apocalyptic scenario in which they will disappear into a Christian millennium are hardly acceptable to Jews in the US, Israel or elsewhere.

What unites the three groups is a devotion to a hard-line politics of expansionism in the State of Israel and to a vision of American economic and military world hegemony in which Israel plays a key supporting role. For the Christian Zionist premillennialists, Israel's return to the Promised Land means an exclusive right of modern Israeli Jews to the whole of Palestine, including the West Bank and Gaza, perhaps parts of Jordan, Lebanon and Syria. Palestinians, including Palestinian Christians, are infidels, who have no right to the land and should be expelled for exclusive Jewish rule. Any proposals to turn over land to the Palestinians in return for peace is a betrayal of this exclusive divine gift of the land to the Jews.

Citing Genesis 12:3 ('I will bless those who bless you and curse those who curse you'), the United States is seen as blessed as a world power through its support for exclusive rights of Jews to all of the 'promised land.' Christian Zionists also support the takeover of the Old City for exclusive Jewish residency and an eventual destruction of the Muslim sites of the Haram al-Sharif in order to build a Jewish temple on the site. That this establishment of expanded and exclusive Israeli power is for Falwell and others a mere transition to Jewish conversion to Christianity, the destruction of all remaining Jews in the battle of Armageddon and the reign of Christ is ignored in the light of the power and wealth such evangelicals mobilize for neo-conservative politics in the US and Israel here and now.

EVANGELICAL CRITICS OF CHRISTIAN ZIONISM

From the 1980s and particularly from 2000, with the consolidated alliance of the Christian Right, neo-conservatives and the Pro-Israeli Right in American politics, there has emerged an increasing critique of Christian Zionism and its political effects. American and British evangelicals, often those previously schooled in these views who have come to repudiate them, have taken the lead in this critique. Among the leading evangelical critics of Christian Zionism and its politics are Donald Wagner, author of *Anxious for Armageddon* (1995) and *Dying in the Land of Promise* (2003), Gary M Burge of Wheaton College and author of *Whose Land? Whose Promise?* (2003), and the Reverend Stephen Sizer, a British pastor and author of *Christian Zionism: Road Map to Armageddon* (2005).

These evangelical writers are responsible for making the history and theology of Christian Zionism better known among main-stream Protestant, Catholic and Orthodox readers, including Palestinian Christians, to whom its theology is bizarre and alien. These writers have carefully detailed how this view arose, what its ideas are and how it has become a political force today. But their purpose is to discredit it. While taking Biblical authority seriously, they seek to propose a different Biblical theology based on a God who supports all nations and peoples equally. They denounce a view of God as a tribal war God as incompatible with the teaching of Jesus.

These evangelicals are sympathetic to the Palestinians who they see as having been unjustly deprived of their lands and homes. Some kind of two-state solution allowing both Israel and the Palestinians to forge a peaceful coexistence is assumed by these writers. Wagner, Burge and others have developed alternative networks of Evangelicals, such as Evangelicals for Middle East Understanding, and have been behind major international conferences critical of Christian Zionism, such as the conference sponsored by the Palestinian Christian Liberation Theology Center, Sabeel, in Jerusalem in April of 2004, 'Challenging Christian Zionism: Theology, Politics and the Palestine-Israel Conflict.' In such conferences Christian Zionism is called a 'false ideology,' a 'heresy' and 'idolatry'.

Mainline Churches, Pro-Israel Views

In the aftermath of the Second World War, with the horrific revelations of the Nazi death camps, many mainline Christian bodies, both Protestant and Roman Catholic, sought to probe Christian responsibility for the atrocity and to reform Christian theology and pastoral practice to eliminate anti-Semitism. Some Christians felt the need to overcome any supersessionary relation of Christianity to Judaism, and to affirm the equal validity of both faiths as vehicles of redeeming relation to God. The extent to which any continued effort to convert Jews to Christianity should still be pursued proved controversial for many Christians. The views of such church bodies and theologians will be discussed primarily in terms of their implications for relationship to the Israeli-Palestinian conflict, rather than changes in Christian theology of Jewish-Christian relations.

Already in 1942 theologians Reinhold Niebuhr, Paul Tillich and William Albright had formed the Christian Council on Palestine to help Jewish refugees migrate to Palestine. Their view was primarily humanitarian. Jews were displaced and needed some place to settle and be secure from anti-Semitic hostility. The fact that Palestine, rather than some other land (such as the United States), was seen as the place for such secure residency reflected an assumption that Jews had a unique relation to this land as their historical homeland. Also Christians should repent of anti-Semitic hostility and thus owed Jews this help.

In the 1980s the development of Jewish-Christian dialogue suggested a deeper revision of the theology of Jewish-Christian relations to purge Christian theology of anti-Semitism. Jewish spokesmen at these dialogues generally insisted that Jews are not just a religious community, but a nation and so have a necessary relation to a Jewish nation state, so anti-Zionism is anti-Semitism. Thus many Christians involved in the dialogues felt they should accept some unique relationship of Judaism to the State of Israel. Several Christian theologians emerged who supported this view that anti-Zionism is anti-Semitism and hence Christianity must support a Jewish state as integral to the Jewish faith.

Among these theologians are husband and wife couple, Roy and Alice Eckhardt, Paul Littell and Paul Van Buren. The Eckhardts claimed that all people have a right to security within a state of their own. Any denial of this for Jews would be a continuation of the Christian view that the Jews are reprobate and should be a wandering stateless people. Palestinian rights to a state are ignored by claiming that Palestinians already have a state in Jordan and Palestinian Israelis already have equal citizenship rights in Israel. Paul Littell takes the view that Jewish election and God's gift to them of the Promised Land give Jewish unique rights to a Jewish state, different from any other nation. The Palestinians are ignored.

Paul Van Buren attempts a more radical revision of Jewish-Christian relations. God's election of the Jews is the only covenant of God with an elect people and is eternal and unchangeable. The election of the Church is dependent and auxiliary to the election of the Jews, for the purpose of extending that election to the conversion of the gentiles. Jesus is not the Jewish Messiah, but simply the embodiment of the covenant of God with Israel for the gentiles. Israel, Van Buren believes, has a unique religious witness to the nations. This means that it should not be a secular state, but one governed by the Torah. Christians have a responsibility to the Jews to encourage them to be Torah observant and also to defend the state of Israel against its enemies. The Arab world is responsible for the Palestinian refugees and should integrate them into their societies. They have no claims within Israel, for Van Buren.

Although Van Buren's more radical revision has not caught on, there remains within the theology of Jewish-Christian dialogue a general assumption that God's gift of the Promised Land exclusively to the Jews means the Jews have a right to a Jewish state, also that Christian guilt for the Holocaust means Christians should be uncritical of this state, supporting it as a necessity for Jewish security against further outbreaks of anti-Semitism. Many Christian pastors and theologians, having spent many years trying to amend their world views through such dialogue, are reluctant to learn much about the Palestinian plight lest any attention of Palestinian grievances sour their relations with their Jewish colleagues. In effect, fear of being called anti-Semitism causes many Western Christians to either be silent on the Palestinians or to mute any criticism of Israel.

An example of such pro-Israel Christian theology of dialogue was the address of Rowan Williams, Archbishop of Canterbury, delivered by a proxy at the Fifth Sabeel conference in April, 2004. In this address

Israel as the covenanted people with God is called to be a paradigmatic people for all nations who exemplify what it means to be obedient to God and just toward one another. The State of Israel is described as the needed homeland for this people, 'the sole place where the Jewish people have a guaranteed place.' Rowan calls on Israelis to better exemplify this calling to obedience and justice by being more just to the people around them (i.e. the Arab states around Israel) as well as to the 'stranger in their midst'. Palestinians are unnamed and their rights to a state within Palestine are ignored. This address created great indignation among both Palestinian Christians and Western Christians with a more sympathetic view of Palestinian rights at the conference. Christian Palestinian civil rights lawyer, Jonathan Kuttab, wrote an extended critique of the address.

From the 1980s into the first decade of the twenty-first century, Christian denominational views of the Israel-Palestinian conflict evolved from a pro-Israel view based on Jewish election, God's gift of the Promised Land, need for refuge from anti-Semitism and compensation for Christian guilt, to one that sought to balance Israel's right to security with the rights of Palestinians to a state. These statements become less Biblical and theological and more based on a calculus of social justice due all people equally. Both Jews and Palestinians have historical roots and affinities with the land of Palestine. Both have suffered injustice. There needs to be some way to 'balance' the claims of each, to give each a secure place where their civil and economic needs can be met, where reconciliation and peaceful co-existence can be forged.

These evolving perspectives of mainline Protestants will be illustrated through the development of the statements of the World Council of Churches. The World Council of Churches, and various Christian denomination bodies, were involved in refugee work with Palestinians from 1948, but were reluctant to propose political solutions, such as a Palestinian or a bi-national state, lest they be prevented by the Israeli government from giving humanitarian aid in the camps.

These limitations began to shift after 1967 as Israel occupied the West Bank and Gaza. This occupation came to be seen increasingly as unjust. At the same time the PLO emerged as the political representative of the Palestinians, and the Middle Eastern Council of Churches was created as a vehicle for Arab Christians to speak for themselves. Moreover the politics of the WCC, influenced by liberation theology, leaned more to the side of supporting the political rights of colonized and oppressed peoples to struggle for their liberation.

In 1969 the student arm of the WCC, the World Student Christian Federation, recognized the PLO, the first Christian international body to do so. That same year the WCC's body on Inter-Church Aid, Refugee and World Service, declared that the Palestinians had an equal right to a state, along with the Jewish State of Israel. By failing to recognize Palestinian rights to self-determination, along with the rights of Israel, 'injustice has been done to the Palestinian Arabs by the great powers and this injustice should be redressed.'

In 1974 the WCC made explicit its view that guarantees of the existence and secure borders of the State of Israel should be 'balanced' with affirmations of the rights of Palestinians to self-determination. 'What we desire is equal justice for both Palestinian people and Jewish people in the Middle East.' This has remained the view of the WCC. Its statements have also been models for those of other world Protestant bodies, such as the Lutheran World Federation and the Alliance of World Reformed Churches, as well as national denominational bodies.

Thus mainline Protestant Churches have come to assume that the framework for a just peace is a two-state solution with a Palestinian sovereign state within the 1967 borders, a sharing of Jerusalem as the capital of both nations, the return of refugees or compensation for loss or damage to their property and the dismantling of the settlements. The chief changes in WCC and other mainline Protestant statements has been increasingly sharp criticism of Israel's violations of Palestinian human rights and their continued promotion of settlements, closures, targeted assassinations, the building of the 'wall of separation' and other such impediments to negotiating a just settlement. In 2004-5 some denominations, such as the Presbyterians and United Church of Christ, also began to suggest that economic pressure in the form of economic boycotts might be exercised to pressure Israel to make a just settlement of the conflict.

THE VATICAN

The Second Vatican Council's (1962-65) 'Statement on the Relationship to Non-Christian Religion' declares that God's election of the Jews is the root into which the Gentile Church as been engrafted and that this covenant has not been rescinded. Any collective guilt of the Jews for Jesus' death is repudiated and anti-Semitism condemned. This laid the basis for Catholic-Jewish dialogue institutionalized in 1970 with the Catholic-Jewish Liaison Committee. However, the Vatican has also insisted on separating religious relation to Judaism from political relation with the state of Israel. It has particularly expressed concern for equal access to the holy places in Jerusalem for all three religious faiths.

The Vatican has also maintained major institutions that support Palestinian human rights. The Pontifical Mission for Palestine, established in 1949, oversees a large number of schools and charitable works on a non-sectarian basis. In 1982 and again in 1988 the Vatican received Yassir Arafat as the representative of the Palestinian people. After the second meeting the Vatican affirmed that the Palestinians and the Israelis 'have an identical fundamental right to their own homeland in which they could live in liberty, dignity and security, in harmony with neighbouring people.' This same view of parallel rights was affirmed by the US Bishop's Conference in 1989, stating that the Palestinian homeland should have 'sovereign status recognized by Israel.'

The Vatican delayed granting full diplomatic recognition to Israel on the grounds that there were not yet secure borders for both states. After the signing of the Oslo Accords between the PLO and Israel in 1993, which appeared to grant such a secure homeland for the Palestinians, the Vatican signed a 'fundamental agreement between the Holy See and the State of Israel', focusing on religious freedom to be upheld by both. In 1994 this agreement was balanced by establishing official relations with the PLO. As hopes for a just peace have faded, the Vatican has joined with the World Council of Churches and the Lutheran World Federation to denounce Israeli violence and repression of Palestinians. Palestinian delegate to the Holy See, Afif Safieh, says 'the Pope's views on the Middle East always receive much attention and approval from the Arab media.' Particularly with his strong opposition to the American-led war against Iraq, Safieh claims the Pope 'has saved the future of Christian-Muslim relations.'

The Orthodox Churches and Arab Christians

The Orthodox Churches, many of them members of the World Council of Churches, have generally followed similar views to those of the WCC in upholding equal rights of Palestinians to a secure state. Since Greek Orthodoxy is the historical majority Church in Palestine and holds large properties there, it has a particular concern for the protection for these properties. At the same time the Greek Patriarch of Jerusalem has been faulted by other Palestinian Christians for allowing Greek Orthodox properties to be sold to Israelis.

Other Orthodox leaders, such as Patriarchy Alexy II of Moscow and all Russia, has joined his voice with other Christian bodies in denouncing the violence against both Jews and Palestinians in the second Intifada. The Holy Land is described as a place of many ethnic groups and all three religions, Christianity, Judaism and Islam. 'One national or religious group cannot prevail in this sacred land. The Holy Land must become a hospitable home for everyone.' The Patriarch called for the world community (the Russian Federation, the United States, the United Nations and the European Union) to become involved in stopping the bloodshed and restoring negotiations for a peace.

Among Middle Eastern Christians, the Orthodox Youth Movement played a major role in revitalizing these churches and linking them with international bodies, such as the WCC. Metropolitan George Khodr, one of the founders of this movement and its general secretary for many years, helped organize the 1967 statement by Middle Eastern theologians, 'What is required of the Christian Faith concerning the Palestine Problem.' The perspective of this statement is one of an inclusive universality. Christians are called to be witnesses to God's salvific love for all human beings. So they must reject any nationalism based on religious, ethnic or cultural exclusivism.

Separation of religion and state is a primary means for distinguishing religious and political allegiances and thus allowing for equal citizenship of people of all religions. Both Israel as a Jewish state and Islamic states are condemned. Zionism and Muslim nationalism are seen as parallel distortions of monotheistic religions into religious states. Secular, pluralistic states are necessary so Christians, Jews and Muslim can live together as equal citizens. Jews in Israel are called upon to overcome racism and to affirm the universal vocation of Judaism. Palestinian refugees who have been thrown out of their homes should be integrated into Israeli society and reparations made for the damages they have suffered. All inhabitants of Palestine should be considered full and equal citizens. Thus the Middle Eastern Christian statement follows the lines of early PLO views that Palestine should become one secular pluralistic state for all its citizens.

Palestinian Christians

Palestinian Christians, like other Christians in the Arab world, have historically been a minority religion in Islamic societies. Unlike Western Christians, they have not lived in Christian-ruled societies since the seventh century. In modern times they have been strong supporters of a secular Pan-Arabism. All religions should be equally respected, but political status should be separated from religion.

Palestinian Christians are generally well educated and urbanized. They have benefited from the many schools which Western Churches, Protestant and Catholic, have founded in the Holy Land, as well as from cultural ties to Europe and the United States. Many have been educated in the West. Afif Safieh, for example, came from a cultured and well-to-do Catholic family from West Jerusalem. He was educated at the French College des Frères in English, French and Arabic, and then at the University of Louvain, Belgium.

Yet these cultural ties have facilitated immigration, scattering Palestinian Christians around the world. Today Palestinian Christians in Israel and Palestine have decreased to under 2 percent, raising fears of the disappearance of indigenous Christianity from the Holy Land.

Christians have been disproportionately represented among Palestinian intellectuals. Edward Said, professor of literature at Columbia University in New York for many years, has been an outstanding example of such a critical intellectual, notable for his sharp criticism of Western 'orientalism' and indefatigable defender of Palestinian human rights. But it is hard to trace particular Christian influences on the thought of such intellectuals, who tend to be predominately secular, and even somewhat disgusted with the spectacle of Christian competition against one another in Jerusalem. Their pan-Arabism and support for a secular nationalism of equal citizenship follows the general views of Arab Christians, related more to the social location of Arab Christians as a minority group than to Christian tradition.

However, there has also emerged a significant sector of Palestinian Christian theologians and pastors who have defined a distinctively Palestinian contextual theology. Among these are Naim Ateek, Anglican priest and founder of the Sabeel Center for a Palestinian Ecumenical Christian Liberation theology, Mitri Raheb, pastor of Christmas Lutheran Church in Bethlehem, Munib Younan, Bishop of Jerusalem of the Evangelical Lutheran Church of Jordan, and Elias Chacour, Melkite priest and creator of the Mar Elias schools in Ibillin, Israel.

These Palestinian Christians articulate an attractive vision of inclusive universalism. God is seen as the God who loves and seeks the wellbeing of all peoples. God speaks through all religions, although, in practice, these theologians are primarily concerned with the three Abrahamic faiths, Judaism, Christianity and Islam. A God of exclusive nationalism who chooses one people against others is denounced as a tribal idol. Palestinian Christians are called to reject the temptation to hatred of Jews because of the injustices they have suffered and to steadily insist on the equal humanity of Jews and Palestinians who must learn to respect and love one another as members of one extended family.

The Jerusalem Sabeel Document, 'Principles for a Just Peace in Palestine-Israel' (2004) articulates this Palestinian Christian vision for a just peace. Theologically this vision is based on a universal God who loves all people equally and demands that justice be done between them as the basis for true peace. The woundedness of both peoples should be acknowledged, the Holocaust in the case of the Jews and the 'catastrophe' by which Palestinians have been displaced from their land and kept under harsh military rule in the case of the Palestinians.

The document supports a two-state solution with a sovereign, viable and democratic state of Palestine on the whole of the Gaza Strip and the West Bank including East Jerusalem. The Jewish settlements in the occupied territories must become part of Palestine, and Palestinian refugees must be guaranteed the Right of Return. Once these two sovereign states are established and the two peoples become used to working together as equals, perhaps some larger federation between them and with neighbouring states could develop.

Our vision involves two sovereign states, Palestine and Israel, who will enter into a confederation or even a federation, possibly with neighbouring countries and where Jerusalem becomes the federal capital. Indeed the ideal and best solution has always been to envisage ultimately a bi-national state in Palestine-Israel where people are free and equal, living under a constitutional democracy that protects and guarantees all their rights, responsibilities and duties without racism or discrimination. One state for two nations and three religions.

This vision has been further expanded and reaffirmed in the *Kairos Palestine* document issued by an ecumenical group of Palestinian Christian leaders in December, 2009. This document concludes with the visionary statement: 'In the absence of all hope, we cry out our cry of hope. We believe in God, good and just. We believe that God's goodness will finally triumph over the evil of hate and death that still persisting in our land. We will see here "a new land" and "a new human being", capable of rising up in the spirit of love for each one of his or her brothers and sisters.'

BIBLIOGRAPHY

Naim Ateek, *Justice and Only Justice: A Palestinian Theology of Liberation*, Orbis Press, Maryknoll, NY, 1989.

Naim Ateek and Michael Prior, *Holy Land, Hollow Jubilee: God, Justice and the Palestinians*, Melisende, London, 1999.

Gary M Burge, *Whose Land, Whose Promise: What Christians are Not being Told about Israel and the Palestinians*, Pilgrim Press, Cleveland, OH, 2003.

Elias Chacour, *Blood Brothers: A Palestinian Struggle for Reconciliation in the Middle East*, Kingsway Publications, Eastbourne, 1985.

Larry Elkin, *Enduring Witness: The Church and the Palestinians*, WCC, Geneva, 1985.

Herzel Fishman, *American Protestantism and the Jewish State*, Wayne State University, Detroit, 1973.

George E. Irani, *The Papacy and the Middle East: The Role of the Holy See in the Arab-Israeli Conflict*, Notre Dame University Press, Notre Dame, IN, 1986.

Michael King, *The Palestinians and the Churches, 1948-56*, WCC, Geneva, 1981.

Andrej Kreutz, *Vatican Policy on the Palestinian-Israeli Conflict: The Struggle for the Holy Land*, Greenwood Press, NY, 1990.

Jonathan Kuttab, 'Open Letter to ArchBishop Rowan Williams', www.FOSNA.

Presbyterian Church-USA: 'Mission Responsibility through Investment', www.pc-usa: Social Justice.

Mitri Raheb, *I am a Palestinian Christian*, Fortress Press, Minneapolis. MN, 1995.

Rosemary and Herman Ruether, *The Wrath of Jonah: The Crisis of Religious Nationalism in the Israeli-Palestinian Conflict*, Fortress, Minneapolis, MN, 2002, 2nd edition.

Russian Orthodox Church News: 'Statement by Patriarch Alexy II of Moscow and all Russia and the Holy Synod of the Russian Orthodox Church on the Situation in the Middle East', www.russian-orthodox-church.org.ru/ne204052.htm.

Sabeel Document: 'Principles for a Just Peace in Palestine-Israel' 2004, www.FOSNA

Afif Safieh, 'Interview: God and I', *St Anthony's Messenger* March, 2004, pp. 6-8.

Edward Said, *The Question of Palestine*, Vintage, London, 1992, 2nd edition.

Regina Sharif, *Non-Jewish Zionism: Its Roots in Western History*, Zed, London, 1983.

Stephen Sizer, *Christian Zionism: Road Map to Armageddon*, Intervarsity Press, Downers Grove, IL, 2005.

Rowan Williams, Archbishop of Canterbury, 'Holy Land and Holy People', www.archbishopofcanterbury.org.

Munib Younan, *Witnessing for Peace: In Jerusalem and the World*, Fortress Press, Minneapolis, MN, 2003.

Kairos Palestine Document, December 11, 2009, Friends of Sabeel, North America, PO Box 9186, Portland, OR 97207.

HEALTH CARE IN THE OTTOMAN HOLY LAND AND MOUNT LEBANON PRIOR TO WESTERN PROTESTANT MEDICAL MISSIONARY ENTERPRISE

Ramsay F Bisharah

INTRODUCTION

In the early sixteenth century in the year 1516 the Ottoman Turks occupied the Holy Land releasing it from the rule of the Mamluks and for nearly four hundred years ruled it in a most stifling, restrictive, and stagnating fashion. Although the Ottoman province of the Holy Land *per se* exhibited a rather mediocre demographic and socio-economic growth and development best demonstrated during the reign of Sultan Suleiman the Magnificent (1520-1566), Jerusalem, in particular, underwent an upsurge in construction and development for both secular and especially religious and sacred purposes and motives. However, by the end of the seventeenth century, the Ottoman Empire, as a whole, 'The Sick Man of Europe' as it was to be called, began to rapidly decline and the process of this decline adversely affected the standard of what heretofore had been an extremely mediocre, substandard, and unremarkable medical care system in the Holy Land and beyond.[1]

Even immediately prior to the advent of Western medical missionary and philanthropic intervention in the Ottoman Holy Land and Mount Lebanon in the late eighteenth and early nineteenth century (by Britain, continental Europe and America), medical care in this region was most notable for its abysmal standard or its blatant absence.[2]

---

1 Amar, Zohar and Lev, 'Efraim An Early Glimpse at Western Medicine in Jerusalem 1700-1840: The Case of The Jews and The Franciscans' Medical Activity', *Vesalius* XI, 11, 2005, pp. 81-87, p. 81.
2 Khairallah, Amin A, 'A Century of American Medicine in Syria', *Annals of Medical History* Vol. 1, 1939, p. 460.

The first ever reported observations and remarks which were noted concerning the medical care system in the Holy Land under the sterile rule of the Ottomans came from a lay French pilgrim named Monsieur Constantine Francois Volney. This lay French pilgrim visited the Holy Land in 1785 at which time, although not a physician by profession, he did describe the standard of medicine in Egypt and Syria in what was considered at the time to be drastic, radical, and controversial terms; although as it turned out, he was fortuitously very near to the sad truth: he wrote in his personal notes the following profound words: 'Scarcely can we meet with one of the latter [physician] who knows how to bleed with a fleam; when they have ordered a cautery, applied fire, or prescribed some common recipe, their knowledge is exhausted; and consequently the valet de chambre of an European is consulted as an Esculapius; where indeed should physicians be formed, since there are no establishments of the kind?'[3]

Reviewing such bare-knuckle, aggressive remarks and humiliating observations concerning the medical care system of these times in the Holy Land only serves to re-emphasise how dismal and substandard it was.

A Rabbi named Rafael Malki (d. 1702) portrayed yet another ghastly and harsh description of the this very medical system and the physician's status in seventeenth-century Jerusalem. An astonishing and bewildering 150 years before Titus Tobler's visit (on whom see below) it sorrowfully and profoundly indicated that, within the duration of 150 long years of stagnating Ottoman rule, the medical care system had hardly made any appreciable or remarkable advancement which is again yet another most devastating indictment. Rabbi Malki comments in very poignant words: 'A physician in Jerusalem is hard to find, a knowledgeable one you cannot find at all, others that are not learned or knowledgeable are everywhere. This is because medical knowledge of the eastern countries, the Turkish Empire ... is poor ... This is why it is impossible to be a physician in Jerusalem—its inhabitants and its scholars do not believe in real medicine and its practice. In their eyes, anyone who claims to be

---

3   Amar, Zohar and Lev, Efraim, 'An Early Glimpse ...', p. 81, and Lev, Efraim, and Amar, Zohar, 'The Turning Point from an Archaic Arab Medical System to an Early Modern European System in Jerusalem according to the Swiss Physician Titus Tobler (1806-1877)', *Canadian Bulletin of Medical History* Vol. 21: 1, 2004, pp. 159-180, p. 162.

a doctor and a real physician are equal ... In these circumstances, and considering the level of the physicians in the city, one must not turn to any of the doctors of Jerusalem, and whoever follows their instructions is a killer ... Better that such doctors be absent than present, and rather ... leave the sick in God's hands than place them in the hands of such a one.'[4]

Accordingly, it is quite apparent that during the long and tiresome reign of the Ottomans in the Holy Land the prevalent medical care system in the province comprised a hybrid system combining ancient Hippocratic Galenic-grounded principles and fundamentals with the somewhat slightly improved medieval Islamic medicine.[5]

Yet another early coverage of the prevalent medical system in the Ottoman Holy Land came from the outstanding, comprehensive and factual reports of the world-famous Swiss physician Titus Tobler. Dr Titus Tobler was born in 1806 in the village of Wolfhalden in the Swiss canton of Appenzel. He pursued the study of medicine and practised the discipline in Zurich, Vienna, and Wurzburg (Germany) and by 1827 was awarded his medical doctorate.

Dr Tobler was a man of extraordinary and rare qualities possessing extremely diverse capabilities and expertise besides his medical knowledge and skills. Thus the distinct importance and great value of his expert documentation on observations, interviews, and eye-witness experiences gained in the Holy Land.

His rare aptitude to research in different locations and critical objective observations enabled Tobler to review the facts he observed diligently and accurately and to publish his conclusions with an error-free accuracy unrivalled for the period.

In Switzerland he delved into politics, becoming a member of parliament, availing him to directly concern himself with communal affairs of his immediate society; he acted for a number of professional societies, personally forming a prominent one to fight against cholera.[6]

Tobler spent his life practising medicine and in addition his linguistic skills allowed him to become an outstanding author. Dr Tobler died in Munich in 1877 and was laid to rest in a cemetery in

---

4   *Ibid.*, p. 163.
5   *Ibid.*, p. 159.
6   *Ibid.*, p. 160.

his beloved native village. His distinctive and superior legacy is made up of his precious contributions to personal and expert knowledge of the Holy Land in the nineteenth century. He is sometimes labelled as the 'father of German scholarship in the Holy Land'.

This work is based on the details drawn from his multiple visits and pilgrimages to the Holy Land in 1835, 1845-6, 1857, and 1865 respectively, with each visit resulting in expert articles and books reporting on his observations, researches, studies and scholastic experiences, especially his writings and findings on the situation and status of the medical care system in the Holy Land in the nineteenth-century as witnessed first hand by a distinguished physician with standard European knowledge and skills.

His first visit to the Holy Land in 1835 was taken as a holy pilgrimage and out of personal curiosity. His second journey in 1845-6 was purposely directed at studying the Holy Land, and concentrating mainly on the Holy City, Jerusalem.

He lodged with Dr Simon Fraenkel (1809-1880), a native of Germany and the first Jewish physician of the Jewish community in Jerusalem, sent on his mission by the Jewish millionaire and philanthropist Sir Moses Montifiore. During this stay the two physicians became good friends resulting in Tobler's reports being extremely reliable on account of the first hand experiences he witnessed and observed. In 1853, Dr Tobler put pen to paper and published his first document entitled: 'Recollection of Jerusalem', a report based on his earlier pilgrimage to the Holy City. In one chapter Tobler provided a detailed description of the various medical institutions in Jerusalem. By 1856 he had published a second document entitled: 'A Description of Medical Conditions in Jerusalem'. This particular document presents a distinctive and remarkable account and picture of medical care in the Holy Land. Written by a notable and outstanding physician, the main topics expertly depict the true prevailing medical conditions along with the major diseases and problematic medical conditions, injuries and disabilities.

His detailed accounts and relevant information provide full details of the common medical methods and procedures practised, local traditional cures, medicinal substances, medical facilities, primitive medicaments, birth rates, death rates, and family dynamics.

Thus it is in all a near complete and comprehensive description of the medical system as witnessed by an expert immediately prior to the advent of modern Western missionary medicine to the Holy Land.[7]

Dr Tobler even describes personal meetings and interviews with many local healers of various faiths, Muslims, Jews, and Christians, thus witnessing a diversity of medical procedures and treatments commonplace among the different inhabitants. He was stunned and astounded by their medical methods and techniques employed to remedy various ailments and complaints. He was shocked and promptly condemned an old Jewish woman for the treatment she administered to a patient with an eye inflammation on account of the severe damage she was causing in the process.

Another method of treatment popular at the time was the practise of bloodletting. He reported witnessing Jewish, Muslim, and Christian healers piercing open blood vessels using a variety of devices, implements, and other special instruments.

When these medical practices were first used, it was reported that such treatments were administered in the main streets in ignorance of the dire dangers of infection or contamination; however, later on such treatment began to be administered indoors. Such remedies were usually provided gratis for poor patients and for small fees for those able to pay.

Barbers, as self appointed 'glorified surgeons' practised bloodletting procedures or rather blood sucking, for they sometimes used medicinal leeches for this process.

Tobler carefully described the procedures practised by several Arab and Jewish barbers; he witnessed them scratching the skin, placing the base part of an animal's horn over the wound, and then sucking the blood from the cut in the top of the horn as though it was a straw. In this way, they avoided any contact with human blood. This suction procedure would last some thirty minutes in duration. During this procedure the barbers would use a piece of leather covering the suction hole to preserve the vacuum pressure allowing them a period of respite so they could breathe between each sucking action. This technique was commonly performed on the arms and the neck of the patient. Such a procedure, he related, was once upon a time used in Switzerland in some health spa clinics.[8]

---

7   *Ibid.*, p. 161.
8   *Ibid.*, p. 162.

What aggravated and magnified the wretched state of the medical care system in the nineteenth century in the Ottoman Holy Land was the very deleterious and worsening use of the deep rooted power and absolutely negative influence deriving from a system of superstitions and curious idiosyncratic beliefs which held the entire population without respite under its spell. Jew, Muslim and Christian, man, woman, and child, were under these powerfully binding, socially destructive and mystical irrational beliefs.

These medical superstitions and magical cures were strongly believed to be achieved through incantations, sorcery, witchcraft, mascots, charms, and the use of mystical and paranormal artefacts.

Tobler described how amulets were artefacts of choice for bringing on cures; one could hardly find one Arab inhabitant in Jerusalem who did not own an amulet.

He reported that orthodox Jews acquired help in these matters from Arab sheikhs or imams.

Cautery, a frequently used procedure in treatments was performed by heating a stone or a piece of iron to a red hot state and then placing it on the skin; other practitioners set light to a piece of cotton for cauterising the skin. In contrast bathing in spring water was also a popular form of treatment.[9]

One can only get to the bottom of this sorry state of affairs in the medical system of the Ottoman Holy Land by noting the various reports which repeatedly state the reality that there was a severe shortage of physicians in this era; the fact was that initially there was not one single resident doctor or qualified medical practitioner to be found from Gaza to Antioch, from Hebron to Hawran, or from Beirut to Damascus or Homs or Hamah. In addition there were no hospitals, dispensaries, infirmaries or public charities to cater for a patient whether they were diseased, injured, or disabled, or for an orphan or helpless mother or widow.[10]

In general the Ottoman Holy Land was extremely vulnerable to illnesses and diseases. The physical geography and topography of the region did not allow for an easy existence. The territory was right on the Islamic pilgrim's path to and from the Muslim Holy Cities of Mecca and Medina for their annual Holy Hajj—availing itself and

---

9 *Ibid.*, p. 163.
10 *Ibid.*, p. 164.

its unsuspecting inhabitants of a steady influx of various and sundry disease-carriers and diseases such as malaria, smallpox, leprosy, trachoma, cholera, dysentery, tuberculosis, typhus, typhoid and many others.[11]

Based on their patterns of life the local Arab Palestinian inhabitants were classified into three distinct groups: rural peasants *(fellaheen)*, nomads or semi-nomads *(badu)* and urbanised *(hadar)*. All these groups and others relied on local traditional medicine, including the use of herbs, bone-setting, cauterisation, blood-letting, leeching and cupping; all were administered by barbers, butchers, traditional birth attendants, and male religious or lay healers of sorts.[12]

As indicated earlier, many infectious and communicable diseases were prevalent in the Ottoman Holy Land and, aside from the role of superstition, accordingly many distinctive, disparate, and extremely controversial theories and beliefs existed among the inhabitants as to the aetiology, causation, origins, and methods of spread throughout the region; again these depended on ethnic, religious, racial, or other human factors.

Theories, beliefs and the like rested on controversial arguments derived from earlier traditions. Some believed that certain diseases originated in an act of God, drawing their thinking from the Qur'an and declarations in the Hadith attributed to the Prophet Mohammad; other ideologies referred to Biblical mythology or legends implying that God was imposing an ethical-moral lesson as a punishment.[13]

Others took the argument of translating the contagion theory into a form of miasma—an infectious unhealthy, poisonous vapour, acting as the causative agent of an infectious or communicable disease entity. Others believed that diseases were natural, spontaneous and autonomous entities or phenomena distinctly independent and utterly unrelated to human behaviour or mortality dynamics.

Another controversial idea proposed that some diseases associated with miasmas were caused by earthquakes or other geographical disasters or disturbances in the earth's crust.[14] This belief had been popular

---

11 Davidovitch, Nadav and Greenberg, Zalman, 'Public Health, Culture, and Colonial Medicine: Smallpox and Variolation in Palestine During the British Mandate', *Public Health Reports*, May-June; 122 (3), 2007, pp. 398-406, p. 398.
12 *Ibid.*, p. 399.
13 Mossensohn, Miri Shefer, 'Communicable Disease In Ottoman Palestine: Local Thoughts and Actions', *Korot*, Vol. 21, pp. 19-49, 2011-2012, p. 27.
14 *Ibid.*, p. 28.

among Christian's physicians in Spain, for example, who attributed the aetiology of diseases to a relationship between earthquakes and other geographic or terrestrial disturbances and reverberations themselves setting off miasmas which helped trigger a disease entity of some sort.[15]

Other groups of doctors attributed the causation of disease to the action of certain heavenly bodies, and still others implied that the scourges of disease entities originated with bad human behaviour, straddling immoral crimes and misdemeanours including rebelliousness, aggravated assaults on fellow men, fornication, committing homosexual acts or other illegal social acts.

Accordingly those guilty of such acts were to be punished by divine acts through His jinns, angels, stars, and other heavenly bodies. An impending plague may be signified by many stars falling from the sky, or by jackals, dogs, or other beasts roaming the land immediately prior to the outbreak of disease.[16]

During this same era, the relatively few doctors in the Ottoman Empire were reserved exclusively for and catered solely to the Turkish Empire's military ranks and their immediate families in the province of Ottoman Turkey proper.[17] This cadre of medical practitioners originated predominantly from eastern European countries such as Poland, Italy, Bulgaria, Greece and Turkey. The level of medical training they had received would be considered inadequate by modern standards and the care they provided to the military ranks and their families was often minimal.[18]

As such, the majority of inhabitants of both the major cities and rural districts of the Ottoman Holy Land and Mount Lebanon relied for medical care upon self-appointed local unqualified healers, barbers, butchers, elder females, and traditional birth attendants.[19]

GENERAL HEALTH CARE

In every city and inhabited area, there were one or more 'traditional healers' who had absorbed experiential knowledge of the common

---

15 *Ibid.*, p. 29.
16 *Ibid.*, p. 31.
17 Khairallah, Amin A, 'A Century of American Medicine in Syria', p. 460.
18 *Ibid.*, p. 460.
19 *Ibid.*, p. 460.

endemic ailments and diseases and the appropriate prescribed forms of treatment.[20] In most cases, this rather non-scientific knowledge would be passed down within the immediate or secondary family from elders to their children or grandchildren, with the female elders providing knowledge regarding childbirth. This information was often enhanced by consulting ancient reference books.[21] In some cases—such as those involving barbers and elders females—some degree of inherited knowledge was combined with the astute observations and experiences in one's life which would permit one to assume the role of dentist, bone-setter, herbalist, traditional healer or midwife. Dental work, tooth extraction and minor dental surgery were performed by local barbers, who were also known to nurture, stock, and apply medicinal leeches to patients needing bloodletting as a remedy for high blood pressure conditions. It was common to encounter cases of severe infections and cross-infections brought about by repeated use of the same leeches, either on different sites on the same patient or by using the same contaminated leeches on other patients. Frequent epidemics of smallpox, cholera, typhus fever and other diseases were also common in those days and, with very little or no appropriate medical care available, death tolls were high, especially among younger and more susceptible children.

INTERNAL MEDICINE

In the late eighteenth and early nineteenth centuries, barbers were thus regarded as a source of specialised knowledge concerning venesection, wet and dry pressure cupping (i.e. applying pressure cups on the body of the patient at the site of the medical ailment), application of medical leeches for bloodletting and blood pressure treatment, and many other common ailments including skin diseases, especially those involving the area of the scalp.[22] For all internal pains, cautery was the universal treatment and, in order to bring about a chronic discharge into the cauterised area, a raw pea or green bean was secured to the healing area. This procedure was universal for all joint aches of the body. For

---

20 *Ibid.*, p. 460.
21 *Ibid.*, p. 460.
22 *Ibid.*, p. 460.

the treatment of fevers, bloodletting with a razor-blade was performed, with or without the deployment of pressure cups.[23]

Various mixtures of herbs were combined with olive oil, butter or animal fat to form pastes or ointments which were then applied to wounds and aching body parts. Other herbs and certain varieties of spices were mixed with honey and taken as syrups for various indicated treatments. Similarly, fresh, dried, or boiled herbs were ingested for a variety of specific complaints and the leaves of certain plants were dried and powdered to aid in the healing of ulcers. Writing scripts of certain maxims on ornamental pieces and then wearing them on one's person was another common method used for fighting disease and treating other specific medical problems.[24]

ORTHOPAEDICS

Butchers, goat-herders and shepherds were, from life experience and absorbed knowledge alone, ascribed a detailed knowledge of animal anatomy and were also known in rural circles to assume the role of setter/healer of fractured bones.[25] Butchers, in particular, often applied their knowledge of bones, joints, cartilage, ligaments and muscles in the treatment of bone fractures and dislocations.[26]

PHARMACY

Certain families were known by the local population to have acquired various pharmacological formulae which had been handed down through the generations by family elders. These formulae were considered appropriate and effective treatments for a range of ailments and medical conditions including skin diseases, ulcers and common infections. Tradition in those days allowed such families to keep such medicinal formulae secret within the family, but they would often

---

23 Bishara, Nakhleh E, 'A Medical Pioneer in Nazareth', *Korot* Vol. 12, 1996-1997, p. 129.
24 *Ibid.*, p. 130.
25 Khairallah, Amin A, 'A Century of American Medicine in Syria', p. 460.
26 *Ibid.*, p. 460.

grant the relevant remedies to a needy neighbour or local resident at no charge.[27]

Usually in common practice medicinal treatments for the patient meant taking a specific drug and grinding it up with a pestle and mortar. If the medicine were in a liquid or semi-liquid state it would be pressed through a cheesecloth. After the grinding or sieving, the processed drug would be mixed with some suitable, easily ingestible medium, such as olive oil, beer, wine, or milk.

Drinking the processed drug was the most common methods of administration, helping absorption into the body as well as providing purgative and/or emetic effects. A second popular mode of administration of a drug into the body was by means of enemas.[28] Other forms of suppositories consisted of crushed drugs mixed with supposedly inactive material such as sheep's kidney extracts as a medium for administration.

Tampons, filled with a drug placed in a woollen mesh soaked in an oily medium, were inserted into the nose, ear, vagina or rectum for treatment. Other dry mixtures of drugs were used to treat the lungs; this entailed heating the drug in a pot of oil, beer or ghee and then having the patient bend over the hot pot inhaling the resultant vapours.

Among other remedies for external use were salves, poultices, drops and powders used mostly for treating the ears, eyes, and the nose. Salves comprised drugs mixed in oils or fatty substances and the mixture applied to body parts from head to toe. Poultices comprised drugs spread onto cloths or leather straps and applied to various body parts as necessary. Liquid ingredients used as media of administration for drug suspensions were usually ingredients such as milk, vinegar, olive oil, beer and wine.[29]

PHYSIOTHERAPY, OBSTETRICS AND GYNAECOLOGY

Some women applied their skills in massage to the treatment of dislocated bones, in addition to treating the chronic swellings and

---

27 *Ibid.*, p. 460.
28 Powel, Marvin A, 'Drugs and Pharmaceuticals in Ancient Mesopotamia, A Paper', pp. 47-67; in Jacob, Irene and Walter, eds, *The Healing Past, Pharmaceuticals in the Biblical and Rabbinic World*, E J Brill, Leiden, 1953, p. 61.
29 *Ibid.*, p. 63.

aching joints of both upper and lower limbs.[30] Other women, typically family elders, frequently assumed the role of birth attendant or midwife, having learned the art and science of childbirth from their own mothers or grandmothers. Such women had invariably acquired a considerable amount of valuable experience in matters regarding childbirth and common ailments by other women and their progeny.[31] However, they used primitive childbirth instruments comprising nothing more than a pair of household scissors and a piece of string, with which they tied and secured the umbilical cord prior to cutting it off the attached placenta with scissors. All women of the day gave birth at home surrounded by their immediate mature female family members; the expectant mother-to-be would straddle a specially designed wooden 'maternity chair' which was brought in by the birth attendant as part of her equipment. In the centre of the maternity chair was a large oval hole and, immediately under that, a basin full of warm water was placed.

After giving birth, the mother would be provided with nourishing food, usually comprising meat and/or chicken broth. The new-born would be breast-fed and, in cases where this was impossible due to lack of milk from the mother, a close relative or friend of the mother who was capable of acting as a wet nurse would breast-feed the newborn.[32] In that era, giving birth was a process which routinely placed both the mother and the newborn in severe jeopardy, as dangerous complications (resulting from the relatively primitive standard of medical care) often resulted in death for one or both.

Historical Armenian Church records in Jerusalem attest to the dangers associated with childbirth. These records indicate that, in the 1850s, approximately three out of four young women from the Armenian community died during their first childbirth; in reality, this meant that most newly married women would die in the first year of marriage. Many of the children who survived childbirth went on to die in early childhood.

---

30 *Ibid.*, p. 460.
31 *Ibid.*, p. 460.
32 Rose, John H Melkon, *Armenians of Jerusalem: Memories of Life in Palestine*, The Radcliff Press, London 1993, p. 17.

MEDICINE, OPHTHALMOLOGY, MINOR SURGERY

Other traditional healers included the numerous practitioners who were either native to the country, or itinerant healers originating from North Africa who were known locally as 'moughrabies'. Of these individuals, some were highly skilled in tooth extraction, stone extractions, cupping and even performing cataract operations on the eyes.[33] In addition to these specialised skills, they dispensed secret formulae of extracts of culinary or medicinal herbs, which were prescribed as common laxatives, expectorants or diaphoretics. Still others among these itinerants were skilled as oculists, administering cures for the treatment of catarrhal conjunctivitis and trachoma, ailments which were very common in those days. The most common treatment involved an ingredient known as 'kuhl', a black substance which was also used by women as a form of eye-shadow for eye make-up.[34] Human milk was also used as eye-drops for all types of infectious diseases of the eyes.[35]

NINETEENTH-CENTURY HEALTH CARE

Many of the above methods were used in the emergency treatment applied to the American missionary Reverend Pliny Fisk in an attempt to relieve him of the severe injuries he received as a result of a bludgeoning attack he had suffered at the hands of highwaymen near Nazareth in 1825 during his last trip to the Holy Land.[36] The various treatments administered to him included:

- Medicinal leeches which were applied to his forehead to absorb the blood emanating from his skull;
- An Italian-speaking doctor who was hurriedly summoned from Sidon to assist in the emergency treatment proceeded to prescribe mustard poultices

---

33 *Ibid.*, p. 460.
34 *Ibid.*, p. 460.
35 *Ibid.*, p. 130.
36 Gabrill, Joseph L, *Protestant Diplomacy And The Near East: Missionary Influence On American Policy 1810-1927*, University of Minnesota Press, Minneapolis, 1971, p. 8.

(i.e., soft and moist masses of flour placed on the skin to reduce inflammation) for his feet;
- Warm wet cloths were applied to his stomach, in addition to frequent draughts of rice-water.

Regrettably, all such treatments proved to be of no avail as Reverend Fisk died in Beirut on 23 October 1825 as a result of his injuries.[37]

Immediately after the invasion of Ottoman Syria (i.e., Palestine, Mount Lebanon, Jordan and Syria proper) by Ibrahim Pasha, the son of Mohammad Ali of Egypt in 1832, the Pasha began sending young Egyptian men to France to pursue medical studies. He also had sent to Egypt a number of other equally studious men to pursue medical studies at the Qasr El Ain medical school in Cairo.[38] Many of these men, upon graduating from medical school, returned promptly to their homeland and these newly qualified medical practitioners, together with the aforementioned doctors among the Turkish military ranks, formed a corps which was later augmented and strengthened by the Western medical missionaries who were beginning to arrive in the region and this constituted the first medical practitioner corps of the Levant.[39]

It was not until the earliest pioneer Protestant missionaries from America, Britain and continental Europe began to suffer early deaths among themselves, their wives and children, did those pioneering missionary societies begin to dispatch qualified doctors as medical missionaries. Initially this dispatch of Western missionary doctors to the region was primarily aimed at looking after the Western missionary flock, although later it was also aimed at establishing accredited missionary dispensaries, clinics, hospitals, schools, colleges, and universities.[40] This arrangement saw the first arrival of the founding fathers of medical missionary enterprise in the Levant, including Dr George Post of Mount Lebanon and Beirut, Dr Pacordi Kaloust Vartan of Nazareth, Dr David Watt Torrance of Tiberius and Dr Alexander Paterson of Hebron, to name some of the most eminent. Upon the

---

37 Finnie, David H, *Pioneers East: The Early American Experience in the Middle East*, Harvard University Press, Cambridge, Massachusetts, 1967, p. 152.
38 *Ibid.*, p. 460.
39 *Ibid.*, p. 460.
40 Kaplan, Robert D, *The Arabists: The Romance Of An American Elite*, The Free Press, 1993, p. 23.

arrival of Dr Vartan as the first medical missionary in Nazareth in 1861, he initially faced difficulties as a modern Edinburgh-trained physician applying his newly acquired medical knowledge. The local native healers, barbers and midwives of the town initially opposed him and prevented him from carrying out his medical practices. Traditional beliefs, superstition, ignorance and minimal education among the local people took considerable time to overcome; however, once his practices were accepted, he was eventually accepted as their 'Hakeem al-kabeer' ('the big, good, wise doctor').

Psychiatry

Persons suspected of manifesting psychiatric disorders were treated by being shunned from their homes, isolated and imprisoned in underground caves or grottos and often tied down by heavy chains to nearby rocks. As part of their routine treatment, they would be subjected to severe beatings in order to drive out the evil spirits from within their bodies. This treatment, which was often sanctioned by the patient's immediate family members, would be administered by monks and priests of the monastery or convent, which usually housed these caves and dungeons. In the 'Mysterious Orient', insanity or a deranged state of the mind were diagnosed as 'demon mania' (i.e. devil obsession) and the prescribed treatment of the times was exorcism.[41]

Deep in the region of Mount Lebanon, the monastery of Kuzhayya had a specific cave reserved for casting out evil spirits. It was dedicated to St Anthony of Padua who had lived there for 40 years as a hermit and who was, at the time, believed to have imparted special healing powers to the resident monks of the monastery. Persons suspected of 'demon mania' were typically chained and beaten for three days, after which time St Anthony would be expected to appear and cast out the demon or evil spirit, thereby restoring the patient to full health and reason.[42] In cases where the patient died during this ordeal, the monks would report to the family that St Anthony had loosened his chains and had taken the patient straight to heaven,

---

41 Khatchadourian, Herant, 'The Historical Background of Psychiatry in the Lebanon', *Bulletin History of Medicine* Vol. 54, 1980, pp. 544-553.
42 *Ibid*.

thereby entitling the monastery to a generous donation from the family on behalf of the deceased.[43]

Several other caves in different regions of the Holy Land were reserved for similar 'treatment' of the mentally ill. These archaic practices were brought to the attention of the authorities by the German-Swiss Quaker missionary Theophilus Waldmeier (founding father of the famous Quaker Boarding School, Barman High School) who was supported by Sir Thomas Smith Clouston (1850-1915), the physician superintendent of the Edinburgh Royal Asylum. In an attempt to bring a halt to such treatment of the mentally ill, Waldmeier related his personal observations from his journeys through Palestine and Syria at the historic meeting convened on 17 April 1896 at the home of the American Missionary Revd Henry Harris Jessup, one of the pillars of the American Board's Syrian Mission in Beirut.[44] Of the ten individuals present at that meeting, John Gregory Wortabet, Professor of Anatomy at the Medical School of the Syrian Protestant College, was elected as chairman.

Shortly thereafter, a campaign was launched to establish a hospital for the insane in the Ottoman province of Syria and Theophilus Waldmeier immediately travelled to Europe, Great Britain and the USA to generate interest and acquire funds for the purchase of land and the construction of the proposed hospital in Beirut. The first meeting of the London General Committee was convened at the Bethlem Royal Asylum on 11 March 1897, with medical superintendent Dr Percy Smith designated as the chairman who would act as advisor to the Beirut Executive Committee. In 1898, a plot of land was purchased approximately six miles from Beirut and on 6 August 1900 the 'Asfuriyeh Hospital' admitted its first ten patients. The hospital prospered and expanded periodically; it treated 150 patients in 1924, 350 in 1935 and 410 in 1936. In 1938, the hospital was renamed as the Lebanon Hospital for Mental and Nervous Disorders. By 1949, approximately 14,000 patients had been attended to and treated on the site.[45]

In addition to its clinical work, the hospital served as a training centre in psychiatry after having become affiliated to the American

---

43 *Ibid.*
44 Jessup, Henry Harris, *Fifty-Three Years in Syria*, 2 Vols, Flemming H Revell, New York, 1910, Vol. 2, p. 521.
45 http://www.mundus.ac.uk/cats, p. 1.

University of Beirut Medical Centre. In 1939, the hospital gained recognition from the Royal Medical Psychological Association as a training centre for a certificate programme in mental health nursing—the first of its kind in the Near East—and by 1948 the World Health Organisation recognised it as a suitable training centre for its purposes in the region. The hospital advanced rapidly with the times and, by 1952, had developed departments specialising in insulin coma therapy, cardiazol convulsion therapy, chemotherapy, occupational therapy and electric convulsion therapy (ECT). Such progress placed this hospital on an international standard of excellence until it was largely destroyed during the Lebanese Civil War in 1975. Despite appeals for funds for its rejuvenation and reconstruction, the hospital's occupation by the Israeli army in 1982 condemned it to a very tragic end.[46]

Thus the year 1982 saw the utter destruction of a most eminent hospital for mental and nervous disorders in the Near East which had served the region for nearly nine illustrious decades. Regrettably to this very day no attempt has been made to replace this hospital, which in itself reflects a very sad state of affairs for the region, let alone Lebanon.

In the midst of all this substandard activity in health care circles in the Holy Land in the nineteenth century one must not forget to mention the work of the Franciscan Order representing the Catholic Church in Jerusalem. Their medical activity especially in the seventeenth and eighteenth centuries was of a most commendable and high standard.[47]

The Franciscans' primary duty was to provide medical care for Catholic pilgrims to the Holy Land. They were pre-qualified as physicians, pharmacists, surgeons, and nurses and were sent to Jerusalem for this special purpose. Most were from Italy, and a few came from France, Spain and Czechoslovakia.

Their Catholic pilgrim patients were treated at a boarding house for the poor sited in the Christian quarter of the Old City. The location was named Dar Ishak Bek in Arabic and Casa dei Principi in Italian. Tobler mentioned that the premises contained about twenty rooms accommodating nearly one hundred patients who were poor and sick Catholic pilgrims. Only a few serious cases were admitted to the monastery.

---

46 *Ibid.*, p. 2.
47 Amar, Zohar and Lev, Efraim, 'An Early Glimpse …', p. 81.

Besides this premises the friars had access to a European-style pharmacy, a satellite dispensary and an outstanding medical library also at their disposal.

The dispensary became world famous for the innovative concoctions produced in it, most notably the secret formula containing forty different pharmaceutical ingredients for the world famous 'Jerusalem Balsam'. It is curious that such outstanding medical and pharmaceutical activity was taking place right under the noses of the unsuspecting Holy Land inhabitants who had no access to such modern medical care with European qualified physicians and surgeons.

The medicines were prepared by special modern European means and with modern equipment imported from Europe. However, controversial comments refer to all this activity in rather derogatory terms; with the Franciscans and even the Jewish medical physicians in pharmacies so to speak just down the street, Jerusalem was accused of not having succeeded in bringing about any significant changes and developments in the condition of medicine in the Holy Land or beyond. It is claimed that their influence was actually marginal and of course very limited in its scope or extent in the Holy Land proper.[48]

Conclusion

The inhabitants of the Ottoman province of the Holy Land from the sixteenth to nearly the mid-nineteenth century suffered severely from a stifling if not stagnating and neglectful rule by the Ottoman Turks. This affected many aspects of their existence and most notably the medical care system they had to endure for nearly four centuries. What scarce medical knowledge the very few physicians in the Ottoman Empire possessed was restricted to Ottoman Turkey proper and only for the Turkish army and their immediate families. The inhabitants of the Holy Land proper were left to their own devices, suffering under a medical care regime which was firmly ancient and substandard, lacking in knowledge, structure, function and procedure. This paper aims to highlight the medical care system endured by these nineteenth-century inhabitants, relying on self-appointed lay healers or misguided religious figures or itinerant travellers, shamans and/or charlatans under whose

---

48 *Ibid* p. 86.

ill-advised treatments and procedures the local population were a submissive and captive audience.

Acknowledgement

The author would like to thank Dr Rohan Borschmann of the Institute of Psychiatry, London, UK, for thoroughly reviewing this paper and for his valuable observations, comments, guidance and technical assistance thereof.

CHRISTIAN SYRIA*
Ignace Dick

> *'Remember in your prayers the Church in Syria.'*
> Saint Ignatius of Antioch

The present Syrian Arab Republic carries within itself the destiny of historic Syria. Though its capital was transferred from Antioch to Damascus and it lies at the heart of the Arab and Islamic world, it does not repudiate its Christian past.

Since Christ was born in Bethlehem, Syria is the cradle of Christianity and Syria's Christians are still a proud, lively and united community, despite their reduced numerical strength and the diversity of their rites and denominations.

We shall briefly outline the principal features of Syria's Christian history and the current situation of its Christians.

Syria in the New Testament

Palestine used to be part of the Roman Province of Syria. Jesus was born during the census of Caesar Augustus 'when Cyrenius was governor of Syria.' (Luke 2: 2)

Jesus began his ministry in Galilee, preaching and healing, but 'his fame went throughout all Syria.' (Matthew 4:24) Going beyond Galilee, Jesus traversed the southern regions of today's Syria, the district of Caesarea Philippi in the Golan. That is where Peter proclaimed his

---

* Translated from the French by V Chamberlain.

Christian Syria

faith in Jesus as Son of God and received from Christ the promise of primacy. (Matthew 16:13-20 and Mark 8:27-30) The Canaanite woman whose daughter Jesus healed of possession by an unclean spirit was Syro-Phoenician Greek by birth.

Saul, the future Paul, was converted on the way to Damascus, when he was coming to apprehend the followers of Christ, who were already numerous in Damascus, less than five years after Christ's resurrection. (Acts 9:2-25) He preached in Damascus and in the southern region (Arabia) for three years. (Galatians 1:15-18)

A pious tradition reported by Eusebius of Caesarea (a fourth-century historian) tells how Abgar, King of Edessa, heard talk of Jesus and invited him to come and stay with him to escape the snares of the Jews. Jesus promised to send him one of his disciples, Addai (Thaddeus), who evangelised Edessa.

The Christian community of Antioch was founded by those who fled Jerusalem after Stephen's martyrdom. (Acts 11:19-21) Barnabas, delegated by the Church of Jerusalem to organise that community, 'departed ... to Tarsus, for to seek Saul: and when he had found him, he brought him unto Antioch. And it came to pass, that a whole year they assembled themselves with the church, and taught much people.' (Acts 11:25-26) The Book of Acts adds a very important piece of information, 'And the disciples were called Christians first in Antioch.' (Acts 11:26) Paul was linked to the Church of Antioch, which assigned him to various missions in Asia Minor and Greece. After his various journeys, he came back to Antioch as to his home base. That is where Paul recruited as his companion Luke, a cultured physician, who went on to write the third Gospel and the book known as the Acts of the Apostles. There too he confronted Saint Peter over his weak attitude with regard to the Judaisers. (Galatians 2:11-14) Saint Peter stayed for quite a long time at Antioch and is considered its first bishop. That perhaps is the source of the affinity we find between the two Apostolic Sees of Antioch and Rome.

SYRIA OF THE MARTYRS AND FATHERS

The seed of the Word sown by Christ himself and the Apostles was watered by the blood of martyrs. They were countless during the persecutions of the first three centuries, before Constantine proclaimed religious freedom. Nonetheless we should mention the following saints: Ignatius, Bishop of Antioch, given to the lions in Rome under Trajan, in 107; Babylas, Bishop of Antioch, martyred under Decius in 250, and whose tomb venerated at Daphne was profaned by Julian the Apostate; Sergius and Bacchus, two Roman officers, martyred towards the end of the third century during the Diocletian persecution and venerated at Rasafa, near the Euphrates in the basilica built over their tombs; the two unmercenary physicians, Cosmas and Damian, buried in the city of Cyr.

Christianity spread during the course of the second century in various circles. Pope Anicetus (150-168) was a native of Homs in Syria. In the third century, Christians formed a substantial community which attracted the interest of emperors, notably those of the Syrian family. The Emperor Philip the Arab was Christian. Zenobia named one of her friends, Paul of Samosata, to the see of Antioch. With Constantine, Syria took on a Christian appearance and paganism went into decline. Thanks to bishops and monks, the countryside was evangelised and the nomadic Arab tribes embraced Christianity in the fifth and sixth centuries, forming two bishoprics.

Syria gave celebrated theologians and writers to the Church: Ignatius of Antioch, Theophilus of Antioch, Tatian, Ephrem, John Chrysostom, Diodore of Tarsus, Theodore of Mopsuestia, Theodoret of Cyrus, Romanos the Melode, Severus of Antioch, Philoxenus of Mabbug, Jacob of Saruj, Dionysius ... The official language was Greek, but the language of the people, Aramean, became a literary language (Edessa dialect). A theological school developed in Antioch with Lucian of Samosata and another at Edessa with Ephrem (+373.)

The liturgical rite of Antioch, already put together in outline, spread and influenced that of the Church of Persia and Armenia and the rite of Constantinople.

Syrian monasticism developed, taking on an austere aspect in its various forms, coenobitic (community living), hermits, stylites etc. The most famous of stylites was Saint Simeon, who died in 459, and whose fame reached Saint Genevieve of Paris, and gave us the great basilica built around his column, and which remains a masterpiece of Syrian art.

Syria is strewn with monuments that witness to the flourishing of Christianity in Syria from the fourth to the sixth centuries (both in the limestone high plateau to the west of Aleppo and the basalt massif of the Hauran, south of Damascus).

The Church of Syria was organised around its centre Antioch, whose primatial role was attested at the Council of Nicaea. Then the patriarchal form of government took shape. Antioch became the fourth patriarchate after Rome, Constantinople and Alexandria. Jerusalem was detached from Antioch at the Council of Chalcedon in 451, to form a fifth patriarchate, grouping together the three provinces of Palestine. Antioch had under its jurisdiction twelve metropolises and one hundred and fifty-three bishoprics, two of which were for nomads. Greeks, Hellenised Arameans of the cities, Arameans from the countryside and nomadic or semi-settled Arabs lived in fellowship in complementary pluralism. Unfortunately, theological, Christological quarrels, the disaffection of the Ghassanid Arabs in relation to the Empire and the awakening of Syrian special interests, led to the rupture of the unity of the Church of Antioch. Advocates and opponents of the Council of Chalcedon (451), which had defined Christ as one divine person with two natures, clashed head-on. The Emperors Zeno and Anastasius gave some breathing space to the opponents of the Council and even favoured them. The backlash of Justin and Justinian who drew closer to Rome did not succeed in re-establishing unity. Over against the Chalcedonian hierarchy recognized by the Empire there was established a parallel, opposing hierarchy which rejected the Council and had its own adherents. It owed its organisation to Jacob Baradeus, supported by Theodora, the Syrian wife of Justinian. That is why it received the name of Jacobite. The advocates of the Council who stayed in communion with Rome and Constantinople were called 'Melkites' (supporters of the emperor.) The trial rapprochement with the opponents of Chalcedon brought about by the Second Council of Constantinople led to nothing.

Besides this still unrepaired breach, the Church of Syria was weakened by the various calamities that struck Syria: earthquakes which destroyed Antioch several times and Romano-Persian wars that laid waste and bankrupted the country. The Persians of Chosroes II occupied Syria for nearly twenty years (609-628). The reaction of Heraclius came, late. He succeeded in driving out the Persians and bringing back the relic of the true Cross to Jerusalem. Wishing to re-establish religious unity, he supported the doctrine of monergism and monothelitism (a single action and single will in Christ, though possessing two natures). That doctrine of compromise did not succeed in re-establishing unity. During that period the Maronite Patriarchate was established in Syria, later taking refuge in Lebanon.

CHURCH OF THE ARABS

The conquest of Syria by Muslim troops come from Arabia (634-640) did not put an end to Christianity in Syria, but gradually weakened its numerical strength and curtailed its freedom and influence.

Many Christians emigrated into Byzantine regions or to Rome. From that Syrian colony there came five popes during the seventh and eighth centuries: John V (685-686), Sergius I (687-701), Sisinnius (708), Gregory III (731-741) and Constantine (708-715.) Those who remained were considered as second-class citizens, forced to pay a special tax in return for the limited freedom of worship guaranteed to them. The liberal attitude of the first conquerors gradually gave way to a stricter form of government with regard to Christians; restrictions and humiliations were imposed on them, which were not according to the spirit of early Islam.

Up until the middle of the ninth century, Christians remained in the majority and continued to enrich the universal Church through their theological and hymnographic contributions (Saint John of Damascus, James of Edessa, Saint Andrew of Crete, Cosmas of Mayouna etc). In the tenth century, they represented no more than half the population.

The Arab conquest cemented the division of Syria's Christians and gave equal rights to Jacobites and Melkites. The Jacobites were centred on Mesopotamia and southern Anatolia; they dropped Greek from their liturgical use and led an independent ecclesial life. The Melkites remained in communion with Rome and Constantinople and sent representatives to the Ecumenical Councils meeting in the Byzantine capital: the Sixth Council (681), the Seventh Council (787), the Constantinopolitan Councils of 869 and 879. The caliphs sometimes used Melkite patriarchs as emissaries to Byzantine emperors. In the tenth century, the saintly Melkite patriarch, Christopher, was the friend and confidant of the famous prince of Aleppo, Sayf al-Dawla, who was treacherously assassinated in 967, through jealousy.

Christian Syria

The Church of Syria adapted to the new situation. The use of Greek was soon lost. Syriac was more tenacious. However, Arabic became the language of culture and the mother-tongue of all the Christians in Syria, both Melkites and Syro-Jacobites. The Melkites especially made a great effort to Arabise Christian culture. They translated the Bible, the liturgy, the Church Fathers and composed original works in Arabic.

The Christians, on the fringes of political and military life, played a considerable role in the economic development of the country and in all the wheels of the civil service. They were in positions of service and trust, not positions of prestige and command. They co-operated actively in the flowering of culture and civilisation called Islamic. They put across in Arabic the key elements of Greek philosophy and learning and themselves composed many academic works and chronicles in Arabic. Very many Arab poets were Christian, including the well-known poet of the Umayyads, al-Akhtal. With Christians and Muslims living together as neighbours, a certain Islamic-Christian dialogue developed. Christians had to strengthen the faith of their fellow-Christians and offered a defence to Muslims who took issue with them. The principal controversists were: Theodore Abu Qurrah, Abu Raita, Qusta ibn Luqa, Elia of Nisibi and Paul of Sidon.

This still tolerable situation lasted (bar sudden crises) until nearly the end of the eleventh century. Political power was until that time in the hands of Arabs who saw in the Christians of Syria blood-brothers of the same stock. At the end of the eleventh century, the hegemony passed to Seljuk Turks who lacked Arab sympathies and had no common denominator with Syria's non-Muslims. Christians became a marginalised and humiliated minority.

The occupation of Antioch in 1098 and Jerusalem in 1099 by the Crusaders did nothing to redress the situation, but rather the contrary. The Crusaders had not come to help local Christian groups, but carved out for themselves fiefdoms and principalities and any Christians in regions not occupied by the Crusaders found themselves in an awkward position. The Byzantine cathedral of Aleppo was transformed into a mosque in 1124. During the capture of Antioch in 1098, the Melkite patriarch was John V. At first he was recognized as the only patriarch of all the Christians. But soon he had to give way to a Frankish prelate and take refuge in Constantinople. The long stay of the Melkite patriarchs in the Byzantine capital during the period of the Crusades, which came after the Byzantine re-occupation of Antioch between 969 and 1084, accentuated the Byzantinisation of the Melkites with regard to liturgical and canonical practices. The Jacobites and Armenians drew closer to the Crusaders, but complete unity was not achieved.

The liquidation of the Frankish presence by the Mamluks of Egypt was accompanied by coercive measures against the Christians. Antioch was razed to the ground in 1268. Many monasteries suspected of connivance with the Crusaders were laid waste. Christians were driven out of coastal cities, for fear of their contact with Cyprus.

The Melkite patriarchs fixed their seat definitively in Damascus. The invasion of Tamerlane in 1400 managed to wreck whatever historic monuments had hitherto survived.

The first concern of the Church was to survive. The patriarchal institution allowed this survival to take place, since patriarchs were able, without any intervention from abroad, to ensure apostolic succession by filling vacant bishoprics, with married priests being placed locally to provide the sacraments in the most out of the way places, and the liturgy being in the language of the people, which enabled folk to learn the essentials of the faith from the doctrinally rich Eastern liturgical texts.

The Ottoman conquest of Syria in 1516 did not change the situation of Christians at all, but a spectacular readjustment took place from the seventeenth century onwards. Syria's Christians came out of their isolation. The northern frontiers fell and they were again in contact with Constantinople and the Eastern Greek world. The Ottoman Empire maintained diplomatic and commercial relations with the West. Colonies of European merchants were established in Syria, notably in Aleppo and Damascus. Local Christians were able to establish contacts with foreigners more easily. They learned the bases of trade and a rich Christian middle class was formed. At the same time, Catholic missionaries settled in Aleppo between 1625 and 1627 (Capuchins, Jesuits, Carmelites, besides the Franciscans already established there in 1571) and thence, swarmed towards Damascus, Sidon and Tripoli. Syrian Christians made trips into Europe for study (Greek College, Maronite College and Urban College) and for trade. As a result of those contacts, Syrian Christians became more wealthy and educated. They then experienced a more significant population growth than that of their Muslim fellow-countrymen. A movement

Christian Syria

sympathetic to Rome, with ideas and forms of Western piety introduced by missionaries, introduced internal disagreements into the heart of the traditional Melkite, Syro-Jacobite and Armenian communities (Armenians had begun arriving in Syria just after the medieval period and their community grew during the seventeenth century as a result of the Armenian flight from Persia to Syria.)

Pro-Roman Eastern Christians and Christians in opposition to Rome lived for some time in the same Church, but due to the ideas of the period, they ended up forming distinct Churches. The definitive split of the Melkites into two branches was in 1724, that of the Armenians in 1740 and that of the Syro-Jacobites in 1783. The Ottomans refused to recognize Eastern Catholics and they had to live in secret while their hierarchy took refuge in Lebanon. They endured persecution and harassment and were only recognized as a distinct group in 1830, under the pressure of Catholic powers.

Despite this Christian recovery from the demographic, cultural and economic perspective, the political situation had not changed. Christians were deprived of full civil rights and subjected to all sorts of slights. However, the ideas of the French Revolution and the pressure of the Western powers on what was usually called 'the Sick Man' led the sultans to issue various liberating edicts concerning Christians (1839, 1856), which repealed the *dhimmi* status of Christians and recognized them as equal citizens. They remained exempt from military service, in return for payment of the *badal 'askari* and were only compelled to do it after the promulgation of the new constitution by the 'Young Turks' in 1908.

Christians outstripped their Muslim fellow-citizens in cultural terms thanks to the many schools founded by pious foreigners and local Churches. Syrians founded the main religious congregations in Lebanon in the eighteenth century, both among Melkites, Syrians, Armenians and Maronites. They played a great role in the literary renaissance movement called *Al-Nahda*, and were the chief promoters of Arab nationalism, in contradistinction to Pan-Islamism and the expansion of Turkish culture. On the eve of the outbreak of the First World War, Syrians started to dissociate themselves from the Ottoman Empire. In 1913, the Syrian Congress met in Paris.

In the time of the French mandate (1920-1945), Christians experienced a regime of liberty and equality such as they had not known under Ottoman rule. They were even rather favoured because of their knowledge of French and their higher level of education. Christianity in Syria was buoyed up by three waves of emigrants fleeing the Turks, survivors of the massacres perpetrated during the First World War (1915), those who left Cilicia in 1922 during the withdrawal of the French army and those who chose to live in Syria when the *sandjak* (governorate) of Alexandretta was ceded to Turkey in 1939.

Christians became integrated into the national life of Syria and affiliated to different political parties. Christians had a fixed number of representatives in parliament, proportionate to their number in each district. The new Ba'athist constitution suppressed this clause; Christians being treated like other citizens and not having the right to special seats. But, given the mind-set of the Muslim majority, they were thus disadvantaged.

Present Situation

Current legislation in Syria is a compromise between secularism and Islamic *shari'a*. Christians, in 1950, banded together so that Islam did not figure as the state religion in the constitution. However, the constitution declared Islam as the religion of the head of state and Muslim *shari'a* as the main source of law. Islamic law regulated questions of inheritance, until Law 31 (2006) was introduced, modifying the rule of *shari'a* for Catholic Churches. For issues to do with marriage and personal statute, Christians are governed by their own legislation, unless there is the matter of a Muslim party. There is no mention of religious affiliation on one's identity card, but it remains in the records of one's civil status. That mention determines the authority and legislation governing personal status, as well as the religious education lessons that the student must attend at school. Changing religion is only allowed for the purpose of going over to Islam.

The former prerogatives of the heads of Christian communities, inherited from the Ottoman period, are recognized by the Syrian state and pertain to the Presidency of the Council of Ministers. No obstacle is placed in the way of building places of worship, which are exempt from taxation, just as mosques are.

The Church owns very prosperous schools, although freedom to teach has been considerably restricted. Christian religious education is guaranteed in schools for Christian pupils, just as lessons in Islam are guaranteed for Muslims. Christian religious education for young people is rounded off by religious lessons outside school hours through various youth movements. The Church also carries out a remarkable programme of charitable and social action.

The feasts of Christmas and Easter are officially holidays. Christians can in principle gain access to all government posts, except that of Head of State. In the army, there is no limit on their promotion.

Christians and Muslims generally live together on good terms. The Christian presence is unevenly distributed across the various regions. Certain regions, for example the Valley of the Christians west of Homs, are dotted with completely Christian villages, so one could imagine oneself in a Christian country. Near Damascus, Saidnaya, Maara and Maaloula, like certain villages of the Hauran, are completely Christian. Other villages are mixed. In the cities, Christians are grouped together in predominantly Christian quarters. In various regions, Christians are not represented and many Muslims have no opportunity to get to know Christians. University and the army, however, produce some degree of mixing.

Christians feel completely at home in Syria, as Christianity was the majority religion of Syria before Islam and Christians are just as much Arab as their Muslim fellow-citizens and have contributed to Arab civilisation and national prosperity, both in the classical period and in modern times.

The Christian presence has effectively diminished as a result of emigration and a reduction in the birth rate.

Syria's Christianity best attests to the possibility of living freely in a country of ancient Arab and Islamic culture.

From that point of view, it is more significant than Lebanon's Christianity which lives on an equal footing with Islam. Emigration and the brain drain have to be stopped by dissipating fear of the future, by helping young people to find work and set up their homes, and by supporting Church institutions of social service and training.

CHURCHES AND ECCLESIAL COMMUNITIES

Christians represent some eight percent of the population, or about 1,675, 000. They belong to various communities and traditions.

Up until the sixth century, they formed just one Church, presided over by the Patriarch of Antioch. Alongside Greek, the official language, Syriac was used in the liturgy, mainly in the countryside. The dispute over the Council of Chalcedon led to the internal split of the Patriarchate of Antioch. The supporters of the Council were called Melkites and its opponents Jacobites, then Syrians. Melkites gradually adopted the Byzantine Greek rite and celebrated in Greek and Arabic. Syrians retained the ancient rite of Antioch and abandoned the use of Greek in order keep to Syriac. Melkites became the best represented numerically, alone accounting for more than half the total number of Christians.

Each of the two Melkite and Syrian communities split in the eighteenth century into two branches, because of their attitude to the Church of Rome. So there obtained the (Melkite) Greek Orthodox Church and the Melkite Greek Catholic Church, the Syrian Orthodox Church and the Syrian Catholic Church each having at its head, a patriarch with the title *of Antioch*, the first three residing in Damascus.

In the seventh century, there was constituted another Antiochian offshoot from the Melkite stem, the Maronite community, which did not accept the Sixth Ecumenical Council condemning monothelitism and did not undergo Byzantine influence, remaining faithful to the Syriac tradition. Established in Syria, it was not long before it took refuge in Lebanon. During the Crusades, it affirmed its communion with Rome and underwent strong Latin influence. The Maronite expansion reached the Syrian coastal region, where many villages were Maronite. Many families, especially in north Lebanon, settled in Aleppo between the sixteenth and seventeenth centuries and formed bishoprics. More recently, the capital attracted a large number of families. The Maronite Patriarch also has the title *of Antioch* and resides in Lebanon. Maronites do not have an Orthodox branch.

The Armenians came to Syria especially from neighbouring Little Armenia (Cilicia) at the end of the medieval period. Their community grew in the seventeenth century, through families fleeing the persecution of Shah 'Abbas of Persia and especially the survivors of the massacres of 1915 and those who left Cilicia after the withdrawal of French troops in 1922. The Armenians of Syria belong to the Catholicosate of Sis (Cilicia.) In the course of the eighteenth century they split, like the Melkites and Syrians, into two branches: Armenian Orthodox and Armenian Catholic.

The Chaldeans are a Catholic branch of the Eastern Syrian Church (that of the former Persian Empire, Iraq and Iran). In the seventeenth century, they were represented in Aleppo by some families and Franciscans provided their spiritual service. In the second half of the nineteenth century, their number was augmented by elements from the Mosul region. Their patriarch, resident in Iraq, sent them a priest and helped them build a church. In 1957, they became constituted as a bishopric. The Assyrians (a branch of the Ancient Church of Persia not united to Rome) were welcomed into Syria when they were partly driven out of Iraq by King Faisal I in 1933. The majority of them are in the Jezireh. They now have a bishop.

From the sixteenth and seventeenth centuries onwards, the Latin community was made up of European traders and diplomats based in Aleppo and Damascus. They were served by Franciscans. Gradually, the Franciscans built up parishes for themselves from elements taken from Orthodox or Eastern Catholic communities. They are led by an apostolic vicar having the title *of Aleppo*. The size of the Latin community is due above all to the considerable number of male and female religious working in the country.

In the course of the nineteenth century, the Protestant missions succeeded in gaining members who formed the Arab Evangelical Church. Among the Armenians who had arrived in Syria in 1915, there was a group of Armenian Protestants. Both groups maintained an independent organisation. Recently, a little group of Baptist tendency has gained recognition as a distinct community.

Below is a table of the different Churches or ecclesial communities in Syria:

A	Catholics
1.	Melkite Greek Catholics: almost 350,000 faithful Five eparchies: the Patriarchal Eparchy of Damascus, the eparchies of Aleppo, Homs, Lattakieh, Bosra (Hauran)
2.	Syrian Catholics: nearly 50,000 faithful Four eparchies: Jezireh (Hassakeh), Aleppo, Homs, Damascus
3.	Maronites: almost 45,000 faithful Three eparchies: Aleppo, Lattakieh (Tartous) and Damascus
4.	Armenian Catholics: nearly 40,000 faithful Three eparchies: Jezireh, Aleppo, Damascus
5.	Chaldeans: almost 20,000 faithful Single eparchy of Aleppo
6.	Latins: nearly 20,000 faithful One district, the Apostolic Vicariate of Aleppo
B	Orthodox
1.	Greek Orthodox: nearly 700,000 faithful Seven dioceses: the Patriarchal Diocese of Damascus, the dioceses of Aleppo, Hama, Homs, Hauran (Suweyda), Lattakieh, Akkar, straddling Lebanon
2.	Syrian Orthodox: almost 150,000 faithful Four dioceses: the Patriarchal Diocese of Damascus, Aleppo, Homs and Jezireh (Hassakeh)
3.	Armenian Orthodox: nearly 250,000 Two dioceses: Aleppo, Damascus and the Vicariate of Jezireh depending on Aleppo
4.	Assyrians: almost 25,000 faithful Single diocese of Jezireh (Hassakeh)
C	Protestants
1.	Nearly 25,000 faithful spread among three groups: Arab Evangelical Protestants
2.	Armenian Evangelical Protestants
3.	Union Church (Baptist tendency)

Inter-community relations have improved with the renewal of the ecumenical spirit. Catholics meet in the Assembly of Catholic Patriarchs and Bishops of Syria and the three Patriarchs resident in Damascus, the Greek Catholic, Greek Orthodox and Syrian Orthodox meet fairly often. Despite all that, lack of unity and co-ordination at local level remain a great handicap, partly overcome through the participation of them all in the Middle East Council of Churches.

Syria's Christianity represents one of the oldest Christian traditions of apostolic origin and it is the seat of three patriarchates which have played an important role in inter-Church relations. The Melkite Greek Catholic Patriarchate played a considerable role in Vatican II in opening the Catholic communion to the traditional values of the East and to ecumenism. The Greek Orthodox Patriarchate plays, in the concert of Byzantine Orthodox Churches, a moderating role between Slavs and Greeks and bears witness to an Arab Church on good terms with Muslims and Catholics in the region. The Syrian Orthodox Patriarch is the supreme leader of his denomination and exercises his jurisdiction as far as South India.

The Christians of various communities feel themselves to be Christian above all. For the visit of the pope to Syria (5-8 May 2001), the Orthodox were keen to take part in the preparatory committee and to receive him in the same way as Catholics.

We think that that visit made Syria and its Christianity better known, that it gave back hope and strength to Christians to maintain their presence in the country and that it fired progress towards unity in full ecclesial communion. It also affirmed national understanding and Islamic-Christian dialogue.

The Church of Syria, proud of its past, is attentive to the present and trusting of the future.

CAN WE RE-IMAGINE ISLAM AS SOLELY WITH A MECCAN IDENTITY, AS SET OUT IN THE WRITINGS OF KENNETH CRAGG?
David Derrick*

In Cragg's partly autobiographical book *Faith and Life Negotiate*, he demonstrates how his long engagement with Islam allows him to be positive regarding Christian-Muslim relations, while remaining able to critique both Christianity and Islam (1994b). Thus, when noting distinctions between the Meccan and the Medinan surahs in the Qur'an, he feels able to question its original intention. Is it to give a theology of Unity based on the Meccan surahs, or to give a political Islamic authority based on the Medinan surahs? Although many would say that both are intertwined, Cragg questions if it is possible for 'divine Unity' to be bound to politics, particularly those relating to war (2001b, 96).

To establish a solely Meccan identity it would be necessary, through 'gentle negotiation' to evaluate the Islamic understanding of the Qur'an alongside that of modern scholarship. These include the problems of translation, Qur'anic criticism and interpretation, the role and status of Muhammad, the problems of abrogation, and the lack of a central authority in Islam. Cragg's own approach to Islam is the overarching consideration. His disdain of power in relation to religion is evident in his misgivings concerning the Anglo-Catholic Movement within Anglicanism (Cragg being an Evangelical Anglican). In *Faith and Life Negotiate*, Cragg becomes uncharacteristically exercised about a book he purchased as a young student while at Oxford. *Northern Catholicism* was published to commemorate the centenary of Keble's Assize Sermon, the accepted signal of the Oxford Movement. Cragg asks whether 'Samuel was not at odds with himself in peevishly denouncing fledgling Jewish

---

* The author would like to thank Anthony O'Mahony for his assistance in this research and also that of Christopher Brown, particularly his article 'Kenneth Cragg on Shi'a Islam and Iran: An Anglican Theological Response to Political Islam', in *ARAM: Society for Syro-Mesopotamian Studies*, Vol. 20, 2008.

kingship yet loftily accommodating it?' He concludes by apologising for speaking about this 'turbulence' of his mind (1994 b, 74). These questions and feelings concerning the relationship between religion and power stayed with him.

Cragg's Engagement with Islam

Christopher Lamb, in *The Call to Retrieval*, gives a comprehensive account of the influences which have moulded Cragg's thought. He sees as one of Cragg's greatest gifts the 'ability to search out from the most uncompromising material the unexpected evidence which indicates that the Spirit of God is never inactive' (1997, 165). Carefully assessing Cragg's 'vocation' to Islam he finds that there has been no significant change in Cragg's viewpoint across a long and extensive literary career. One theme that Lamb claims is evident throughout Cragg's work is the need for rapport to overcome alienation from one another and also from God. Lamb argues that this 'theory of relationships' and Cragg's appreciation of the spiritual dimension in interfaith relationships, counters the claims that Cragg's approach leads to an eccentric understanding of Islam which avoids certain theological issues. He also shows Cragg's awareness of the danger of appearing to be without a theology of religions (23-24). Lamb regards Cragg's over-riding mission to Islam is the acknowledgment of Jesus as the Christ, as understood by Christians (114). It is this prevailing sense of mission that leads to distrust by some authors.

The line Cragg draws between Muslim orthodoxy and heresy is vague. It is in *The Event of the Qur'an* that Cragg is at his clearest when stating his own position regarding Islamic orthodoxy. Here he covers such doctrines as the 'illiterate prophet' and the 'total inaccountability of the Qur'an'. By adopting a pragmatic approach, acknowledging and respecting the orthodox position, while not agreeing with it 'creedally', i.e. not accepting the professed system of religious beliefs, he proceeds to engage with Islam. Cragg is aware that making a distinction between 'the reality in the shape of belief and the shape of security in it' may cause 'alarm or suspicion' (1994 a, 21).

Working in Lebanon from 1939-47 Cragg developed his interest in philosophy. This knowledge was inevitably deepened when he became acting Head of the Philosophy Department at the American University of Beirut. Here he began to see philosophy rather than theology as the investigative methodology. Importantly, he began to question the role of the evangelist and the nature of mission. Charles Malik (then Head of Philosophy at AUB, before leaving to become Lebanon's first Ambassador in Washington) by accident or design, was to play an important role in this development. Cragg was clearly impressed with Malik, likening him to the ancient Greek statesman and orator Demosthenes (1994b, 102). Cragg gives a fuller evaluation of this fascinating man's life and his country in *Charles Malik and the meaning of Lebanon*, one of the last papers Cragg published (2011).

AUTHORITY AND ISLAM

Cragg considers how far the Islamic mind can be regarded as corporate. (2001a, 309) Whereas the Roman Catholic Church has a formal hierarchy and a Magisterium to make final and binding decisions regarding articles of faith, Islam has no such system of authority. In attempts to find a systematic authoritative system within Islam, writers like Jacques Waardenburg (a former teacher of Arabic and Islamic history at the University of California etc) have used such analytical categories as 'official', 'popular' and 'normative Islam' (Waardenburg 2002). Richard McGregor of Vanderbilt University argues that these terms are no longer helpful (2008, 220-222). He sees more promise in the approach of Norman Calder (formerly of the University of Manchester). Calder shows Islam being involved in an on-going process of interpreting its past instead of having a rigid hierarchy with defined articles of faith (Calder 2000, 66-86).

Calder initially examines creeds as the indicators of orthodoxy but finds this approach unsatisfactory. Referring specifically to Sunni Islam, he identifies the basic categories of thought in Islamic orthodoxy. He claims that the whole intellectual tradition of Sunni Islam is encapsulated in a comprehensive list of literary genres and argues that 'the limits of Islamic orthodoxy are expressed in this list' (2000, 75). Calder demonstrates how scholars, through the notion of 'intertextuality', articulate orthodoxy by exploring the boundaries that separate orthodox tradition from those traditions that are acknowledged to deviate from it (2000, 79). McGregor feels that Calder pushes his analysis too far when trying to show the relationship between the orthodox Sunni perspective and the rejected concepts of the Mu'tazili, Shi'i and Sufi. He also criticises Calder's list for being too disparate; that it is 'equivalent to simply saying that "orthodoxy" is drawn from a variety of belief options available to Muslims' (McGregor 2008, 222).

However, Calder's approach corroborates the 'yes-but-no' attitude that pervades Muslim-Christian themes. He shows that a great deal of philosophical terminology became absorbed into the tradition but, because of other writers' dislike of philosophy, it was not absolutely internalised. Thus 'inside Sunnism we have a kind of "yes" and "no" with regard to both the philosophers and the Mu'tazila' (2000, 81). While many writers would say 'yes', those who say 'no' would include the Indian Muslim scholar Hasan Askari who disallows any notion of such a discourse that would result in an evolving Islam (Siddiqui 1997, 111).

TRANSLATING THE QUR'AN

In Muslim countries where Arabic is not spoken, translation of the Qur'an becomes essential. Cragg gives this as an example of Islam adapting to modernity (1965, 168-9). Cragg looks behind the arguments regarding translation and considers the importance of 'luminous Arabic' to the Qur'an arguing that by being written in Arabic, Muhammad's position as a prophet was strengthened. He notes that the Qur'an frequently uses the formula, 'We have sent it down, an Arabic Qur'an,' fulfilling the tradition that prophets were 'to their own country' (2004a, 21). Translation difficulties have shown that while there has been some movement concerning orthodox attitudes towards Qur'anic translation, elsewhere traditionalists feeling attacked are reactive rather than proactive. Being mindful of Cragg's considerable Arabic scholarship, his own translations are used herein wherever possible.

QUR'ANIC CRITICISM

Although Cragg makes use of 'Virtuoso catenas of quotation', he equivocates on the question of the relationship of poetry to the

Qur'an (Lamb 1997, 6). This may be because of the treatment by Muslims of writers like Taha Hussein. Cragg may be identifying with, rather than reacting against, the Muslims' anguish resulting from the treatment of their tradition. In *Islamic Surveys* (1965), Cragg observes that critical textural study of the Qur'an has come mainly from outside Islam. With great foresight, he argues that further study should be made of primary sources, such as pre-Islamic poetry and patterns of speech (170-177).

Mohammad Ali Amir-Moezzi (Directeur d'études, Section des sciences religieuses, Sorbonne) observes that 'for more than a decade Michel Cuypers patiently worked on his meticulous system of rhetorical analysis of the Qur'an' (2007). Cuypers obtained a PhD in Persian literature at the University of Tehran. In 1986 he became a researcher for the Dominican Institute of Oriental Studies in Cairo. Amir-Moezzi, briefly outlining Cuypers rhetorical analysis, explains that the Qur'an is structured on a Semitic rhetoric which has been forgotten or overwhelmed by the later Hellenistic rhetoric. This makes it impossible to resolve the questions of the organisation of the text. In an interview in 2007 Cuypers points out that the Qur'an has no linear structure; its subjects are mixed together and some passages introduce topics extraneous to the context, thus giving the impression of complete incoherence (Strazzari 2007). The challenge is to find order within the text. Cuypers argues that fragmentation of the text forces classical scholars to comment on the Qur'an verse by verse, ignoring their literary context. He demonstrates that when a verse is put back into its context and enclosed within its proper textual structure, its true meaning becomes apparent. Cuypers maintains that rhetorical analysis, which presupposes that the Qur'an be regarded as a literary text, allows a contextual reading. Nevertheless, he insists that these foundational texts are alive and are still relevant to humanity's moral and spiritual development. Although Cuypers' work has yet to be fully developed and assessed, Anne-Sylvie Boisliveau, in her review of *Le Festin* by Cuypers, is generally supportive. She concludes that he is not dogmatic in employing Biblical exegesis to the Qur'an when using 'semitic rhetoric and a respectful intertextual analysis' (2007, 123). When asked if his work affects the traditions surrounding the Mecca and Medina surahs Cuypers declined to comment, stating that this was a matter for historians and he was not an historian. An English translation of *Le Festin* is available (Cuypers 2009).

Those resisting any literary approach to the Qur'an include Shabbir Akhtar (Assistant Professor of Philosophy at Old Dominion University, Norfolk, Virginia, USA) who has written widely on Islam, Christianity and current affairs. He unwaveringly affirms the traditional position that the Qur'an is the actual word of God which cannot be viewed as poetry. (2008, 141). Commenting on such certitude, Anthony O'Mahony (Director of the Centre for Eastern Christianity, Heythrop College, University of London) cites Cragg, 'While it [Islam] has not been rich in sceptics, there are aspects of the present that more readily evoke them' (2001, 117-118).

However, Peter von Sivers, (Associate Professor, History Department and Middle East Centre, University of Utah) claims that John Wansbrough was the first to systematically enquire as to the historicity of the Meccan and Medinan surahs using Biblical criticism (Von Sivers 2003, 9. Wansbrough 1997). Von Sivers suggests a way forward when considering the main constituents of Islam's 'story of origin': Mecca, the Hijrah, Medina, the Prophet, the early Muslim community and the expansion out of Arabia. By challenging the tradition that this is history, scholars question whether the 'story' should be considered as 'salvation history', or perhaps better described as 'a theology' which is not dependent on a history of Islamic origin. Von Sivers argues that scholars can only trace firm historical ground from the beginning of the seventh century onwards. Citing Michael Cook (Cook, 1981), von Sivers claims that 'all scholars are agreed that this horizon does not reach back into the pre-609 period' (Sivers, 2003, 7). A way through such conflicting views could be to regard the Qur'an as theology rather than history, while being cognisant of von Sivers observation that, 'no one knows for sure how to separate history from theology' (2003, 7).

By presenting the Qur'an as theology and not history the place and method of transmission of its message, the date of the material and the date of codification become of secondary importance. Equally so, such questions as the historicity of the Meccan and Medinan surahs and whether or not these were arbitrarily defined become less imperative. The feasibility of attaining the real facts of history and definitions of historical truth are also subject to academic debate. Of prime importance, is the interpretation of the text. Here there is a similarity to Cragg's position as outlined above. However, whereas von Sivers separates history from theology, Cragg argues for a different separation by accepting that Muslims have certain creedal beliefs, while not acknowledging the validity of those beliefs. Von Sivers' methodology might appear to be more honest, though not the most gentle by Cragg's standards.

Qur'anic Interpretation

Commenting on the study of Christianity by Muslim intellectuals, Katherine P Zebiri (Senior Lecturer in Arabic, SOAS, University of London) argues that the intricate relationship between Islam, Christianity and secular humanism is ambivalent and ironical. This is partly because humanist scholarship mainly contests Christianity, not Islam. She also laments the tiny minority of irenical Muslim writers (2003, 173-174). However, Abdulaziz Sachedina, Professor of Religious Studies at the University of Virginia, maintains that the early Muslim Empire used certain Qur'anic passages to justify toleration towards other faiths. Subsequently, different passages were commandeered that allowed expansionist wars against non-Muslim powers. Sachedina shows the relevance of, and some dangers associated with, asserting the primacy of the Meccan surahs. He notes that intellectuals fail to see how the hermeneutics of the Qur'an change over time. This allows outsiders to misconstrue and fear Islam and Muslims (2006, 291-292). Despite this, liberal Muslims have continued to write and publish; Esack for example, argues that a contextual approach to the Qur'an can be vindicated. Like Cragg, he insists that current events be considered when interpreting the Qur'an (Esack 1997, 49. Cragg1994a, 17).

Muhammad from a Christian Perspective

Christian W Troll SJ (chosen by the Vatican to participate in the dialogue with Muslim scholars) observes that the absolutism surrounding Muhammad and his teachings is a difficult concept for Christians (2007a, 292). He hopes that the efforts of certain theologians to find new approaches may allow recognition of Muhammad's prophethood. A good example would have been David Kerr (formerly at the centre for ecumenical study at Lund University, Sweden).

Kerr claims that Cragg's *Muhammad and the Christian,* motivated by Cragg's quest for 'a community in truth' to reconcile Christianity and Islam, is the most insightful essay of recent times concerning Christian assessment of Muhammad (Kerr 1996, 435). Kerr notes that Cragg first differentiates between 'Messiahship and Prophethood', and then distinguishes between Muhammad's 'prophecy' and the method of 'prophethood'; thus 'affirming the former while criticising the latter' (436). Kerr concludes that this can appear problematical, reflecting the ambiguous positions in Christianity and Islam, having to say 'yes' and 'no' at the same time. Kerr hopes that reinterpretation of different forms of liberation theology will advance Christian understanding of Muhammad (441). In *Muhammad: Prophet of Liberation*, Kerr develops this theme, citing Farid Esack, whose understanding of the Qur'an and Muhammad, advances dialogue on political theology between Muslims and Christians (Kerr 2000, 143). Kerr concludes that as Jesus in Jerusalem prayed for peace in that city, [Luke 19: 41-42] Muhammad made peace *(salam)* in the city *(madina)*. Kerr writes that Esack advocates a Christian-Muslim dialogue of alliance, following the liberative missions of Jesus and Muhammad (170).

Muhammad and the Qur'an

Joel Beinin and Joe Stork assert that 'the divine origin of the text has never been the topic of legitimate debate' (Benin 1997, 3). Cragg has never regarded this topic as proscribed, although he has always approached it with care and respect. Nevertheless, Cragg has not been without criticism. Quoting Akhtar, Esack observes that:

> Anything seen remotely conceding any aspect of Qur'anic revelation is summarily dismissed as making (Esack 1997, 62) 'conceptual room for posing a potentially dangerous question about the authority of scripture' (Akhtar 1991, 102).

Akhtar criticises Cragg for his opinion that, 'the traditional Islamic view about the nature of inspiration and revelation is strange, misguided in motivation and in any case, mistaken' (95). Noting that Cragg sees the model of revelation as 'mechanistic', puzzling and unnecessary, Akhtar abhors his insistence that a Christian assessment of Muhammad must focus on Muhammad's inner experience (97-99). Akhtar claims that Cragg is influenced by the Incarnation and that:

> The Islamic account, jejune and barren as it seems to Cragg, of the human contribution to the divine project of revelation, raises large questions about the whole nature of the relationship between the human and the divine (98).

Akhtar misses the essence of Cragg's argument that a Christian 'acknowledgement' of Muhammad would examine his inner experience; this being more important than his temporal power as expressed through Qur'anic revelation (Cragg 1999a, 6). Cragg turns the argument from the authorship of the Qur'an to the contrast between Mecca and Medina, observing that a Christian recognition of Muhammad becomes a response to the Islamic Scripture. 'It is safe to say that Muhammad himself would not have it otherwise. Nor would any faithful Muslim' (6). Akhtar frustratingly concludes that whilst Cragg appears impartial in his treatment of the Qur'an his motive is to undermine its authority (Akhtar 2008, 134). Obviously, Cragg denies such charges. It is ironic that Akhtar's next chapter heading is *The book as 'the frustrater'*.

Zebiri is critical of Akhtar's approach on a number of counts, particularly his simplistic view that the difference between Christian and Muslim thought is passivism versus activism. Akhtar thus ignores Christian thought on the relationship between faith and politics or power which is of the greatest concern to Cragg (Zebiri 2003, 171). The main disappointment of Akhtar's criticisms of Cragg is that almost two decades later Akhtar, in *The Quran and the Secular Mind*, rehearses the same criticisms(2008, 127-134).Yet, considering the negative Christian attitude towards Muhammad's prophethood, Cragg asks if after almost two decades, 'should there now be some different verdict?' He answers tantalisingly, 'Essentially no, but partially yes!' (1999 a, xi)

As already shown, this 'yes, but' approach is not uncommon. Another example being that of David Marshall (Associate Professor of the Practice of Christian-Muslim Relations and Director of the Anglican Episcopal House of Studies at Duke Divinity School NC USA). He writes that regarding Jesus, 'there is a Qur'anic 'Yes' and a Qur'anic 'But': an affirmation and a rejection.' Marshall observes a similar 'Yes, but' attitude towards Biblical scripture, concluding that there is a 'Yes, but' Qur'anic attitude towards Christianity (2006, 92). Such attitudes hamper a comprehensive overview of many of the aspects here under discussion. Nevertheless, Cragg happily regards paradox and irony as challenges.

MUHAMMAD'S ROLE

As shown above, Cragg questions the tradition that Muhammad played no role in the transmission and reception of the messages that form the text of the Qur'an. Elsewhere, his approach has been similarly probing. In *Muhammad and the Christian* Cragg's stated aim is to show how to remain, 'loyal to Christian criteria while outlining a positive response to Muhammad' (1999 a, viii). In *Muhammad in the Qur'an* he examines 'the soul of the *Sirah*', a topic not dealt with fully in any of his previous books. He explores 'the psyche of Muhammad in the incidence of a sacred text to which he was the unique party.' Such a study is part of Cragg's 'interfaith hope' to bring together an Islamic and a Christian understanding of God (2001b, 2-5).

In *The Weight in the Word,* Cragg attempts to find commonalities in the understanding of prophethood in the Bible and the Qur'an. He notes that although Muslims have 'always insisted on a long prophetic sequence anticipating its culmination in the Prophet,' (i.e. the Patriarchs), the Qur'an does not mention 'the goodly fellowship' that 'stretched from Hosea, Isaiah, and Jeremiah to Ezekiel and Malachi.' For Cragg these prophets are the summation of 'Hebrew ethicism', the critical conscience of patriarchs and priests. This supplants earlier understandings of prophets as seers and soothsayers (1999b, vi). While Cragg finds this omission mysterious (1999b, 71), Troll believes emphatically that the omission is not accidental, but is in keeping with the spirit of the Qur'an. If Jeremiah and all 'the suffering servants' were included in the Qur'an, this would bring into question basic Muslim convictions (Troll 2007a, 299).

Cragg sees no such subterfuge and attempts to link Muhammad with the Biblical prophets by first showing their differences (1999b, 6-16). The contrast for Cragg is that Muhammad becomes 'head of state' whereas the Biblical prophets remain the kings' mentors. Another difference is the broken covenant of the Jewish exiles, as opposed to the persecution of Muhammad and his followers in Mecca that preceded their voluntary 'exile' to Medina, the *Hijrah*. This latter does not represent God's forgiveness but the resolve of Muhammad in the context of his politics.

Cragg argues that accepting the differences between the Biblical and Qur'anic prophethood allows one to understand both traditions 'under the single category of prophethood' (1999b, 9). He calls for a discernment of a Hebraic role in the Qur'an's formation suggesting that the Qur'anic phrase 'The people of the Book' shows the link between a Scripture and an identity. Muhammad's people initially lacked both 'book' and 'apostle'. Thus, Cragg claims they were excluded from a Judaic identity, being *ummiyyun*, 'illiterate', in the sense of not having an Arabic Scripture. Judaic precedent drew the feuding Arab tribes into unity by being 'scripturized' in the vernacular. Cragg believes that this theme is clearly expressed in the Qur'an through such phrases as 'an Arabic Qur'an'. If so, this aspect of Biblical tradition is a factor in the origin of Islam. Cragg argues that disparities between the Biblical text and that of the Qur'an do not affect this link and observes that while the Qur'an merits its own originality, it whispers its own historical incident. He further asserts that the setting in which the Qur'an was received does not affect its claim to a divine origin, noting that the Qur'an refers back to Biblical patriarchs. Cragg concludes, 'Muslim orthodoxy, then can have no quarrel with the inter-association of Bible and Qur'an that *The Weight in the Word* assumes' (1999b, 10).

Troll, while not admitting to the prophethood of Muhammad, feels that by recognising the context of Muhammad and the Qur'an there is more hope of Christian-Muslim communication (2007, 300). This approach resembles von Sivers' methodology (as outlined above) more than Cragg's, although Troll does not stress the Qur'anic qualities of 'patient and courteous manner' that Cragg advocates.

Cragg asserts that the Qur'an makes it clear that Muhammad's experience of *wahy* (the way in which, as a tool of God, Muhammad received the words without mental forethought), is free from 'the skills or vagaries of professional poets' (1999b, 10). This, Cragg interprets as Muhammad's urgent disavowal of professional prophets, i.e. soothsayers. Cragg compares this experience to that of Amos, 'I was no prophet nor a prophet's son' (Amos 7:14). Claiming that both were despised for pretending to be prophets they had to deny that charge and then affirm their true prophethood, Cragg justifies 'associating things Qur'anic with things Biblical' (11).

While accepting that the two prophethoods diverge and entwine Cragg hopes that by being shown their similarities, Muslims will consider the range of prophetic experience and appreciate the qualities of Amos, Jeremiah, and Micah with his 'spears into ploughshares'. Troll's argument would require Muslims to see, as a condition of prophethood, the integrity of the word's superseding power, with honourable failure preferable to dishonourable success. But, as Troll remarks, 'this does not correspond to the norms and values of the Qur'an' (2007, 299).

MUHAMMAD IN MECCA

Conceding the tradition that Muhammad is 'merely' a messenger, there is also a Muslim tradition and philosophy contemplating his status. As Cragg writes, these endow Muhammad's passivity with greater 'cosmic and ontological dimensions', justifying viewing Muhammad's experience as akin to those of the Biblical prophets (1999b, 23). Yet, while Biblical biographies of the prophets enhance understanding of the 'inner psyche of prophetic experience', the Qur'an is subtly different. Cragg observes that although the Qur'an is rich in its imagery of the Hijaz and the markets of Mecca, there is no biographical prelude for the reader to locate the incidence of Muhammad's self-awareness. He is seldom depicted in any personal capacity, nor are there any 'Jeremiah-style soliloquies'. There are no birth narratives like those ascribed to 'Isa (Jesus). The closest the Qur'an comes to depicting Muhammad's calling are allusions to being 'wrapped in a mantle' and being 'enfolded'. The Qur'an shows all the previous prophets of whom Muhammad is their 'ultimate seal', underscoring Muhammad's role. They denounced idolatry, affirming the divine unity.

In *An Introductory Essay* Cragg gives a concise traditional overview of Muhammad's experiences in Mecca (*Readings in the Qur'an* 2004b, 20-23). The most important elements being, that when Muhammad was born in Mecca (570 AD), it stood on a trade route between Yemen and the Levant, an area of tribal feuding and raiding of caravans. Mecca was commercially important and a place of (pagan) pilgrimage. The sacred *haram* (enclosure) surrounded the Ka'bah; it was built by Abraham but degraded by pagan rites. Control of commerce and the pilgrims belonged to a tribe called the Quraish. Muhammad, orphaned early in life, was raised initially by his grandfather and then his uncle (Abu Talib), his 'stout protector' (2004a, 39). Cragg casually points out that history is not decisive regarding Muhammad's early influences, but notes that, 'A habit of meditation intensified around his fortieth year' (2004b, 21). He received his summons to:

> arise and warn, Your Lord magnify, your garments purify, and shun defilement. Give not with a view to self-increase and turn patiently to your Lord (Surah 74, 1-7)

Through his developing sense of prophethood Muhammad proclaims to Meccans the worship of the one God, rejection of idols and preparation for 'the day of judgement'. Understandably Mecca and the Quraish, their interests challenged, reacted against his preaching. Cragg reasons that a sense of the rejection and loneliness of Muhammad's mission comes through in such surahs as:

> They have seen some chance of commerce and amusement they have gone off and left you standing (Surah 62.11) (Cragg 2008, 52).

Cragg contends that Muhammad, although left standing by the indifferent vilifiers, has Allah standing with him. He concludes, 'In fact, if not in essence, what is Allah's suffers inside what is the Messenger's.' As if anticipating accusations of trying to Christianise the Qur'an, Cragg asks:

> Whether we can think of fact as separate from essence since God is One will always be the supreme question for the '*ulama*' (2008, 53).

Cragg now asks how far suffering enters into prophethood and how far it enters into God, which Cragg admits is a very Christian question (2008, xiii). From another angle Cragg pursues this point.

Noting that one of Allah's paramount names is *Al-Sabur*, 'the Patient', he asks if this should not be linked with *sabr*, 'enduring with patience' which is enjoined on the 'burdened messengers'. Cragg gives several examples from the Qur'an where patience belongs to Allah and is required in the prophet. Reasoning that the Qur'an commands the use of patience when spreading the word, not force or compulsion, Cragg argues that words carry no swords, that words are 'the hallmark of the Meccan Qur'an' (2008, 53).

From this Cragg is able to state that Muhammad's 'pain and travail of bearing' is the reason for the question:

> Do you think you can compel them to believe? (Surah 10.99)

As Cragg observes, no Biblical prophet (with the possible exception of Elijah) thought this possible. In the Qur'an there are six occasions when 'the confinement of his mission to words is strictly enjoined on the Prophet.' For example:

> We have not sent you as guardian, or warden, over them (Surah 42.48).

Muhammad is frequently reminded that hostility and indifference was the fate of prophets:

> The apostle said: 'Lord, my people have been altogether dismissive of this Qur'an.' It has been Our way in the case of every prophet to have him experience enmity from these who are hell-bent (Surah 25.30-31).

Surah 42.6 adds, 'It is not your job to be responsible for them.' (Cragg 2008, 54) Cragg's translation of this surah shows a hint of his enduring Lancastrian bluntness; Tarif Khalidi gently translates it as, 'you are not a guardian over them' (2008).

Over the thirteen years of Muhammad's mission in Mecca (609-622), the confrontation hardened. The Qur'an assures Muhammad that the hostile reaction to him is in keeping with that of previous prophets. These are Biblical parallels, Cragg maintains, that come from the middle of the Meccan period when Muhammad was ridiculed. These were used as precedents to show that adversity signalled veracity: Muhammad's tribulations were a sign of authenticity.

Cragg cautiously links the predicaments and the solutions of the Biblical prophets with those of Muhammad in Mecca, in particular the last prophets of the Biblical canon whose self-scrutiny might have given way to a religio-political vision. Muhammad, Cragg maintains, conducted such self-interrogation prior to the Hijrah. But whereas Hebrew prophethood in giving way to the apocalyptic 'sought comfort in the sober realism of the Wisdom writers or submitted to the melancholy muse of Qoheleth', Muhammad sought his answer in the Hijrah (1999b, 83).

The burden on Muhammad and his few followers was magnified by personal tragedy; the death of his first wife, Khadijah, whom Cragg describes as 'his wife and mainstay in vocation', perhaps evokes the role of Cragg's own wife, Melita (2004a, 39). The death of Muhammad's guardian uncle in 619 left him to ponder 'on the mystery of the incontrovertible message denied by entrenched perversity' (2004b, 22). Cragg claims that the deepening pattern of Muhammad's rejection gave rise to the reasoning that resulted in the Hijrah. 'It therefore underlies the entire historic polity of Islam' (1999b, 72).

The Hijrah

In *The Readings in the Qur'an* Cragg states that, 'The Qur'an makes little actual reference to the event of the Hijrah in narrative terms.' There may be oblique references to the Hijrah in Surahs 9.40 and 36.9 but the event nevertheless marks the beginning of the Islamic calendar in 622 CE, rather than, say, Muhammad's birth (2004b, 23). Cragg is surprised that being so pivotal, the Hijrah is not explicitly commanded in the Qur'an (2004a, 40). In an interview with this author, when pressed on this matter, Cragg affirmed that Muhammad had not been sent down any message about leaving Mecca. This move was entirely Muhammad's own decision. By contrast, the Islamic scholar Syed Abul Hasan Ali Nadwi argues that the Prophet was 'commanded' to leave Mecca although Nadwi gives no reference for this 'command' (1983, 128). Cragg further notes that this drastic 'migration' necessitated abandoning Mecca and

Abraham's Ka'bah, thus cutting his followers' tribal bond. Muhammad's reception in Medina by the Yathribites was potentially precarious, as they could not ensure the safety of all of his followers.

In a disdainful tone Cragg maintains that while the Hebrew prophets experienced exile, this was not Hijrah. They coped with adversity through Messianic hope, not the 'self-help of some Hijrah' (1999b, 20). In contrast to the cross, Muhammad was vindicated in 'manifest victory' uniting faith and power. The cross however, represents both the will to suffer un-coercively and the malignancy of the world as 'a crucifying place'.

MUHAMMAD IN MEDINA

Cragg pictures a process by which the town of Yathrib came to be called Medina (*Medinat un-Nabi,* meaning 'the city of the Prophet') (2001b, 91). At first Muhammad, still powerless, was given sanctuary by a minority of the Yathribites. In *Muhammad in the Qur'an* Cragg is concerned with how the story developed 'within the personal self of Muhammad' (2001b, 94). The Qur'an dissertates on the requirements for the liturgical life of Muslims, their legal duties, and their campaigning against Mecca.

Cragg notes the comments in Surah 8 on Muhammad's first victory in battle against the Quraish at Badr:

> Go on taking the fight to them until there is no more subversion and religion is wholly God's (Surah 8.39-40).

This surah mentions the *Yaum al-Farqan* (the 'time that discriminates') which Cragg interprets as discriminating the 'precarious *islam* of pre-Badr from the new *élan* and prestige that the "Day of Decision" at Badr set in train' (2001b, 92, note 3). Cragg's choice of the word *élan* (an impetuous rush) suggests that he is disdainful of the whole enterprise. Circumstances became 'vigorous, robust, forthright, assertive, even ugly and violent.' Interpreting the consequence on Muhammad's personal psyche, Cragg shows that the Qur'an reflects a 'strident, harshly peremptory and necessarily aggressive' mood. However, he argues that reluctance to fight was overridden by 'sterner readings of duty and valour' and by seeing war as divinely legitimised (2001b, 96-97). Yet Cragg's approach in *Readings in the Qur'an* is more sympathetic. He notes that the passages in the Medinan Qur'an show the fighting was not gratuitous but punctuated with a searching of conscience and a longing for peace, though these were trounced by claims that God and Muhammad gave authority for war (2004b, 39).

Cragg argues that the more strident tone of the Medinan Qur'an can be demonstrated in the transitions of the word *fitnah*, a tribulation or a test (2004a, 41). In Mecca where Muhammad was oppressed, *fitnah* meant persecution. When in Medina with the onset of hostilities, *fitnah* became 'timidity' in face of martial claims. Later, when Muslims were the dominant power, *fitnah* meant 'sedition' or 'subversion' practised by the opposition, no longer able to oppress but still, conspiratorially, trying to harm. Cragg gives Qur'anic examples:

> ... subverting is a greater [evil] than *qatl* (slaying) (Surah 2.271).

Surah 2.191 is in the same vein:

> Fight them until there is no more subversion and religion is wholly God's.

This goal being achieved, Cragg argues that the justification for force ceases:

> The politically submissive society vindicates both the message and the policy of the successful faith. It is the forthright logic of the Qur'an ... (1999a, 34)

Bassam Tibi, a German political scientist who critiques Islam as a cultural system, writes that Muhammad founded the first Islamic political structure, its fundamentals being stated in the 'municipal code of Medina' (1991, 34-36). He cites W Montgomery Watt for whom this code represents a treaty of alliance following traditional Arab principles. Tibi notes that the Muslim community asserts that there can only be one concept of Islam. He observes that those early Muslims of Medina who did not submit themselves to the Prophet were called 'the hypocrites' *(munafiqun)*, yet he sees that there are two conflicting concepts in Islamic doctrine. The first looks backwards to the original Muslim community in Medina as the enduring model, constraining development to a utopian past. The other looks forward to the future when all humanity will be united under the banner of Islam.

Other writers see more positive factors in the Medinan period. Michael Nazir-Ali, former Anglican Bishop of Rochester, sees the 'Constitution or Covenant of Medina' as a remarkable document, which ought to have greater influence on Islamic polity. Noting that there are many projects for an Islamic state in different parts of the world, he asks why such a state could not be modelled on the Constitution of Medina. (2006, 61) By contrast he comments that a number of scholars, including Mahmud Taha, call for '"abrogation in reverse", that is for a return to a purely Meccan form of Islam' (151).

Abrogation

The Arabic word *naskh* (usually translated as 'abrogation') is a term for Islamic legal exegesis which deals with seemingly contradictory material in the Qur'an and the Prophetic Sunna. It employs the logic of chronological and progressive revelation. The situations encountered during Muhammad's prophethood necessitated new rulings to meet the Muslim community's changing circumstances. The often-quoted example is the early community's increasing militancy towards pagans, Jews and Christians. The Meccan Surahs urge patience in the face of mockery and rejection whereas the Medinan Surahs incite warfare against unbelievers.

Sachedina comments that judgements made in the past regarding abrogation of the text are the principal problems facing modern academics when dealing with interfaith relations. He argues that earlier scholars ignored the sense of those verses regarded as abrogated, or applied a loose meaning of the term abrogation in its lexical sense. Consequently, chronologically late (Medinan) verses, which are hostile to disbelievers of Islam abrogate the more tolerant earlier (Meccan) ones (2006, 300).

The following two examples show the range of opinion that exists. The former chief justice of the High Court of Cairo, Muhammad Sa'id al-'Ashmawy, argues that many verses were temporary. But militants cite verses regarding *jihad* and the treatment of non-Muslims as immutable and ahistorical, rather than specific to a historical context that no longer exists (Fluehr-Lobban 1998, 20). Muhammad Mustafa al-Azami, was born in India in the early 1930s. He now holds Saudi citizenship, is Professor Emeritus at King Sa'ud University (Riyadh) and is considered a leading scholar of Hadith. He claims Cragg's proposal to abrogate the Medinan surahs implies that politicised Islam is at odds with Western democracies. Al-Azami then affirms that the Prophet is the only sanctioned expounder of the Qur'an. It is difficult to trace Cragg's actual words, as al-Azami's references seem to be corrupt (Al-Azami 2005).

CRITIQUE OF CRAGG'S APPROACH

David Kerr notes that the distinction made between the Meccan and Medinan surahs by contemporary Christian apologists began with Medieval Latin polemics in Spain. He writes that Blaise Pascal summarised this in his aphorism:

> Muhammad chose the path of human success, while Jesus Christ chose that of human suffering (Kerr 2000, 160).

Kerr reasons that compared with Jesus' death and suffering, Muhammad transgressed the requirements for prophethood by gaining political power, either from an overbearing vision of his righteousness or to promote God's word against determined opposition. Kerr does note a 'sharp rebuke from Fazlur Rahman' that Christian scholars are so fixated on such distressing accounts as the crucifixion that achieving political success appears repugnant. If God is a God of history, then historical forces can be used when ethically and morally feasible. Finally, Kerr shows that Rahman sees the Meccan prophethood being fulfilled in the socio-political application of spiritual and ethical principles in Medina (Kerr 2000, 160).

Lamb observes that a familiar theme in Cragg's writing is that the Hijrah is the 'hinge' of the Muslim story, enabling Muhammad's 'transition from prophethood to rulership' (Lamb 1997, 89). He also detects 'gaps in Cragg's writing about the Qur'an compared with that of Fazlur

Rahman.' Lamb shows that while Cragg accepts the significance of the Qur'an for a modern writer like Rahman, this differs from that which Cragg portrays. Rahman sees the Qur'an as a purely functional 'socio-political order in human society' disregarding any spiritual dimension. Lamb argues that Cragg sees such concepts as the dangerous use of power in the service of religion and that 'we are only at the beginning of this kind of reading of the Qur'an outside its own community' (Cragg 1973, 194). Lamb reasons that omissions in Cragg's explanation of the Qur'an show an individualistic view of Islam (1997, 145).

Cragg's own experience and 'vision' of Islam is unique. Nevertheless, there are also difficulties with his interpretation of Muhammad's use of power, particularly when considering Cragg's own disdain of power. Kerr argues that this leads to Cragg's 'sense of antithesis between the ministries of Muhammad and Jesus'. Kerr sees this antithesis as problematic given Cragg's desire to see 'the essential unity of their conviction about the rule of God' (Kerr 1996, 436). Here Cragg is at his most vulnerable to the charge of 'judging Islam by its external history but Christianity by its inner spirit' (Lamb 1997, 126). Lamb observes that Cragg sees those liberal Muslim thinkers who support the primacy of Islam's Meccan surahs as 'a self-correcting mechanism within Islam' (Lamb 1997, 113).

Conclusion

Cragg has identified a 'harsh' Islam. He has suggested that the Islam set out in the Meccan surahs is not only non-belligerent but also truer to its original ideal. In the Introduction to *The Qur'an and the West* Cragg summarises his argument for a Meccan Islamic identity. He describes this identity as:

> the peace-held Islam that first was, and ever remains, the *raison d'être* of the whole, the Islam to which in the Qur'an, Muhammad was rigorously bound as only 'a preached summons' to submission to Allah.(2006, 10).

While understanding the rationale behind the Hijrah Cragg argues that, facing constant opposition, Muhammad closed off this 'peace-held' identity with the use of force, 'thereby seeming to abrogate the Meccan "innocence".' Cragg observes that historic Islam is left with the ongoing dilemma of the 'two minds of Islam': the Meccan 'faith-care' and the Medinan 'sense of legitimate belligerence'. Philip Lewis (Principal of Bradford Churches for Dialogue and Diversity and a specialist in Christian-Muslim relations) explains this belligerency in a more positive manner:

> The Sunni majority belong to a religious tradition which in its classical development took power for granted (2003, 88).

Cragg concludes that as a 'preached religion' Islam has survived for fifteen centuries into an era of global order; 'what was once a rationale for recourse to armed belligerence is quite superseded' (2006, 11). There can be no 'compulsions' to belief. He continues:

> Muslims addressing their own vocation need to be enlisted, but only on their own principles, not as if recruited for Western interests. ... Its [Islam's] potential to be enlisted, not in the West's cause, but in humanity's and their own, is not in doubt ... (19-20)

If the Meccan surahs prioritise the Medinan then a generally agreed 'principle of interpretation will be needed to permit applying some verses of the Qur'an and accompanying Sunna instead of others' (An-Na'im 1996, 34). Cragg demonstrates that the Meccan surahs are an 'antidote' to the harsher Medinan surahs. Therefore a 'yes' can be given to the question this paper sets because the Meccan surahs show the true heart and non-violent side of Islam.

If, as Cragg also argues, Muslims themselves must address this matter (though with the support of non-Muslims) then a 'no' must be given, as the Medinan surahs are an essential part of the current Islamic identity. Calder writes:

> Contemporary Muslims are ... offered by their tradition a massive, complex, sophisticated heritage, a generous profusion of modes of religious fulfilment,

and any step towards making that heritage smaller must
be a bad thing (2000, 84).

Thus, given this sense of 'yes-and-no', it is possible to re-imagine
an Islam which has a solely Meccan identity. Bishop Kenneth Cragg
asserts also that this is a Christian mission and a human duty. Therefore
the question of a Meccan Islamic identity conjoins all, not just those
involved in Christian-Muslim relations.

REFERENCES

Akhtar, Shabbir. 1991. An Islamic model of revelation. *Islam & Christian Muslim Relations* Vol. 2, no. 1, (June): pp. 95-105.
Akhtar, Shabbir. 2008. *The Quran and the secular mind: A philosophy of Islam.* Routledge, London.
Al-Azami, Muhammad Mustafa. 2005. *The history of the Qur'anic text: from revelation to compilation.* Suhail Academy, Pakistan.
Amir-Moezzi, Mohammad Ali. 2007. Préface to *Le Festin, une lecture de la sourate al-Mâ'ida,* Michel Cuypers. Lethielleux, Paris, p. iii.
An-Na'im, Abdullahi Ahmed. 1996. *Toward an Islamic Reformation: Civil Liberties, Human Rights, and International Law.* Syracuse University Press, Syracuse.
Beinin, Joel, and Joe Stork. 1997. 'On the modernity, historical specificity, and international context of political Islam'. In *Political Islam: essays from Middle East Report.* I B Tauris, London.
Boisliveau, Anne-Sylvie. 2007. Review: 'Le Festin, une lecture de la sourate al-Mâ'ida, by Michel Cuypers'. *Journal of Qur'anic Studies*, 9 (1), pp. 119-123.
Calder, Norman. 2000. 'The limits of Islamic orthodoxy'. In *Intellectual traditions in Islam.* Ed. Farhad Daftary. I B Tauris, London, pp. 66-86.
Cook, Michael. 1981. *Early Muslim dogma: a source-critical study.* Cambridge University Press, Cambridge.
Cragg, Kenneth, 1965. *Islamic surveys, counsels in contemporary Islam.* Edinburgh University Press, Edinburgh.
Cragg, Kenneth. 1994a. *The event of the Qur'an: Islam in its scripture.* Oneworld Publications, Oxford. Orig. pub. 1971.
Cragg, Kenneth. 1994b. *Faith and life negotiate: A Christian story-study.* The Canterbury Press, Norwich.

Cragg, Kenneth. 1999a. *Muhammad and the Christian: a question of response.* Oneworld, Oxford. Orig. pub. 1984.

Cragg, Kenneth. 1999b. *The weight in the word: prophethood: biblical and qur'anic.* Sussex Academic Press, Brighton.

Cragg, Kenneth. 2001a. 'Commonweal ahead?' In *Christians and Muslims in the Commonwealth: A dynamic role in the future,* eds. Anthony O'Mahony and Ataullah Siddiqui. Altajir World of Islam Trust, London, pp. 308-30.

Cragg, Kenneth. 2001b. *Muhammad in the Qur'an: the task and the text.* Melisende, London.

Cragg, Kenneth. 2004a. *A certain sympathy of scriptures: biblical and qur'anic.* Sussex Academic Press, Brighton.

Cragg, Kenneth. 2004b. *Readings in the Qur'an.* Sussex Academic Press, Brighton. Orig. pub. 1988.

Cragg, Kenneth. 2006. *The Qur'an and the West.* Melisende Publishing, London.

Cragg, Kenneth. 2008. *Mosque sermons: a listener for the preacher.* Melisende Publishing, London.

Cragg, Kennth. 2011. 'Charles Malik and the meaning of Lebanon', *Journal of Eastern Christian Studie*s 63 (1-2), 221-232.

Cuypers, Michel. 2007. *Le Festin, une lecture de la sourate al-Mâ'ida.* Lethielleux, Paris.

Cuypers, Michel. 2009. *The Banquet.* Convivium, Florida.

Donner, Fred M. 2008. 'The historical context'. In *The Cambridge Companion to the Qur'an,* Jane Dammen McAuliffe. Cambridge University Press, Cambridge, pp. 23-39.

Esack, Farid. 1997. *Qur'an, liberation & pluralism: an Islamic perspective of interreligious solidarity against oppression.* Oneworld, Oxford.

Fluehr-Lobban Carolyn. 1998. *Against Islamic extremism, the writings of Muhammad Sa'id al-'Ashmawy.* University Press of Florida, Florida.

Kerr, David A. 1996. ' "He walked in the path of the Prophets." Towards Christian theological recognition of the Prophethood of Muhammad', *Christian-Muslim Encounters,* eds. Yvonne Yazbeck Haddad and Wadi Zaidan Haddad, University of Florida Press, Florida, pp. 426-446.

Kerr, David A. 2000. 'Muhammad: Prophet of Liberation—a Christian perspective from Political Theology', *Studies in World Christianity* Vol. 5, pp. 139-174.

Lamb, Christopher 1997. *The call to retrieval: Kenneth Cragg's Christian vocation to Islam.* London, Grey Seal.

Lewis, Philip. 2003. 'Christians and Muslims in the West: from isolation to shared citizenship?' *International Journal for the Study of the Christian Church* Vol. 3, no. 2, pp. 77-100.

Marshall, David. 2006. 'Heavenly religion or unbelief? Muslim perspectives on Christianity', *Anvil*, Vol. 23, no. 2: p. 92.

McGregor, Richard. 2008. Book Review: 'Defining Islam', *Journal of the American Academy of Religion* 76 (1), (January), pp. 220-222.

Nazir-Ali, Michael. 2006. *Conviction and conflict: Islam, Christianity and world order*. Continuum, London.

Nadwi, Syed Abul Hasan Ali. 1983. *The Message of the Mission*. The Islamic Foundation, Leicester.

O'Mahony, Anthony. 2001. 'Christians and Muslim-Christian relations: theological reflections'. In *Christians and Muslims in the Commonwealth: a dynamic role in the future, eds.* Anthony O'Mahony and Ataullah Siddiqui. Altajir World of Islam Trust, London, pp. 90-130.

Sachedina, Abdulaziz. 2006. 'The Qur'an and other religions'. In *The Cambridge Companion to the Qur'an,* ed. Jane Dammen McAuliffe. Cambridge University Press, Cambridge.

Siddiqui, Ataullah 1997. *Christian-Muslim dialogue in the Twentieth Century*. Palgrave Macmillan, Basingstoke.

von Sivers, Peter. 2003. 'The Islamic origins debate goes public', *History Compass* Vol. 1, no. 1, (January-December), pp. 1-16.

Strazzari, Francesco. 2007. 'The Bible, the Qur'an, and Jesus: how to reach the heart of the Muslim Creed', in Il Regno, issue no 4, (original in French). In Sandro Magister, *For a renewed interpretation of the Qur'an,* http://chiesa.espresso.repubblica.it/articolo/145581?&eng=y (accessed Sept 13 2013)

Tibi, Bassam. 1991. *Islam and the cultural accommodation of social change*. Trans. Clare Krojzl. Westview Press, Boulder.

Troll, Christian W. 2007 a. Muhammad—Prophet auch für Christen?' ['Muhammad—Prophet for Christians also?'] *Stimmen der Zeit* (5 May), pp. 291-303.

Waardenburg, J. 2002. *Official, popular, and normative religion in Islam*. Walter de Gruyter, Berlin.

Wansbrough, J. 1997. *Qur'anic studies: sources and methods of scriptural interpretation,* London Oriental Series, 31. Oxford University Press, Oxford.

Zebiri, Kate. 2003. *Muslims and Christians face to face*. Oneworld, Oxford. Orig. pub. 1997.

DIALOGUE: WHAT IS THE POINT OF IT?
Hugh Boulter

The original version of this paper was presented to the Living Stones theology group in September 2012. With a few minor amendments the original text remains much the same. However, it has been expanded partly to take into consideration various comments made in and after the original meeting concerning the nature of dialogue itself and the implications for a theology of change. In addition I became conscious that while most of my comments are drawn from experience in Britain; several members of the group are from a background in the Middle East with a very different context. I have therefore looked more closely at some of the papers in the *Living Stones Yearbook 2012* and in particular the first and second papers, 'The Current Situation of Christianity in the Middle East'[1] and 'The Synod for the Middle East: First Results and Future Possibilities'.[2] In the light of these two papers, I then reflect on their extensive comments about dialogue in relation to my underlying thesis.

There is a general consensus that dialogue is 'a good thing' and several people have put forward typologies of dialogue. For everyday use I find a modified version of Michael Barnes's typology, drawing on *Redemptoris Missio,* most helpful: the dialogue of theological exchange; the dialogue of friendship (Barnes has 'life'); the dialogue of action; and the dialogue of religious experience.[3] However, less has been written about what happens in dialogue and what it may achieve. In

---

[1] Audo, Antoine, 'The Current Situation of Christianity in the Middle East, especially Syria, after the Synod of the Middle East's final declaration (September 2012) and the Papal Visit to Lebanon', *Living Stones Yearbook 2012*, pp. 1-17.
[2] Bouwen, Frans, 'The Synod for the Middle East: First Results and Future Possibilities', *Living Stones Year Book 2012*, pp.18-37.
[3] Barnes, Michael, *Theology and the Dialogue of Religions*, Cambridge, 2002, p. 21.

this paper I want to look at three texts written over twenty years ago, which have not received the attention they deserve but which may help to answer the question posed in the title of this paper. The first is *The Dialogical Imperative: A Christian Reflection on Interfaith Encounter* by David Lochhead.[4] The second is *Postmodernism and Islam: predicament and promise*[5] by Akbar S Ahmed and the third is *The Nature of Prejudice*[6] by Gordon W Allport.

The focus will be on Christian/Muslim dialogue, not least because I shall support the arguments of Lochhead, Allport and Ahmed by reference to my own research and experience in this field, but I believe that the Christian/Muslim experience can be generalised to other areas of dialogue as well. This clearly has implications for the situation in Palestine/Israel and hence the Living Stones theology group.

My starting point is Lochhead. The key section comes in the middle of his book where he writes:

> The agnosticism, which I am suggesting is proper to dialogue, is an agnosticism that is prior to dialogue. In dialogue judgments will have to be made ... In other cases, we will discover the fruit of the Spirit in the midst of other religious traditions. In those cases, a positive response to what we find elsewhere will be appropriate. When we believe that we discern the work of God's Spirit, that too should be named ... We do have a warrant to discern the spirits.[7]

On reflection, a number of points come to mind. First, dialogue can and does take place at many different levels: e.g. the personal, the local, the national and the international. How do these different levels relate and influence each other? Secondly, such a pattern suggests different outcomes in different places and at different times. Thirdly, this approach implies a constantly changing outcome. Fourthly, there are important theological implications. How does this relate to our

---

4 Lochhead, David, *The Dialogical Imperative: A Christian Reflection on Interfaith Encounter*, SCM Press, London, 1988.
5 Ahmed, Akbar, *Postmodernism and Islam: Predicament and Promise*, Routledge, London, 1992.
6 Allport, Gordon, *The Nature of Prejudice*, Addison-Wesley, Reading MA, 1982 ed.
7 *Op.cit.*, p. 45.

Christian understanding of the nature of God, not only to the theology of religions but also to a theology of change?

Lochhead, a minister in the United Church of Canada and Emeritus Professor of Systematic Theology at Vancouver School of Theology, describes himself thus: 'I approach the subject of interfaith dialogue as one who was trained upon the borderline between philosophy of religion and systematic theology.'[8] Theologically he recognises the influence of Karl Barth and Søren Kierkegaard: philosophically he refers in particular to Plato, Martin Buber and Wittgenstein. From Plato and Buber he argues that, 'Dialogue is the means of knowing truth, the way our potential knowledge is made actual.'[9] Following Wittgenstein he argues that, 'The meaning of words needs to be understood from their role in life, from the "language games" in which they are used.'[10] It is what semanticists call 'the contextual theory of meaning'. In other words our understanding of the meaning of words is generated by their usage in specific contexts—what one might call dialogue. An interesting slant on this comes from an interview I conducted with Tim Winter, a Cambridge academic and convert (revert) to Islam. Our exchange ran as follows:

> HB: There is a particular question I wanted to ask you. In the West, in postmodern times—post-Wittgenstein I suppose—a particular understanding of how meaning is generated—what effect do you see this as having on Islam?
> TW: None whatsoever. Islam remains an uncomplicatedly scripture-based way of reading religion.
> HB: What I am trying to get at is that even if you have a fixed text, how it is understood now is going to be different from how it was understood in the first place, over a thousand years ago.
> TW: Unquestionably. Religions are primarily the product of what people wish to read into texts as a result of their own time-bound, socially conditioned needs and insecurities.[11]

---

8   Ibid., p.3.
9   Ibid., p.51.
10 Ibid., p.68.
11 Boulter, Hugh, *The Spirit in Islam: A Study in Christian-Muslim Dialogue and Theology of Religions*, Bristol University, 2003, p. 194.

Dialogue: What is the Point of It?

This raises many issues but clearly represents a 'bottom up' approach to religious understanding and is an outcome of my methodology which is more interested in what people actually believe rather than in what they think they ought to believe. This 'bottom up' approach is a general feature of ethnography. Lochhead does not consider the impact which the social sciences may have upon theology or upon our understanding of dialogue but it is in line with Richard Roberts's view:

> Sociology and theology which embody concerns for the other cannot afford to neglect or express contempt for ethnography, that is the effective representation and interpretation of what is actually happening in human lives.[12]

Another insight from ethnography is that in dialogue or other exchanges we are all changed to some extent by the encounter. The point was nicely made in a talk given by Dr Eleanor Nesbitt, Professor Emerita of Religions and Education at Warwick University. She was addressing a religiously diverse audience of some 200 students at Slough Grammar School on the topic of *Who Am I? Religious Diversity and Young People*. At the end of her talk and before we broke up into discussion groups for the rest of the day, she commented: 'By the end of today we will all be changed albeit imperceptibly by what we have heard and said.'[13]

From my own interviews, which were primarily designed to elicit information but in practice became vehicles for dialogue, there were several examples of how people's perceptions were changed. The most marked example was an interview with Yahya Michot, an Oxford academic. At the beginning of the interview in which I asked him to consider the possible parallels between a Christian understanding of the Holy Spirit and the Islamic concepts of *ruh* and *din al-fitrah* (a natural turning to God), he said, 'That one question of Spirit appears of course, and you would not deny it, as a very, very Christian approach ... so we are not on the same wavelength from the start.'[14]

---

12 Roberts, Richard H, 'Theology and Social Science' in Ford, David, ed., *The Modern Theologians*, Blackwell, Oxford, 1996, 2nd edition, p. 206.
13 Boulter, Hugh *Who Am I? Religious Identity and Young People* (DVD), *The Event*, Art Beyond Belief Slough 2012.
14 *The Spirit in Islam*, p. 198.

At the end of the interview, the following exchange took place:

> HB: It does seem to me extremely important, from a Christian point of view, that the theology is developed in such a way that it enables other religions to be respected and that is really what I am seeking to do.
> YM: I think it is important. I think speaking about the Spirit as you propose to do will be one of the ways, probably a good way to do so.[15]

A third aspect of ethnography in relation to inter-faith engagement is that, because it is a 'bottom up' rather than a 'top down' methodology, it tends to highlight differences rather than similarities. This is a welcome antidote to many theological discussions which tend to think about religions, especially Christianity and Islam, as unchanging reified entities.

An interesting and potentially important example of this difference of thinking within Islam became clear in my interviews. As is widely known, the Qur'an has several references to Christians and Jews, some of them favourable, some unfavourable. For example, Q 2.62 (Arberry's translation) reads:

> Surely they that believe, and they of Jewry and the Christians ... whoso believes in God and the Last Day, and works righteousness—their wage awaits them with their Lord, and no fear shall be upon them, neither shall they sorrow.[16]

By contrast Q 5.57 reads:

> O believers, take not Jews and Christians as friends; they are friends of each other. Whoso of you makes them his friends is one of them. God guides not the people of the evildoers.[17]

---

15 *Ibid.*
16 Arberry, Arthur J, *The Koran Interpreted*, Oxford University Press, Oxford, 1983, p. 8.
17 *Op. cit.*, p. 108.

Dialogue: What is the Point of It?

In my interviews both points of view are reflected: four take the first inclusivist point of view, while six either explicitly or implicitly follow the second exclusivist line. Indeed, it is fair to say that most were too polite to be blunt on the subject, although Tim Winter in his writings, where he follows Jane McAuliffe, writes: 'The conclusion must hence be drawn that the founding documents of Islam intend an abrogationist salvation history.'[18]

Ataullah Siddiqui of the Markfield Centre, Leicester, highlights the issue when I interviewed him:

> In one place the Qur'an says that, yes, among the nearest among you, you will find Christians and then there is a description about how they pray and how sincere they are, and all those things ... Then we also find that there are some negative critical remarks about Christians. Now my question to my fellow Muslims and scholars of religion is, 'How do you understand these two verses in today's context, in the British context?'[19]

These two attitudes are clearly of significance to Christians in Britain today and are but one example of an area for fruitful dialogue.

In this section I have suggested that dialogue is a dynamic process which helps us to engage with religious issues in a constantly changing context and which also helps us to generate new understanding.

I want now to consider the situation of those who do not wish to engage in dialogue, the reasons for it and the dangers of isolation. Following that I will consider some of the theological issues which emanate from engagement in the dialogical process.

I come to my second main text, Akbar Ahmed's *Postmodernism and Islam: Predicament and promise*.[20] Ahmed is a previous Pakistani High Commissioner in London, a former Cambridge anthropologist who currently holds several academic and public posts in the United States. In *Postmodernism and Islam* he reflects in a semi-autobiographical way about his time in Great Britain, offering trenchant comments about

---

18 Winter, Tim, 'The Last Trump Card: Islam and the Supersession of Other Faiths', *Studies in Religious Dialogue*, Peeters, Leuven, 1999, p.145.
19 *The Spirit in Islam*, p. 81.
20 Ahmed, Akbar S, *Postmodernism and Islam: Predicament and Promise*, Routledge, London, 1992.

British society in its relationship to Islam. However, I am concerned here in particular with his historical understanding of Islam's intellectual history over the last millennium, leading to what he sees as the current situation within Islam.

Ahmed argues that Islam was not always hostile to the wider philosophical discourse represented by the classical Greek inheritance but that after the death of Avicenna (d.1037 CE) in the East and Averroes (d. 1198 CE) in the West, for reasons which are not entirely clear, 'the Islamic schools began to close the gates of *ijtihad* or innovation.' He continues:

> Perhaps the difficulties facing Islam in coming to terms with the thinking of modern Europe are not due to its rejection of Greek thought, but to its rejection of the Greek receptivity to new ideas. The Arab crescent was now on the wane.[21]

Whatever the reason for this change of heart, it has had at least two long term implications. First, because 'the Prophet led the prayers ... and the armies' Islam has not been secularised. For Islam, politics and religion are fused. This is in contrast to the West where Christianity engaged with new philosophical ideas, which in turn led to the Renaissance, the Reformation, the wars of religion, the Enlightenment and the division between state and religion. Secondly, Islam has tended to follow a path of isolation and avoidance. Ahmed, whilst recognising this to be the case, also argues that it is fundamentally non-Islamic:

> The main Muslim responses appear to be chauvinism and withdrawal; this is both dangerous and doomed. The self-imposed isolation, the deliberate retreat, is culturally determined. It is not Islamic in spirit or content.[22]

For Ahmed the future lies in a greater engagement both philosophically and theologically between Islam on the one hand and the West and Christianity, on the other. He commends Islamic scholars such as al-Faruqi, Hossein Nasr and Fazlur Rahman for their

---

21 *Op. cit.*, p. 84.
22 *Op. cit.*, p. 47.

engagement in inter-faith dialogue as well as the new breed of Western scholars who seek an impartial study of Islam. He concludes:

> Postmodernism, with its emphasis on globalization and plurality, equality and tolerance, will perhaps encourage such friendships ... Perhaps it will nourish the new breed of scholars. That is one ray of hope in an other wise bleak picture.[23]

We need to remember this was written some twenty years ago and the scene has changed since then. Many in Britain have experienced a reluctance by Muslims to engage in dialogue. For example, an Anglican priest, with wide experience in inter-faith work, when he moved to Bradford none of the local Imams would meet him. I myself was invited to give a talk recently to a Muslim seminar in Maidenhead at which the Home Secretary was also present and at which I suggested that there was a need for Christians to study Islam and for Muslims to study Christianity. The Imam who had organized it was not well pleased, although one or two younger Muslims came up to me afterwards and praised the work of such Islamic scholars as Tariq Ramadan and Tim Winter whom they saw as trying to build bridges with those of other faiths. A recent and counter example of a Muslim scholar prepared to engage in depth with Christian theology is Mona Siddiqui whose *Christians, Muslims, and Jesus*[24] is referred to by Philip Lewis as, 'This splendid work makes clear that mutual understanding requires empathy and courage to move beyond formulaic positions. Any serious theology today has to be interreligious.'[25] Ahmed would have been pleased.

The dangers of isolation, which Ahmed refers to, are well documented. A *locus classicus* in this field is the work of Gordon Allport.[26] His work is based on studies of racial prejudice in relation to blacks and Jews in the United States but has a general application to other situations. He argues that there is a downward movement in attitudes from 'antilocution' (verbal abuse) to 'avoidance' (isolation), 'discrimination, physical attack and extermination;' and that each step

---

23 *Op. cit.*, p. 191.
24 Siddiqui, Mona, *Christians, Muslims and Jesus*, Yale University Press, New Haven and London, 2013.
25 Lewis, Philip, 'Muslim Scholar Engages', *Church Times* 24 May 2013, p. 33.
26 Allport, Gordon W, *The Nature of Prejudice*, Addison-Wesley, Reading MA, 1982 ed.

in this movement is always preceded by the step immediately before it.[27] In Britain we have become much more sensitive to the dangers of racial abuse. For example, Michael Hewstone, when writing about the riots of 2001 in several towns in the north of Britain underlines the strength of Allport's analysis and makes specific reference to the lack of group contact as being contributory to these riots.[28]

Lochhead also writes at some length about what he calls 'The ideology of isolation'.[29] He points out that isolation can be either self-imposed or imposed by outside forces and that in either case, 'The isolated community defines reality for itself.'[30] This can be an understandable defensive mechanism designed to strengthen group identity but it can also leave the community vulnerable to outside pressures. There is also the danger that by sharing a common view that they are right, they may come to regard others as being 'ignorant, deluded, misled, superstitious'.[31] An example of this occurs in my interview with Musharaf Hussain, the Imam in Nottingham and in other ways quite an eirenic figure, where he says:

> When they [imams] are talking to their congregations, they are not going to be too perhaps careful about the details ... and the motives are perhaps different as well as one sees, it could be that, rather than to get understanding, it is actually to inflame and incite people to hatred really in order to get the message across.[32]

There are hopeful signs in Britain that the situation is improving and much of my own inter-faith work has been in deliberately bringing people of different faiths together to engage in dialogue at a significant level. I have already mentioned the *Who Am I?* Project at Slough Grammar School. A particularly significant comment is made by the head of Philosophy, Critical Thinking and Religious Studies where she says: 'Students [Christian, Muslim, Sikh and Hindu] are not moving

---

27 *Op. cit.*, pp. 14-15 and 45.
28 Hewstone, Michael 'Intergroup Contact: Panacea for Prejudice?', *The Psychologist* July 2003, vol. 16 no.7, pp. 352-355.
29 Lochhead, David, *The Dialogical Imperative*, pp. 5-11.
30 *Op. cit.*, p. 7.
31 *Op.cit.*, p. 8.
32 Boulter, Hugh, *The Spirit in Islam*, p. 175.

Dialogue: What is the Point of It?

away from their faith, rather they are moving forward into something new where they are adapting their faith within the context of modern British society.'[33] Another example is the themed study week which the Oxford Diocesan Committee for Inter-faith Concerns (ODCIC) has organised for ordinands at Ripon College, Cuddesdon, and where the students engage with a wide range of people of different faiths. The things that have inspired them most have been the Religious Studies programme at Slough Grammar School and meeting with a mixed group of Muslim men and women in High Wycombe to discuss the problems of bringing up children in British society. I mention these examples because those who wish to engage in inter-faith dialogue often find it difficult to create situations where it can take place. However, when we consider Akbar Ahmed's analysis of a Muslim tendency to isolation we may reflect on to what extent in Britain it is imposed by outside forces or conversely self-imposed. Either way there are real dangers. And, of course, in the context of Palestine/Israel and the Middle East in general, we can see all too clearly the downward trend from antilocution to isolation to discrimination to violence.

I want now to consider some of the theological issues in relation to dialogue. We have already seen that Lochhead suggests that in dialogue we will have to 'make judgments' and 'In other cases, we will discover the fruit of the Spirit in the midst of other religious traditions.' And again, 'When we believe that we discern the work of God's Spirit, that too should be named.'[34] He thus sees the potential of the Holy Spirit working through other religions and in those of other faiths. Furthermore he argues in favour of ethical criteria—the fruit of the Spirit—as the basis for our judgments. This is a reference to St Paul's letter to the Galatians 5. 22-23: 'The fruit of the Spirit is love, joy, peace, patience, kindness, generosity, faithfulness, gentleness and self-control. There is no law against such things.'[35]

It should be noted that in my interviews, at least two of my Muslim respondents reacted strongly against this line of argument. For example, one says:

---

33 Boulter, Hugh, *Who Am I?*, p. 4.
34 Lochhead, David, *The Dialogical Imperative*, p. 45.
35 Galatians 5:22-23 (NRSV translation), p. 188.

> The atheist could very well do good, social good, ethical good and so on and never believe in God. To say that that too becomes a manifestation of the Holy Spirit can sometimes make the whole thing very mushy. Then there are no standards almost.[36]

Yahya Michot makes a similar point:

> And when we see the fruits of the Spirit like patience, kindness, goodness, faithfulness, humility, self-control and those ethical values—the fruits of the Spirit, the Muslim would say: 'No. Those are just basically shared human values.'[37]

Now is not the place to go into the whole issue of virtue ethics which underlies my line of argument, but it is interesting that Michot concedes that there are such things as 'shared human values'. It is of course also interesting that the quotation from Galatians ends with the sentence, 'There is no law against such things,' Islamic ethics being based on *fiqh* (jurisprudence) rather than any ethical system as such. It is an area for very considerable further dialogue between Christians and Muslims.

But to return to Lochhead's argument, he is suggesting that in dialogue we all change and that in doing so we have the opportunity to generate new understanding. This often appears alarming to those involved, but the alternative—isolation or avoidance—is also fraught with danger and if we embark on the course of dialogue we should use the ethical criterion of the fruit of the Spirit as our guiding principle. In other words it is the Holy Spirit himself who will guide us in such exchanges and bring us into a loving relationship with those with whom we disagree whether they are believers or atheists. In relation to Palestine/Israel, I recall a Christian priest from the West Bank saying, at an earlier Living Stones seminar, that this is the only long term solution to the current conflict and we must all pray that it will happen sooner rather than later.

I want now to consider some of the comments made at the original seminar held in September 2012 and also my analysis of the

---

36 Boulter, Hugh, *The Spirit in Islam*, p. 245.
37 *Op. cit.*, p. 243.

first two papers in the *Living Stones Yearbook 2012* about dialogue on the Middle East.

After my original paper had been read in September 2012, it was suggested that 'conversation' might be a better word than 'dialogue'. On reflection I think the force of the two words is slightly different. Might it be that 'conversation' has the sense of something one does for its own sake, while 'dialogue' implies a sense of purpose? If we agree with this, I would be happy to accept that the dialogue of 'friendship' or 'life' has a strong element of conversation in it and is valuable in building trust and breaking down isolation (Lochhead) or avoidance (Allport). Mona Siddiqui, writing from what she admits is a minority Muslim point of view, says: 'Dialogue is a contested term, but for me it has always been about learning, my desire to know more about Christian theology, and through this to be challenged in my own Muslim faith.'[38] Certainly my view is that, in relation to the inter-faith context in Britain, individual Christians and the churches to which they belong have a responsibility to bring together people of different faiths to work towards new ways of understanding and living together in harmony.

At the beginning of this paper I expressed my concern that, while most of my experience and data were based in Britain, many of those in the Living Stones theology group had a background in the Middle East. I decided therefore to look in more detail at the first two papers in the *Living Stones Yearbook 2012* which are concerned with the Papal visit to Lebanon in 2012[39] and the aftermath of the Synod for the Middle East held in Rome in 2010[40] to see what they had to say about dialogue, especially in Syria and Lebanon.

Each of the papers has extensive reference to dialogue or dialogical activities—about twenty references in each. A number of comments should be made about them.

First, most of the examples in the two papers are to do with what one might call the dialogue of theological exchange in the widest sense. That is to say they are inter-religious rather than inter-faith in that they are about dialogue between communities which see their identity as being religious—Muslim, Christian, Jewish—rather than to do with specifically religious issues themselves. Nonetheless nearly

---

38 Siddiqui, Mona, *Christians, Muslims and Jesus*, p. 1.
39 Audo, Antoine, 'The Current Situation of Christianity in the Middle East, pp. 1-17.
40 Bouwen, Frans, 'The Synod for the Middle East: First Results and Future Possibilities', pp. 18-37.

all the references imply the bringing together of different groups in order to generate a new understanding or settlement.

Secondly, most of the references are aspirational rather than reflective of current practice. For example, in relation to the Pope's visit to Beirut in September 2012, Bishop Audo writes: 'The Pope insisted on dialogue as the way towards ending the war and violence [in Syria]'[41] and 'It is time for Muslims and Christians to come together to put an end to violence and war.'[42] Similarly Bouwen writes: 'Christians in the Middle East are called upon to pursue dialogue with the followers of other religions, bringing hearts and minds closer together'[43] and again, 'We say to our Muslim fellow-citizens: we are both brothers and sisters; God wishes us to be together, united by one faith in God and by the dual commandment of love God and neighbour.'[44]

However, on the positive side, it should also be mentioned that Audo lists three examples of the dialogue of action where Christians and Muslims have been working together in Aleppo in order to run quite large scale projects for the good of all. For example he writes:

> A group of Jesuit priests ... together with groups of young scouts, crisscross the city to provide daily meals for five thousand displaced people. Here too Christians and Muslims witness to common values and provide evidence of a Syria of citizenship, a Syria of positive laicity, to the right to difference and respect for alterity.[45]

And Bouwen refers to gatherings of people meeting to discuss the outcomes of the Synod of Bishops: 'In Jerusalem, several interreligious meetings were organised, with the participation of Jewish and Muslim partners.'[46] Such examples of actual dialogue in practice are very much in a minority.

Thirdly, there are several references not only to inter-religious dialogue but also to what one might call intra-religious dialogue: not only between the different Catholic churches but also between

---

41 *Op. cit.*, p. 9.
42 *Ibid.*, p. 10.
43 *Ibid.*, p. 31.
44 *Ibid.*, p. 32.
45 *Ibid.*, p. 16.
46 *Ibid.*, p. 33.

Catholic, Orthodox and Protestant churches. For example, Bouwen writes:'Promoting a deeper awareness of communion as well as a closer collaboration within the various Catholic Churches and between them was certainly one of the most important aims of the Synod [of the Middle East].' Again he writes:'Fraternal Delegates from the Orthodox, Anglican and Evangelical Churches ... were invited to speak in the plenary sessions [of the Synod] and could take part in the small working groups.' 'All churches should resist the temptation to withdraw into their small community in a reaction of self-defence or survival: they will only be able to survive in common.'[47] This is summed up as follows: 'In the East, we Christians must be together or we will not be.'[48]

In relation to my analysis of these two papers, there is much exhortation to dialogue as a means of generating new understanding between different groups but also an awareness that at the moment there is much work to be done not only between Christians and those of other faiths, but between different Catholic churches, among different Christian churches and between clergy and laity.[49] In this sense the specific comments I made earlier about the need for dialogue between those of different faiths in Britain applies with perhaps even greater force in the Middle East.

I come now to the final section of my paper. I have already argued that dialogue implies change and a bringing together of those with different views. Where is God in this process? Reference has already been made to the fruit of the Spirit in Galatians ch.5.[50] Reading earlier in the same chapter, we also see that Paul lists the 'works of the flesh' which include 'enmities, strife, jealousy, anger, quarrels, dissensions, factions, envy'.[51] When we consider the situation currently in the Middle East, and Syria in particular, can we not say that God through his Holy Spirit is at work when we seek to move from the 'work of the flesh' to the 'fruit of the Spirit'? In the discussion, which took place after the paper was originally read, a valuable insight was expressed from Quakerly practice: 'Within the Religious Society of Friends ... we practise stillness in our meetings so that we can listen to where words

---

47 *Ibid.*, p. 26.
48 *Ibid.*, p. 23.
49 *Ibid.*, p. 24.'Communication between the Bishop and his priests, between the clergy and the laity leave at times a lot to be desired.'
50 Galatians 5:22-23.
51 Galatians 5:19-20.

come from ... Movement, change, growth, development, maturity ... may come from the mystical appreciation of the presence of God.'[52] By listening prayerfully to God within us, we may be able to discern how we can help to move from 'works of the flesh' to 'the fruit of the Spirit.'

---

[52] E-mail dated 21.9.2012 from Colin South to members of the Living Stones theology group.

MARY KAHIL:
A LIFE GIVEN FOR MUSLIMS
Sr Agnes Wilkins OSB

Mary Kahil, who was born in Egypt in 1889 and died there in 1979, deserves to be better known as she has something important to say to us today about Muslim-Christian relations. According to Boutros Boutros-Ghâli, a former Secretary General of the United Nations who married her niece Lily Kahil and knew her family well, she is a 'forgotten heroine', yet she 'served Egypt with passion, fervour and courage.'[1] That she is remembered at all outside Egypt is due to her close association with Louis Massignon, the well-known French Islamicist, who has not been forgotten, and even seems to grow in importance as the dialogue with Islam assumes ever greater urgency. However, nothing in Mary's past would seem to have prepared her for such a close collaboration with this outstanding scholar of Islam. They met almost by chance when he was for a time a student of philosophy at the El-Azhar University in Cairo. This proved to be only a short acquaintance, but after a lapse of more than twenty years they met again, this time on a much deeper level, and made a 'vow' together—not in any formal, juridical sense, yet equally as strong, that bound them together in an very close spiritual relationship, which changed both of their lives forever. Although outwardly the second half of Mary's life bears some resemblance to the first half before the vow, inwardly she was totally transformed, and her life was forever bound up with Louis Massignon, whose vision she incarnated in Cairo. Together they founded a movement which was a very Christian way of relating to Muslims; not by trying to convert them, but by praying for them, loving them, and being 'substitutes' for them before God. This *Badaliya*, as it came to be called, is still a Christian spiritual movement today, but it

---

1 See Jacques Keryell, *Mary Kahil: Une grande dame d'Egypte 1889-1979*, Geuthner, Paris, 2010, *Préface,* p. 3 (henceforth *M Kahil*).

derives its meaning from a very Muslim concept, which Massignon found in Al-Hallaj, the Sufi mystic and martyr. For Massignon a *badal* is someone who freely takes the place of others, that is, 'substitutes' him or herself, in order to fend off some evil that threatens them, rather like Abraham and the just men who could have held back the anger of God against Sodom (Gen.18:16-33).

The focal point of Mary's life, around which all else revolves, is the *Badaliya* vow she made with Louis Massignon when she was in her mid-forties. Before describing this, however, something of Mary's background and early life must be told, which will be introduced by a brief description of her country Egypt, and the Melkite Church to which she belonged.

The Egypt of Mary

We think of Egypt today as a Muslim country, one of the most important in the world, yet it has a long and illustrious pre-Islamic history, stretching back five thousand years. We are all familiar with the Egypt of the Pharaohs, and of the Exodus as told in the Bible when Joseph and the children of Israel took refuge there for four hundred years. It is the country at the heart of the revelation of the One God, when Yahweh made himself known to Moses in the burning bush. It also gave asylum to the Holy Family, Jesus, Mary and Joseph when they had to flee from the murderous designs of King Herod. Christian monasticism had its beginnings in its deserts; many followed the example of the great St Anthony whose life was publicised in the biography written by St Athanasius, and it was here that Pachomius began the first experiments in cenobitic monastic life. Damietta on the Nile Delta is Mary's birthplace where the *Badaliya* vow was taken, but is also famous for the encounter between St Francis and the Sultan Malik-al-Kamil during the Crusades, when Francis tried to convert him to Christianity in 1219.

Egypt is also the home of Coptic Christianity which is nineteen centuries old, and still strong today. Originally the word *copt* was not a religious designation, but referred to all Egyptians. Today it refers only to the Christian minority, but they survive strongly in the midst of Muslims. Coptic Christianity is 'more than a tradition and a heritage;

it is about more than patriotism or nationality, it is an instinct, has become a mental category, stronger than persecution ... In truth, it is the Cross ... The life of Copts in the midst of Islam is a miracle of the Holy Spirit.'[2] This is very evident today as they continue to survive strongly in a Muslim country which is not always friendly towards them.

The Melkite Church, to which Mary belonged, is the second most important Christian community. The Melkites are Oriental Orthodox Christians who follow the Byzantine rite, the liturgy of St. John Chrysostom, whose official language is Arabic. They have been in communion with Rome since 1724, but have their own clergy and patriarch, the current one being His Beatitude Gregorius III. Originally they were Christians of Syria and Egypt, who accepted the doctrinal ruling of the Council of Chalcedon in 451 on the two natures of Christ, but as they had adopted the Byzantine rite they were taken up into the general schism of the Orthodox Churches with Rome in 1054, under Michael Cerularius, Patriarch of Constantinople.[3]

Mary's Background and Early Life

Mary was born on 28 January 1889 in Damietta, the city closely associated with St Francis where she and Massignon took the *Badaliya* vow. Her ancestors had emigrated from Syria to Egypt in 1775, and soon came to prominence under the *khedive* Mohammed Ali who ruled from 1806-1848. Conditions were good for Christians in Egypt then, as he saw them as an enterprising minority, and desirous of opening up his country to European ways he abolished all discriminating policies against them and allowed them to occupy responsible positions. One of Mary's forbears, Mikhail Pacha Kahil, became a member of his Council and was entrusted with much responsibility in the country's financial affairs. Mikhail's brother was given similar responsibilities and altogether the Kahil family furnished the national magistrature with no less than three illustrious members. Mary's father Constantin made his fortune in the wholesale lumber industry through running a firm which operated internationally on behalf of the government. He

---

2 Abbas Chalaby, *Les Coptes d'Egypt,*, Cairo 1973, p. 76-77, quoted in *M Kahil*, p. 17.
3 See *Louis Massignon: L'Hospitalité Sacrée. Textes inédites présentés par Jacques Keryell*, Nouvelle Cité, Paris, 1987. Henceforth *L'Hospitalité Sacrée*.

bought several properties in and around Cairo, and the Greek Melkite cathedral was built on his land. His wife was German and bore him five children, two sons and three daughters, Mary being the youngest.[4]

Mary's own account of her life—though far from complete, recorded on tape at the request of Jacques Keryell who had the forethought to visit her for this purpose before she died, is the main source of our knowledge of her life and character.[5] She also shared with Keryell some of her correspondence with Massignon in the belief that the movement they had begun was not just for themselves, but for everybody. She describes an idyllic childhood. We learn from the tapes that she spent the summer months in the family house in Damietta on the Nile, which was large and spacious. A mosque was nearby and she describes hearing the call of the muezzin as she played with her dolls on the balcony of the family house, and its haunting quality gave her a sense of great peace.[6] She describes having a Muslim nurse at this time, and the family also employed a Muslim gardener. Her German mother who was married to her father in Damietta, spoke Arabic well, and frequently paid visits to the local people by whom she was much loved and respected.[7]

Mary describes briefly her school years, which began in Cairo with the nuns of the *Religieuses de la Mère de Dieu*. She was later sent away from home to complete her education in Beirut, again with nuns, the *Soeurs de Nazareth*. She is not ashamed to record that she slept during Arabic lessons; she therefore spoke it well but never learned to read or write it.[8] Even in these years of her adolescence, Mary showed a strong leaning towards feminism. While still at school she and a friend joined forces in rebelling against French, and Western culture in general. They sang revolutionary songs, one of which began: *My Syria, my country, listen and rejoice, because the presence of France is shameful for you.*[9] She describes herself at this time as having become 'a rather distinguished young woman'.[10] Her religious development is not mentioned at all;

---

4 See *M Kahil*, p. 11-12.
5 *L'Hospitalité Sacrée*, p. 11-12.
6 Keryell comments that today it is not so peaceful, the human voice having been replaced, or greatly amplified, by loudspeakers. See *M Kahil*, p. 27.
7 *Ibid.*, p. 29-30.
8 *Ibid.*, p. 31-32.
9 *Ibid.*, p. 32.
10 *Ibid.*, p. 31.

however it may reasonably be assumed that she practised her faith, but possibly not with great fervour, in contrast to the second half of her life.

The next major event in Mary's life was the death of her father in 1905, when she was sixteen years old. She arrived home one day to find her mother in bed, prostrate with grief, and the house full of relatives.[11] Inevitably she had to remain at home for a while but eventually went back to school. She records no emotion about this event of her father's death; it certainly does not seem to have affected her anything like as severely as it affected her mother. Her family's concern, at this time, now that she was on the brink of womanhood and her school days were nearing their end, was that she should marry. 'If only I could recall all the proposals I received', she said, 'There was one who even said he would double my fortune.'[12] A Jesuit friend of forty years, who greatly admired her and valued her friendship over many years, wondered if she had taken a vow of chastity when she was young, in view of the obvious sanctity of her life when seen in retrospect after her death.[13] He says he would not be surprised, but there is no way of knowing, as Mary herself says nothing about it. However it seems very unlikely; such a vow would have had serious religious connotations which would have been alien to her at that time of her life. The more likely explanation is that she just did not meet anyone with whom she would wish to spend the rest of her life; God had other plans for her, which would unfold in due course.

Mary the Feminist

After the death of Mary's father and completion of her schooling, further education does not seem to have been suggested, nor did she seem to have desired it. Wealthy, attractive, in possession of a lively intelligence and outgoing character, she stood on the brink of adulthood and had no need to earn her living. She filled in her time by expending her energy on many charitable activities, but perhaps the one closest to her heart at this time was the Egyptian feminist movement. This paralleled and took its inspiration from the

---

11 *Ibid.*, p. 32.
12 *Ibid.*
13 *L'Hospitalité Sacrée*, p. 80-81.

suffragette movement which was very strong in Britain at that time. Mary's involvement culminated in the founding, with two friends, of the Feminist Union of Egypt, in May 1923. She was a 'convinced and intrepid militant' who campaigned with like-minded friends for such things as the abolition of the veil for [Muslim] women, of polygamy, for divorce only by arbitration, and equal opportunity for both sexes. With her like-minded companions, she would protest in the streets about the British occupation of Egypt. These feminists had two main objectives: to obtain the just demands of women, and to become a point of contact for the worldwide feminist movement.[14] In her own words Mary sums up this period of her life as follows: 'In 1909 (I was twenty years old), I returned to Cairo, full of ideas. I did not want to remain useless, inactive. I wanted to do something. I wrote a pamphlet: *We Arabic women only want to speak the Arabic language. We wish to honour our traditions, our national costume, our language.* She continues in her personal account, 'I had a lawyer friend... he said to me; *Mary, I know a woman who has nothing to do; she could help you.*'[15] Thus she met her great friend Houda Chaaraoui, a woman twice her age who helped her in her ambition to organise conferences etc., thus giving her the experience she needed when she later did this type of work for Louis Massignon. Through her friend Houda she made wide contacts among the rich and well-to-do of Cairo, including the royal princesses with whom she was on familiar terms. One of them asked to see her, and upon making her acquaintance suggested she might like to be the secretary of the 'Mohammed Ali Association', which was concerned with Muslim affairs. She agreed to this proposal and 'thus', she says, 'I found myself mixing in Muslim society.'[16] This too was to give her the preparation she needed when in later life she worked closely with Louis Massignon. One has to wonder, however, at this point, whether she really was such a committed feminist as she appeared to be, or was she just throwing in her lot, and her abundant energy, with the cause of the moment? It was an enjoyable life for her as she had a wide circle of friends and gave herself up to many interesting activities, as well as charitable works. Undoubtedly Mary did great good during these years, and feminism was, and is, a much needed corrective to so

---

14 *Ibid.*, p. 104-6.
15 *M Kahil*, p. 32.
16 *Ibid.*, p. 34.

many aspects of the world that are male-dominated, but for her it was arguably more a 'time-filler' than a real vocation. However, nothing of this first half of her life was to be lost; it was all providentially preparing her for the second half after the *Badaliya* vow.

THE FIRST MEETING WITH LOUIS MASSIGNON

Mary's first meeting with Massignon took place when she was twenty-five years old, still very much involved with feminist activity, and the work of the Mohammed Ali Association whose main concern was Muslims and their welfare. It was 11 December 1912.[17] On this day she happened to be in the house of a Spanish noblewoman, the Countess of Howenwaert, and Massignon, then aged twenty-nine and in Cairo as a student of philosophy at El-Azhar University, was also there. The countess introduced them under the pretext that they could speak Arabic together, and thus they found themselves next to each other at table. She describes a tall, slim young man, dressed all in black, with a monocle in one eye.[18] Their first exchanges were not propitious for their future relationship. Mary, unsurprisingly, was not impressed by the fact that he had just returned from Syria where he had attended the opening of a school dedicated to the much revered French saint, Joan of Arc, and an argument almost ensued. She went so far as to call him her 'enemy', but he, a Frenchman to the core despite his love for and openness to Islam, confessed himself surprised to meet a Syrian who did not have a profound respect for France, or who was not 'prostrate before France', as she records in her own words.[19] Despite their disagreements and apparent incompatibility, their relationship prospered and they continued to meet frequently at the house of Countess Howenwaert.

Mary recounts a rather significant episode which occurred at this period of her life concerning another guest at these evenings. This was a friend of Louis Massignon, whom she also had befriended, Luis de Cuadra, the son of the Marquess of Guadalmino, who had fallen seriously ill with typhus fever and was hospitalised. Luis had converted

---

17 According to Louis Massignon's agenda. See *M Kahil*, p. 35.
18 *Ibid.*
19 *Ibid.*, p. 37.

to Islam much against his mother's wishes, who now begged prayers for him. Massignon responded to this request and asked Mary to join him. 'You are unhappy because he is going to die', he said to her, 'but you must make a sacrifice for him, the sacrifice of your life.'[20] Mary responded, 'What! The sacrifice of my life. Me?'[21] She was naturally taken aback by such extreme language; it would take her some time to understand his thinking on such matters. Massignon for his part was painfully aware of a deep attachment to Luis; he was also very conscious of the fact that theirs was a relationship which included behaviour of which, since his conversion, he felt the need to repent.[22] Sadly Luis did not recover. He did, however, make a pretence of returning to Christianity to please his mother, but he remained a Muslim at heart according to Massignon, who was deeply hurt by this hypocrisy.[23] Sadly, in the end he committed suicide, as Massignon discloses in a letter to Jean-Mohammed Abd-el-Jalil, the Moroccan convert to Christianity who became a Franciscan friar, and was his godson.[24] This 'substitution' of one life for another was to be at the heart of what the *Badaliya* was all about, though it would eventually be something much more mainstream and fundamental to Christianity than was apparent at this stage. At this moment in time Massignon's desire to give himself in such a way was probably at least partly from a motive of repentance after his conversion experience, in which he returned to the Catholicism of his childhood, which had occurred only three years before, and had changed him profoundly.[25] Mary recalls a conversation from earlier in their friendship when Massignon had asked her whether she prayed regularly, and if she went to daily mass. 'But why should I', she asked, 'What about yourself? He replied simply that he was 'a sinner, a great sinner.'[26] She records that a Franciscan who was present on this occasion

---

20 *M Kahil*, p. 37.
21 *Ibid.*
22 See *Louis Massignon: Badaliya au nom de l'autre (1947-1962), présenté et annoté par Maurice Borrmans et Françoise Jacquin,* Les Editions du Cerf, Paris, 2011, p. 37.
23 *M Kahil,* p. 37.
24 *Massignon, Abd-el-Jalil: Parain et filleul, 1926-1962, Correspondance rassemblée et annotée par Françoise Jacquin,* Préface par Maurice Borrmans, Les Editions du Cerf, Paris, 1907. See letter dated 1 May, 1951, p. 213.
25 Maurice Borrmans would also seem to suggest as much: The spirit of *Badaliya* consisted of an offering with Mary Kahil which was a 'thorn in his flesh', a 'reparation' for his past life. See *op. cit.*, p. 37.
26 *M Kahil,* p. 36.

had suggested that she make profession as a Franciscan (of the Third Order, which does not involve entering a religious community). She had demurred but admitted that she did so, without however, at least in this stage of her life, keeping any of its obligations.[27] Mary and Louis Massignon seemed to be on quite different levels spiritually at this time, but through this incident involving the sickness of Luis de Cuadra they did learn to pray together, and it foreshadowed to some extent their later relationship.

It was not long after this that Massignon began to believe that Mary was becoming too attached to him and he returned abruptly to France. In his private notes, retained by his son Daniel,[28] he confesses to being 'surprised by her feminine onslaught onto his sinful misogyny', and rejoiced that he had withdrawn himself before causing suffering. Mary then records:'He fell ill when he returned to France ... then he wrote to the countess of Howenwaert that he had become engaged to a cousin who had loved him for a long time ... Upon this,' Mary concludes simply,'I did not see him again till 1934.'[29] It is arguable, however, that the problem with their relationship was more Massignon's than Mary's. She does not record any distress at his departure, unlike at a later stage in their relationship, to be described later, when he did something similar which caused her acute distress. For the moment presumably she did not expect to see him again, and her life continued very much as before. Massignon, by contrast, was in a process of discerning his future after his rather shattering conversion experience, and was torn two ways; by the pull of the desert and a life of prayer in the company of Charles de Foucauld, on the one hand, and by an academic life in the wake of his growing reputation as a scholar, on the other.[30] It was the latter that prevailed, but his heart always remained in the desert.

Before Mary's second meeting with Massignon in 1934, twenty one years later, little changed in her life. The war years of 1914-18 intervened during this time, soon after their first meeting. These years she spent in Europe with her mother, two brothers and two sisters, with the family of her German mother. She says little about this time, but

---

27 *Ibid.*, p. 36.
28 See *L'Hospitalité Sacrée*, p. 162, note 28.
29 *Ibid.*, p. 94.
30 Massignon's life history, especially his conversion, has been well documented. See for instance *Jardin Donné: Louis Massignon à la recherché de l'Absolu,* Editions St Paul, Paris, 1993, and *L'Hospitalité Sacrée,* pp. 33-123.

life seems to have passed pleasantly enough far from the combat zone. In 1920 she returned to Cairo by boat, and on disembarking kissed the ground of her beloved Egypt. She went on to help in the foundation of the Egyptian Feminist Union, but lamented that it was her older friend Houda Chaaraoui who was doing most of the work, and in her own words, she was 'the sort of person who liked to do everything'.[31] She therefore spent more of her time with the Mohammed Ali Association, which gave her more scope. And so, as Massignon would remark later, she was very involved in Muslim affairs of every description, including charitable works. There was one significant moment for her during this time. It happened that while she was on pilgrimage in Rome during the Holy Year of 1933, she received a personal blessing from Pope Pius XI who said to her, 'I bless your past, your present, and your future.'[32] This was very shortly before her second encounter with Massignon, in the course of which a profound spiritual communion developed between them and the *Badaliya* vow was taken which changed Mary's life profoundly.

THE SECOND MEETING WITH MASSIGNON IN 1934: THE *BADALIYA* VOW

It happened that Massignon was in Cairo again at the Institute of Archaeology, but rather than contact Mary directly he sent a postcard through a third person which simply said *En respectueux souvenirs*. Sometime afterwards, when she was taking tea with a writer friend, her neighbour at table asked her if she knew that Louis Massignon was in Cairo, at the Institute of Archaeology. She said nothing to her companion but slipped out secretly to the said institute, where she found him in the library. She describes seeing a figure 'rather quaint, and a little stooped', whereas when she had known him formerly he was 'very tall and upright'.[33] He was only fifty, and she was now forty-six. She describes how they found a seat outside the library and began to talk, but it seems that it was Massignon who did most of the talking. He spoke about his life for a long time, but Mary admitted that she was

---

31 *M Kahil*, p. 39.
32 *L'Hospitalité Sacrée*, p. 79.
33 *M Kahil*, p. 40.

not really listening, and understood nothing. Then he asked her about herself. She told him she occupied herself with charitable works, and added that she had a car (which cannot have been common among Egyptian women at that time).[34] She offered to call for him at the Institute the next day, and they began this renewing of their relationship by attending mass together at 7.30 in the morning. When time came for communion he turned to her and said, 'Go to communion.' Perhaps she was not in the habit of doing so—we do not know, but she obeyed without question and describes entering a spiritual state 'unknown to her, quite different from happiness, quite strange.'[35] It is significant that this new phase in their relationship should begin with mass. It is at the heart of the *Badaliya* movement they began and would be, thanks to Mary's influence, central to Massignon's spiritual life when he transferred his allegiance to the Melkite Church which allowed ordination for married men. How this came about will be described later.

It was some little time later after they had been meeting regularly, that they decided one day to visit Damietta. Mary describes a former visit to this favourite destination when Massignon had spoken much to her about his earlier life, especially past vices. 'But I understood nothing', she admitted, 'and I was bored.'[36] On this occasion, the day of the vow; it was 9 February 1934, they went straight to the Franciscan church. Mary describes the scene: the little church with three great windows overlooking the Nile through which one could see the swaying palm trees outside. She was praying with great intensity, which was obviously unusual for her, and she found it 'difficult to explain'.[37] She turned to Massignon and said how grieved she was that this beautiful town, to which so many Syrian Christians had come, including her own ancestors, was now completely islamisized. Massignon responded that she was specially chosen to make a vow. It is impossible to know whether he knew he was going to do this beforehand, or if it was completely spontaneous, at the prompting of the Holy Spirit. 'But what vow?' Mary asked. 'To love them,' he replied. 'I told him,' she continues, 'that it was impossible—I hate them.' Massignon responded that nothing was closer to hate than love,

---

34 *Ibid.*
35 *Ibid.*, p. 41.
36 *Ibid.*, p. 42.
37 *Ibid.*, p. 44.

and he urged her to make a vow to give her life for them. Mary then describes very simply in her own words what happened: 'In a state of exaltation impossible to describe, I did so. I made a vow to live for them, to give my life for them, to be in their place before the throne of Jesus, and that for the whole of my life and my eternity I would plead for them to be given light.'[38] Massignon took her hand and made the same vow. There is something about a vow which changes radically the person who takes it, and Mary was no exception. 'We made the vow in a state of great fervour and illumination such as I have never known since,' she continued, 'and when we came out of the church I was transformed, no longer myself. It was as if my life was all flame.'[39] 'And so', she concludes, 'we made a vow. We offered ourselves for Muslims. Not that they should be converted, but that the will of God be done in them and through them. We wished to make their prayer our own, their life ours, and present them to the Lord.'[40]

As they came out of the church Mary found a large iron carpenter's nail, which she gave to Massignon. This very symbolic gesture has profound Franciscan resonances. Massignon responded, 'Why this nail?' She answered that it was to pierce his heart. He took it and put it in his pocket.[41] Such a nail is a very obvious reminder of the Passion of Christ which is at the heart of Franciscan spirituality. Francis himself, after his unsuccessful attempt during the Crusades to convert to Christianity the Sultan Malik-al-Kamil, later received the stigmata, in which the wounds the nails made in the body of Christ were physically present in his body. Francis had rebelled against the very idea of 'crusading', believing that if Muslims were to be 'conquered', it could only be by love. A typical Franciscan image which appears on their letterheads is of two crossed hands, one of Christ, and the other of any Franciscan (or Christian by extension), nailed together to the Cross. It is a very graphic expression of St Paul's theology as expressed in the letter to the Galatians, *I have been crucified with Christ and yet I am alive, yet it is no longer I, but Christ living in me.*[42] Massignon expresses his understanding of this in a letter he wrote to Mary the next day, 10 February: 'Our meeting, after almost twenty-one years, has pierced my heart, renewing

---
38 *Ibid.*
39 *Ibid.*, p. 45.
40 *Ibid.*
41 *Ibid.*
42 Galatians 2:20.

Mary Kahil: A Life Given for Muslims

in me the grace of my conversion ... the wound has broken open my heart which was closed in on itself ... It unites both our sacrifices, indistinct henceforth, forever, like the nail of the Cross which pierces two crossed hands, with which we are familiar as it is the symbol of Franciscan tertiaries. Our two hands are united as one, the other being that of our One Love, Jesus.'[43]

But what is *Badaliya,* this thing that bound them so closely together? In Arabic the word means 'substitution'. Certain Sufi traditions taught that the world owed its salvation to the presence of *Abdāl,* that is, men and women who by their sanctity turned away the evils which threatened humanity from Satan or the vengeful justice of God. Massignon, always on the lookout for anything that would make a link between Islam and Christianity, found this word suited his purposes very well.[44] Abraham was considered to be the first of the *Abdāl,* to be followed by many others right up to the present day. Massignon saw his life, after the vow, as one of 'substitution', as he wished to live for Islam and the Arab world. On another level it was a substitute, in a compensatory sense, for the priestly vocation to which he felt himself called, but was barred (at least for the present) by his marriage. At least he could practise the 'priesthood of the faithful' to which all the baptised are called.[45] After all, for the Christian baptism is nothing less than the entry into the passion, death and resurrection of Christ, on behalf of the whole of humanity.[46]

After the vow Massignon went back to France and involved himself in many things, political as well as scholarly, and had a wide circle of friends and admirers. For her part Mary remained in Cairo where she gave flesh in practical terms to the spirit of *Badaliya.* In 1941 she bought a deconsecrated Anglican church and had it adapted for the Byzantine rite, and in an adjacent house she built up a Centre, the 'Dar-es-Salaam' (House of Peace), where conferences were held on many topics including archaeology, Egyptology, philosophy, ecumenism, theology, hagiography and mysticism. This programme involved a wide variety of speakers including well known authors such as Roger Arnaldez, Louis

---

43 Written from the French Institute of Oriental Archaeology, Cairo. See *M Kahil,* p. 45-6. This is my own, free translation, but captures the sense.
44 See for instance Louis Massignon, *Essai sur les origines du lexique technique de la mystique musulmane,* Vrin, Paris, 1954.
45 See *L'Hospitalité Sacrée,* p. 64.
46 See for instance, St Paul's letter to the Romans 6:3 f, and Colossians 1:12.

135

Gardet, René Voillaume, and of course Massignon himself. Mary was building up and helping to develop a truly Arab-Christian culture, and all her practical and social skills were fully employed.[47]

During this time of great activity, when Mary's life outwardly resembled what she had been doing before, her spiritual life was greatly deepened, thanks in large part to the changed relationship she had with Massignon which was a deep relationship of love that verged on the mystical. Many letters were exchanged, which for Mary were an unfailing strength and support. The spirit of *Badaliya,* in which she gave her life for Muslims, was perhaps for her rather more concentrated than it was for Massignon, being the focus of all she did, whereas for him life was much more dispersed, and he had his immediate family to think of which Mary did not. This of course was the major barrier which prevented him from fulfilling what he thought was his vocation to the priesthood.

THE PRIESTHOOD

It was Mary who helped him overcome that barrier. It happened in the following manner: she describes how one day, not long after their second meeting and the taking of the *Badaliya* vow, she asked him why he had not become a priest. He replied that he had married instead, in obedience to his confessor. She responded with astonishment that a man of his age should obey his confessor. 'And thus he confided to me,' Mary explains,' that he had always wanted to be a priest in order to be closer to the Lord Jesus.' She said to him that it was still possible, to which he responded that he would think about it.[48] The outcome was that Massignon eventually received permission from Rome to join the Melkite Church which permitted married priests, and he was ordained on 28 January 1950 in the Church of Our Lady of Peace, that church so close to Mary's heart—the restored Anglican church built on the land she had purchased—by Mgr Pierre-Kâmel Medawar, auxiliary of the Patriarch Maximos IV, according to the Byzantine rite. Mary herself was present to witness this very significant event in Massignon's life.[49]

---
47 See *L'Hospitalité Sacrée*, p. 112, and p. 143, which describes the aims of the Centre.
48 *Ibid.*, p. 98.
49 *Ibid.*, p. 112.

Undoubtedly the ordination to the priesthood of Massignon was a very significant event in Mary's life too. Although out of discretion Massignon normally only exercised his priesthood privately, Mary seemed to be always aware of the time he was saying mass and loved to join him spiritually from afar. As she wrote to him in a letter dated 9 February, 1950, 'At the consecration I am prostrate, I abandon myself, I lose myself, I exist no longer. This is the Body, this is the Blood, and it is I who am consecrated, transformed. I no longer live; I am annihilated, freed, offered ... and from this day on I am free from the bottom of my heart, offered and given, in a total "Fiat", being constantly renewed. May his will be done in me totally. Health, life, joys, sorrows ... I too consecrate myself to Him ... and I wish to live his presence in me, every morning, at your sacrifice.'[50]

What began in Islam as the substitution of one person for another to fend off some evil has become the offering of Jesus Christ on the Cross for the whole of humanity. This is *the* 'Mystery of Faith', as the celebrant proclaims after the consecration at every mass, a 'mystery' which can perhaps only be understood from within the faith where it is celebrated. Of that faith it is the 'source and summit', as the Vatican II document *Sacrosanctum Concilium* (SC10) tells us, but it is universal in its implication and application. As we say in one of the Eucharistic prayers, 'May this sacrifice advance the peace and salvation of all the world.' Some explicitly give their lives for Islam, as Mary and Massignon did, and the many who follow in their footsteps, but this cause is implicitly included in every mass that is celebrated, whether the participants are aware of it or not.

THE 'FAST OF SILENCE'

Apart from the daily Eucharist, Mary's chief support in her spiritual life was the exchange of letters she had with Massignon. As she wrote to him soon after his ordination: 'A new life is opening up for me, if I respond with fidelity to the interior call of solitude, and the presence of the interior Guest.... and as I do not know how to meditate alone,

---

50 *L'Hospitalité Sacrée*, p. 328. This profound devotion of Egyptians at the consecration was once witnessed by the author, when some members of a congregation of exiled Copts in England literally prostrated in the aisle of their church at this sacred moment.

it is in writing to you, and in my journal, that I put myself in his presence ...'[51] It is not surprising that problems arose in the course of their relationship; it would seem that Mary did attract some criticism on account of her closeness to Massignon, for after all she was wealthy, attractive and single, and he was a married man. With this in mind he wrote to her: 'What does this incomprehension matter, so long as we keep our hands nailed together, with that great nail that you one day gave me at Damietta. The more we are friends the less we will be understood. But He will be our enclosure ...'[52] She could accept this state of affairs while there was this understanding between them but one day, quite unexpectedly, he sent her a letter in which he said he was about to make a 'fast of silence' which he wished her to share with him. It meant that they would not see each other for several years and would exchange letters only rarely. Mary was extremely distressed, feeling she had caused offence in some way she did not understand.[53] Yet despite the pain, with typical generosity she embraces this trial. In her journal she writes, 'My brother, these are new days ... let us run to meet them with open arms, for they are sent by the Lord who permits this terrible trial of silence, of distance, of separation from the spiritual bonds of which Ibrahim gives me a living sense ... But I know he is there, that he prays with me, that he shows me the way ...' [54] And yet in her journal she reveals that she passes though 'great waters of bitterness'. It seems she finds it very difficult to pray without reference to Massignon. She wishes to speak to God of her love, but it is 'closed in, a prisoner ... it is a millstone around my neck which I drag along the dusty roads of life ...', then addressing God, 'I would like to arrive at your presence directly, in response to the coming of your presence to me. Evening is falling, the evening of life, let us begin again with a new heart, let me come to You, let me come.'[55] She gradually achieves this breakthrough, by simply asking God for the grace she needs, 'O my God', she writes in her journal, 'be my only concern, my only preoccupation, my only interest in this life and the next. My only

---

51 *Ibid.*, p. 326. Letter dated 31 January 1950.
52 *Ibid.*, p. 134-5. Letter not dated.
53 *L'Hospitalité Sacrée*, p. 124-5. The author, who is writing from the perspective of his personal visit to Mary before she died, admits that he cannot understand this episode.
54 *Ibid.*, p. 129.
55 *Ibid.*, p. 130.

anguish is that I cannot reach you, my only suffering is that of not loving you enough.' Then she addresses herself, admitting that until now her life has been too taken up with a multitude of activities, and her spiritual life has been 'mechanical'; 'When will you stop running, blind and enraged, and towards what?', she asks herself. 'I must now remain enclosed within this tent, this inner dwelling which for too long I have sought in a mechanical way.'[56]

The painful letter that Massignon had written is not given; an indication of the sacredness of such a relationship, and of ultimately how impenetrable is the mystery of God's love as it reveals itself in the life of two close friends, both of whom had their strengths, but also their weaknesses and failures. During this difficult time Mary was greatly comforted by letters from Louis Gardet, one of the founders of the Little Brothers of Jesus, and a friend both of herself and Massignon. A master of the spiritual life in his own right he said to her, 'He has done it for the greater love of God, and for your common vocation ... the grain of wheat has to die ... He knows that it is a great sacrifice for you but that you will not refuse Jesus anything.'[57] He then suggests that Massignon needs her prayers. 'You must', says Gardet, 'not only pray with him but also for him, and also for those in his life for whom he is responsible. He too has many things to suffer.'[58]

One cannot deny that Mary may have benefitted from this trial for her spiritual growth, in the way that every spiritual journey, as it deepens, encounters darkness and trials on the way to a closer union with God, but there is also some evidence that Massignon had a hidden agenda. This can be found in his letters to Jean-Mohammed Abd-el-Jalil, his godson, who, as their relationship progressed, became for him an occasional *confidant* as well as a spiritual advisor and friend. Massignon, on account of his family circumstances, speaks of living 'in a solitude deeper than that he would have endured had he joined Charles de Foucauld in the desert.'[59] In a footnote Maurice Borrmans comments that 'the spiritual intimacy between LM and MK could not have been anything but painful for Mme Massignon.'[60] It was impossible that an 'outsider' could really understand the relationship

---

56 *Ibid.*
57 *Ibid.*, p. 127.
58 *Ibid.*
59 *Ibid.*; *Massignon/Abd-el-Jalil,* letter dated 27 July 1951, p. 217-18.
60 *Ibid.*, p. 219, footnote 1.

between these two, and it was perhaps inevitable it should cause some tension in Massignon's marriage, whereas for Mary, as a single woman, it was more straightforward.

THE FINAL YEARS

This 'fast of silence' that Massignon asked of Mary lasted a long time, about nine years, and he did not have much time left to live when it was finally broken. Mary wrote to him late in 1959 anticipating what she expected to be one of their final meetings, which she awaited in an 'ardent serenity' as she thought of how they would speak of 'the deeper meaning of their lives, and above all the prospect of death.'[61] Massignon died on 31 October 1962. Mary outlived him by seventeen years, not dying till she was ninety, in 1979. Speaking of the day of his death she writes in her journal, 'but I did not know (he had died) … And on the evening of his death, of his passing, I saw him, in black, reassuring me, passing by like a shadow, fleeting as a star, and sadly I contemplated this vision.'[62] Despite the fact that they rarely met, she felt the pain of his loss intensely, as extracts from her diary show: 'Is it possible that he is dead? He who sowed life everywhere … And then I returned to the little Franciscan chapel that he loved so much, and prayed before the crib, "Jesus, I have suffered so much. I have told you how much I loved him … And you Jesus, allowed me to love him. You planted this love in my heart like a cross … and it is my own cross, this burning love for Massignon." But he also said that Jesus had commanded his love towards me, although it is incomprehensible. It is a divine secret … that we should love each other with a total love, at every instant, always being renewed, because God is love.'[63] Later that year, in August, when she is recalling with pain the letter she received announcing the 'fast of silence', she records, 'I was praying beneath the cross in the Franciscan church … I see Abdel Jalil. He assures me that Louis did not abandon me, ever. He wished to suffer, and asked to be without me. It was harder for him than for me …'[64]

---

61 *L'Hospitalité Sacrée*, p. 131.
62 *Ibid.*, p. 334.
63 *Ibid.*, p. 332-3; the entry reads 'End of the year 1962'—the year of his death.
64 *Ibid.*, p. 336. She refers to Abd-el-Jalil, Massignon's godson, already mentioned above.

Mary Kahil: A Life Given for Muslims

We know little about the years before Mary's death, except that she continued with her charitable work, and the work of the Dar-es-Salam Centre. However, it is recorded that in the final two years of her life she prepared consciously for death by keeping silence, praying much, and listening tirelessly to recordings of the Byzantine liturgy in Arabic. On her ninetieth birthday mass was celebrated in her house by Fr Georges Anawati OP, a lifelong friend, in which she partook fully. She died later that year, 28 June 1979.[65]

Finally, what is her legacy for today? Jacques Keryell has accurately described her as 'the extension of Massignon in Cairo; she gave flesh to his ideas, lived his faith.'[66] One could add that she also incarnated the spirit of St Francis, not only in his approach to dialogue with Muslims, but also in his poverty. She was wealthy, as St Francis was in his youth, but 'she practised a remarkable personal poverty ...' but of course 'the poor used to knock on her door, and she received them with great kindness.'[67] External poverty, however, is not of much value without inner poverty, and undoubtedly Mary had this in abundance. From being rich, self-confident and in control of her affairs, she learned through suffering her total dependence on God and real poverty of spirit. She has left us a remarkable example of holiness of life in a lay person, which in today's Church is much needed. And finally, we owe her a great debt of gratitude for assisting Massignon in his desire to be a priest. This, combined with her own devotion to the Eucharist as the main anchor of her spiritual life, has brought *Badaliya* to the centre of Christian spirituality, and opened it up to all who partake in that sacrament, even if they are not consciously aware of it.

---

65 *Ibid.*, p. 80.
66 *Ibid.*
67 The witness of Fr Georges Zemoknol SJ, who knew her for forty years. *Ibid.*, p. 80.

SHENOUDA III AND THE COPTIC ORTHODOX CHURCH IN MODERN EGYPT: SOME REFLECTIONS

Anthony O'Mahony

The death of Pope Shenouda III (17 March 2012),[1] Patriarch of the Coptic Orthodox Church, was without doubt a significant moment for the Christians in Egypt and Christianity in the wider Middle East. Shenouda, was elected to head the Coptic Church in 1971.[2] Tawadros II was elected the 118th Coptic Pope of Alexandria and Patriarch of the See of St Mark on 18 November 2012.

The death of Shenouda, after four decades leading the Coptic Church, comes at a difficult moment in the transition between different political forces in Egypt.[3] The situation is reminiscent of the moment when the Patriarch of the Chaldean Catholic Church, Bidawid, died as the US-led invasion of Iraq toppled the Baathist régime in Baghdad in 2003, leaving the community leaderless for many months at a moment of great change.[4] For members of the Coptic Church today it will take some time to re-imagine the Church and papacy without Shenouda;

---

1 'Shenouda III', *The Blackwell Dictionary of Eastern Christianity*, Blackwell, Oxford, 2001, pp. 449.
2 Bishop Anagelos, 'The life and ministry of his Holiness Pope Shenouda III', *One in Christ: a catholic ecumenical review*, 2012, Vol. 46, no. 1, 2012, pp. 153-158.
3 See the following studies which give background to the modern situation of Coptic Christianity in Egypt: Vivian Ibrahim, *The Copts of Egypt: The Challenges of Modernisation and Identity*, I B Tauris, London, 2011; Paul Sedra, 'Class cleavages and ethnic conflict: Coptic Christian communities in modern Egyptian politics', *Islam and Christian–Muslim Relations*, Vol. 10, No. 2, 1999, pp. 219-235; David Zeidan, 'The Copts—equal, protected or persecuted? The impact of Islamization on Muslim Christian relations in modern Egypt', *Islam and Christian–Muslim Relations*, Vol. 10, No.1, 1999, pp. 53-67; Randall P. Henderson, 'The Egyptian Coptic Christians: the conflict between identity and equality', *Islam and Christian–Muslim Relations*, Vol. 16, No. 2, 2005, pp.155-166; Paul Rowe, 'Building Coptic Civil Society: Christian Groups and the State in Mubarak's Egypt', *Middle Eastern Studies*, Vol. 45, 2009, pp. 111-126.
4 See A O'Mahony, 'The Chaldean Catholic Church: The Politics of Church-State Relations in Modern Iraq', *The Heythrop Journal*, Vol. XLV (2004), pp. 435-450.

who during his forty-year rule transformed the relationship between the Church and community. For the generation of Copts less than 40-years-old will have not known the Church without Shenouda III.

Shenouda was one of the longest serving religious leaders in the Middle East. During the period of Shenouda III's patriarchate immense religious and political changes transformed not only the region but also Egyptian society.[5] The death of Nasser in 1970 ushered in the slow demise of Arab nationalism. Sadat, an intensely pious Muslim, succeeded him and re-oriented Egypt away from the Soviet Union towards the West, signing the peace treaty between Israel and Egypt which underpinned regional security for three decades. The Islamist movement, encouraged by Sadat in his fight with the left-secular forces, turned on him. Assassinated in 1981, Sadat was succeeded by Mubarak who himself lost power in February 2011. It was these deep political changes driven partly by the Islamic upsurge in society and culture which concerned the Coptic Christians, who make-up 7-10 percent of the Egyptian population,[6] and who feared being pushed increasingly to the margins in the context of Islamist determination towards gaining power and to rule. Coptic Christians have found it a struggle to know how to position themselves in relation to changing times driven by Islamic political forces and economic and political crisis.

Shenouda III died as political change in Egypt took hold. Since the ending of Mubarak's rule the Coptic Christians have been subjected to a high level of violence directed at them by radical Islamist forces

---

[5] Changes in the political landscape in Egypt can be viewed through the relationship between law and religion in society and culture, see Nathalie Bernard-Maugiron, 'Egypt's Path to Transition: Democratic Challenges behind the Constitution Reform Process', in *Middle East Law and Governance*, Vol. 3, 2011, pp. 43-59; 'Which Egypt in the New Constitution': Interview with Nathalie Bernard-Maugiron, Director of the 'Institut de recherche pour le développement' of the Paris Sorbonne University with Michele Brignone [http://www.oasiscenter.eu/articles/arab-revolutions/2012/12/19/which-egypt-in-the-new-constitution]; Nathalie Bernard-Maugiron, 'A Constitutional Declaration that Opens up to the Errors of the Past' 15 July 2013 [http://www.oasiscenter.eu/articles/arab-revolutions/2013/07/15/a-constitutional-declaration-that-opens-up-to-the-errors-of-the-past].

[6] There continues to be a great deal of discussion on the actual size of the Coptic Christian population in Egypt: Cornelis Hulsman: 'Christian Activists' Contributions to Christian Migration from Egypt', in *Mélanges de l'Institut Dominicain d'Études Orientales du Caire*, Vol. 28, 2010, pp. 569-592.

seeking to destabilize political society.⁷ There has also been an attempt to draw in the military either to protect or leave unprotected Coptic Christians their churches and institutions, thus bringing the state and its institutions into the equation in the unfolding inter-communal or 'sectarian' conflict. This strategy might be considered an attempt to compromise government into taking sides as it appeared to be defending Christians in the context of a dominant Muslim society. This strategy was only partly successful as it fed into the general decline of law and order and security across wider Egyptian society. That said, Coptic-Islamist confrontation has become an existential possibility which in turn keeps the issue of violence motivated by questions of the religious identity of the state and society to the forefront as an ever present force in the 'economy' of Egyptian political culture—as highlighted by the controversial policies of the recent Muslim Brotherhood government.⁸

The elections which followed the fall of Mubarak lead to the Islamic movement taking a majority of votes in the elections, although not as a total across the electorate. The Muslim Brotherhood-dominated government proved unable to govern with a vision which included all Egyptian society. In fact the Muslim Brotherhood government seemed not to take full cognizance of how diverse and plural Egyptian society had become, a fact that the Islamist politics had taken account of whilst in opposition.⁹ Within a short time of taking office the new government, dominated by the Muslim Brotherhood, antagonised a growing number of institutions and social groups—in particular secularists, a liberal Muslim class and Coptic Christians—while continued economic hardship alienated many ordinary Egyptians. After only one year in power pressures on Muhammad Morsi erupted in mass demonstrations. The military quickly sided with the anti-Morsi protesters, suspending the new constitution, ousting the Islamist president, and violently dispersing mass protest sit-ins held by the Brotherhood in response.¹⁰ The new government, which is dominated

---

7   Laure Guirguis, *Les coptes d'Egypte. Violences communautaires et transformations politiques (2005-2012)*, Karthala/IISMM, Paris, 2012.
8   Mariz Tadros, 'Copts under Mursi: Defiance in the Face of Denial', *Middle East Research and Information project*, Vol. 43, 2013.[http://www.merip.org/mer/mer267/copts-under-mursi].
9   Laure Guirguis, 'Les Frères, les coptes et la révolution', *Outre-Terre*, 2011/3 (no. 29), pp. 373-387.
10 See the following interesting background comment by Gilbert Achcar, 'Whither Egypt?' [February 2011] http://mondediplo.com/openpage/whither-egypt; G

by the Egyptian military, has started to draft a new constitution away from the Islamic and Shari'a one instituted by the Morsi regime.[11] The question of religion and the place of Islam in the constitution has been the perennial issue for the Coptic Christians in Egypt. Shenouda III early on challenged Sadat on the growing Islamization of society taking place through constitutional change. He opposed Islam being set up as a new form of nationalism, as had happened in Turkey and Iran, which by its very logic would exclude Christians. He objected to the change in Article 2 of the Constitution which made the Shari'a Law the principal source; a view shared by a wide range of interests in Egyptian society.[12]

From a wider perspective Christian-Muslim relations in contemporary Egypt have an importance beyond the Middle East with the decline in societies, during the modern period, in which Christian and Muslims co-habit the same political and societal space. The breaking of these distinct societies' examples can be taken from various post-Ottoman territories and states: for example Cyprus, Bosnia, Macedonia, Turkey and the continuing conflict between religions in Lebanon and Syria—Sunni-Shi'ite and Christian and Muslim. It is against this background that present and future encounters between Coptic Christianity and Islam might be weighed. In Egypt today one of the most important themes is the relationship between religion and politics. This question has been a core issue for the identity and character of the modern Egyptian state which is an overarching contextual question for Coptic Christianity.[13] Meir Hatina has observed:

> The status of religion in the state has been one of the burning issues on the Egyptian political agenda ever since Egypt's encounter with the West in the nineteenth

---

Achcar, 'The Muslim Brothers in Egypt's 'orderly transition' [March 2011] http://mondediplo.com/2011/03/06muslimbrothers; G Achcar, Extreme capitalism of the Muslim Brothers', [June 2013] http://mondediplo.com/2013/06/05brothers.

11 Jean-Jacques Pérennès, 'Et si L'Egypte préparait un avenir post-islamiste?', *La Croix*, 23 August 2013, p. 17; Giovanni Sale, 'La 'Seconda rivoluzione' Egiziana dell'estate 2013', *La Civiltà Cattolica*, No. 3918, 2013, pp. 478-491.

12 Edouard S Sabanegh, 'Débats autour de l'application de la loi islamique (Shari'a) en Égypte' in *Mélanges de l'Institut Dominicain d'Études Orientales du Caire*, Vol. 14, 1980, pp. 329-884.

13 S S Hasan, *Christians versus Muslims in Modern Egypt: the century-long struggle for Coptic equality*, Oxford University Press, Oxford, 2003.

century. Egypt may have become more modernized and westernized than any other Muslim state except Turkey, yet it never renounced the age-old fundamental Islamic unity of religion and state or the dominance of the Shari'a in determining personal status.[14]

Shenouda III and his immediate predecessor Cyril VI radically altered the character of authority between the laity and the clerical leadership. When Cyril VI became patriarch in 1959, the lay notables lost their influence within the community. But their contribution to the movement which had developed towards the end of the nineteenth century and early twentieth century remained central: a new communal self-awareness, based on tradition, echoing that as understood by the European reformists and modernizing intellectuals. The rediscovery of the pharaonic past and the glorious era of Egyptian Christianity opened up a historical foundation to the Coptic community, providing it with an entire heritage on which it could draw in order to sketch out the contours of its new identity. Education, which was at the centre of the reform movement, was based on the important factors of this millennial history, which in turn supported the Copts in their search for national legitimacy. Far from rejecting their tradition, they in fact laid claim to it: it became the point of convergence around which the entire group from that time on constructed what one historian has called its 'collective being'.[15] Fadel Sidarious, a Jesuit scholar from the Coptic Catholic Church in Egypt, has well-described the character of the Coptic Church: 'The contemporary Coptic Orthodox anthropology draws its resources from the first centuries of the Christian era. Its socio-historical foundations reveal: an Apostolic Church, founded, according to tradition, by the Evangelist Mark; a Johannine theology, namely the descending theology of the School of Alexandria; a history of martyrs and minority, all along its history, from the time of the Romans till today; a national Christendom, fundamentally linked with the history of Egypt; finally a unique monastic spirituality, founded by Antony, Pacome, Shenouda.'[16]

---

14 Meir Hatina 'On the Margins of Consensus: The Call to Separate Religion and State in Modern Egypt', *Middle Eastern Studies*, Vol. 36, no. 1, 2000, pp. 35-67, p. 35.
15 Brigitte Voile, *Les coptes d'Égypte sous Nasser: Sainteté, miracles, apparitions*, CNRS Éditions, Paris, 2004, p. 43.
16 Fadel Sidarouss, 'Élements d'anthropologies copte', *Proche-Orient Chrétien*, 2011,

The relationship between the Coptic pope and the community took on a different character under Cyril VI. Brigitte Voile finely describes this in her important study of Cyril VI:

> Excited faithful clustered *en masse* around their patriarch in order to receive his *baraka*, dense crowds gathered around a modest church in the suburbs of Cairo in the hope of seeing an appearance of the Virgin, enthusiastic young people thronging the doors of desert monasteries, these are some of the images of the patriarchate of Cyril VI. Not only did the latter not attempt to curtail these demonstrations of the Coptic faith, but he also provided an example of it himself, by authorising those who spread his reputation as a holy man, encouraging the cult of saints, and creating a new pilgrimage site dedicated to Menas the martyr in the desert region of Mariut, to the South-west of Alexandria. It soon became one of the most important in Egypt, the scene of numerous miracles. These massive demonstrations, during which a religious and communal fervour unprecedented in the modern epoch blazed, characterised the Copts of the 1960s.[17]

If the Coptic Church is currently the most numerous of all the Churches in the Middle East, it had already been so in the time of Cyril VI, Shenouda III's predecessor, although without the influence which the latter gave it. The Copts are indeed more numerous today than they were in the time of Cyril VI; however, many scholars estimate that as a proportion of the entire population their percentage has somewhat diminished. If their numbers have increased, it is simply through the effect of demographic progression common to all Egypt. Their influence is not due their number.[18]

It is not easy to assess the life and contribution of Shenouda III to the Coptic Orthodox Church in Egypt; this is due mainly to the length

---

Vol. 61, no. 1-2, pp. 45-59; p. 59.
17 Brigitte Voile, *Les coptes d'Égypte sous Nasser: Sainteté, miracles, apparitions*, CNRS Éditions, Paris, 2004, p. 43.
18 Cornelis Hulsman, 'Discrepancies between Coptic Statistics in the Egyptian Census and Estimates Provided by the Coptic Orthodox Church', in *Mélanges de l'Institut Dominicain d'Études Orientales du Caire*, Vol. 29, 2012, pp. 419-482.

of his tenure and the closeness to his passing. Shenouda III, however, will be remembered by history as a significant figure in the history of Coptic Christianity but also he will be recalled as an important figure for the wider Eastern Christian tradition.[19] The Coptic Orthodox Church and its traditions are better known to day then at any time for many centuries. Jacques Masson, a Jesuit scholar of the Coptic Christian tradition and long-term resident of Egypt, describes the impact that Shenouda III has had on the public profile of the Copt in Egypt society: 'All the surveys undertaken in recent times note a change in their behaviour. The image of the humble Copt shameful and hugging the wall, a second class citizen as a result of difficulties imposed on him, has changed. Today, Copts speak back, oppose the police, demand their rights, hold their heads high, demonstrate. That they can do so is certainly in part thanks to the policy followed by Pope Shenouda.'[20] We might also go further and suggest that the revival of the Coptic Orthodox Church has made a strong and robust institution that by its renewed presence has helped in no small way in creating the conditions of religious and political plurality in modern Egypt.

Shenouda III/Nazir Gayed Rouphail was born on 3 August 1923 at Salam, a small village in the Abnouth basin, close to Asyut, in Upper Egypt. He entered the monastery of the Virgin at Wadi Natrun on 18 July 1954, and took the name Antonios al-Souriani. He was one of a group of three university graduates greatly attached to their Church but who sought to see it reformed who entered the monastery, since it was from there that its leaders were recruited, and it was therefore from there that reform could and must come. They were the first graduates to enter monastic life. With him were Saad Aziz, who would become Makari and then Anba Samuel, and Youssef Skandar, who would become Matta al-Miskin. Antonios al-Souriani was ordained a priest on 31 March 1958. After his nomination to the patriarchate, Pope Cyril VI summoned these three graduate monks. He first of all chose Makari as his secretary, then entrusted him with the Church's social services, and Antonios al-Souriani was appointed as teacher and director of the seminary. Both were ordained bishops. As to Matta al-Miskin, he would later be called to renovate the monastery of Saint

---

19 *Sa Sainteté Shenouda III patriarche des coptes d'Égypte. La voix d'un Père du desert*, Entretiens Rachel et Alphonese Goettmann, Desclée de Brouwer, Paris, 2006.
20 J Masson, 'Décès du pape Shenouda III: bilan d'un règne', *Proche-Orient Chrétien*, Vol. 62, No. 1-2, 2012, pp. 63-79; p. 65.

Macarius. Antonios al-Souriani was ordained bishop on 30 September 1962, taking the name of Anba Shenouda, a name he retained on being appointed patriarch on 14 November 1971. On 14 November 2011 he celebrated forty years of his reign. He died at the age of 88.

From the outset of his pontificate, Shenouda III sought to build upon the reforms of Cyril VI and the lay movement prior to the 1950s before the renewal of the Coptic papacy.[21]. He increased the number of bishops, undertook numerous priestly ordinations, with a view to a more effective leadership in his Church. Between 1971, the date at which his pontificate begun, and 1981, the date of his deposition by President Sadat and his enforced seclusion in his monastery, he consecrated 39 bishops, increasing the membership of the Holy Synod from 23 to 62. He continued this policy after his return to the patriarchate in 1985, creating auxiliary bishops to serve and lead the districts of the great cities, in Alexandria and Cairo especially, but also at Asyut. Today, between eparchial bishops, monastic superiors, bishops general and bishops in the diaspora, the Holy Synod comprises 92 members. He ordained more than a hundred bishops during the forty years of his pontificate.[22]

'Egypt is not only the land of Christian monastic origins, but also of modern monastic revival.'[23] Shenouda III was a product of the great monastic revival which has taken place in the Coptic Orthodox Church which has increased knowledge and influence of Coptic Christianity on the wider Christian tradition.[24] From the late 1960s onwards large numbers of young Copts have retreated into the desert reviving the ancient monasteries once founded in the fourth and fifth centuries. The monasteries have been enlarged and modernised by these new monks, many educated in schools and universities. Modern technology and means of communication have been introduced and some of the monasteries have close relations with Churches and monasteries in Europe and North America. The

---

21 Magdi Guirguis and Nelly van Doorn-Harder, *The Emergence of the Modern Coptic Papacy*, The American University of Cairo Press, Cairo, 2011.
22 J Masson, 'Décès du pape Shenouda III: bilan d'un règne', *Proche-Orient Chrétien*, Vol. 62, No. 1-2, 2012, pp. 66.
23 Samuel Rubenson, 'Tradition and Renewal in Coptic Theology', in N van Doorn-Harder and K Vogt, *Between Desert and City*, Novus Forlag, Oslo, 1997, pp. 35-51, p. 35.
24 Mark Gruber OSB, *Journey Back to Eden: My Life and Times among the Desert Fathers*, Orbis Books, Maryknoll, New York, 2007.

Coptic monastic revival has received much comment.[25] It reminds a Western Christian of the Cistercian movement in Europe during the medieval period, which through its energy transformed the frontiers of the Christendom and brought new agricultural techniques. The monastic revival has been sourced in the desert tradition itself, where radical hermits during the Second World War began to attract disciples. However, there is also a wider context. Numerous young Egyptians were disappointed with the Egyptian kingdom and its dependence on the British. Muslims rallied in movements of Islamic revival, secularized soldiers in clandestine groups of socialist and Copts in Coptic organizations. While the older Coptic leaders were concerned with integrating their community into the nation as it was being formed and were searching for a lay way of life that was 'liberal', some would say 'secular', in the name of universal democratic principles, the new groups by contrast are concerned first with the life of the Coptic community. 'All authentic service begins and ends with the Church ... has for its aim to link Christ and the community' (Matta el-Meskeen).[26] It could be argued that Arab nationalism, which has continued to root itself in Islam, has not been without influence on the style adopted by the Coptic renewal. Indeed the return to the Arab-Muslim heritage has a strict parallel in the return of the Christian to his Coptic-monastic heritage.

In this context some Copts left society behind and went into the desert. In the monasteries they found not only spiritual leaders, but also libraries with manuscripts containing their spiritual heritage, the writings of the radical monastic leaders of the first centuries, like St Antony, St Macarius and St Issac of Niniveh.[27] But some did not find

---

25 John Watson in his obituary notice of Matta El Meskeen states, 'During the last few decades, a small number of monastics—Catholic, Orthodox and Protestant—have made a significant impact upon many churches and other world religions. The Trappist Thomas Merton of Kentucky, the Russian Orthodox Seraphim Rose of Alaska, the Protestant Roger Shutz of Taizé, and the Benedictine Bede Griffiths of Shantivanam in southern India were all prolific authors. All four of them were also readers of the renowned Coptic (Egyptian) Orthodox monk Father Matta El Meskeeen (Mathew the Poor),' *The Independent*, 27 June 2006.
26 Maurice Martin, 'The Coptic-Muslim conflict in Egypt: modernisation of Society and religious transformation', *Between the Desert and the City: The Coptic Orthodox Church Today*, eds Nelly van Doorn-Harder and Kari Vogt, pp. 31-54.
27 According to Rubenson a great number of texts, relating to the early monastic movement in Egypt, either unknown or fragmentary in Coptic, are preserved in Arabic translations. Given the importance of the monastic tradition for the Coptic

the life in the monasteries radical enough and retreated further into the desert to be able to live the life of the desert fathers of the fourth century. As Samuel Rubenson has reminded us 'Tradition is the heart of this renewal.'

The revival in Coptic monasticism has been encouraged by an unprecedented increase in monks and nuns,[28] the number of monastic institutions has had to multiple to accompany this movement. While some of the new monasteries have been fully sanctioned by the Holy Synod of the Coptic Orthodox Church, others are occupied by a couple of monks since it is the policy of the Church that many of the once abandoned and partly ruined monastic buildings should be restored and subsequently re-occupied. Whereas in 1960 there were 206 Coptic monks living in nine monasteries, in 1986 it was recorded that there were 620 Coptic monks in eleven officially recognized monasteries, distributed as follows: The four celebrated ancient monasteries in Wadi Natroun: Dair al-Baramous (The Monastery of the Romans) 83; Dair as-Surian (The Monastery of the Syrians) 55; Dair Anba Bishoi (The Monastery of St Bishoi) 115; Dair Abu Maqar (The Monastery of St Macarius) 105; the Red Sea: Dair Anba Antonious (The Monastery of St Antony) 45; Deir Anba Boula (The Monastery of St Paul) 45. In Upper Egypt: Dair Anba Samwil (The Monastery of St Samuel) 46; Dair al-Muharraq (The Monastery of the Holy Virgin) 50. In the North: Dair Abu Mina (The Monastery of St Minas) (restored and re-founded by Patriarch Cyril IV) 30; Dair Anba Bakhum (the Monastery of Pachomius)10; Dair Mari Girgis (The Monastery of St.George)25.

Church, and the comparatively rapid transmission from Coptic to Arabic among the Christians in Egypt in the ninth and tenth centuries, this is only to be expected. The Arabic texts and collections are not, however, of importance only as witnesses to lost Coptic originals. On the one hand they give us material for an analysis of the characteristic elements of the type of so-called Middle Arabic used in the Coptic communities. On the other hand the fact that these texts are generally preserved in collections helps us to understand how the monastic tradition grew and how it was transmitted. It is also of interest to note that the theological legacy of the early monastic movement was preserved very much in a context of traditional wisdom literature. Samuel Rubenson, 'Arabic Sources for the Theology of the Early Monastic Movement in Egypt', pp. 33-47.

28 On the female monastic movement see Nelly van Doorn-Harder, 'Following the Holy Call: Women in the Coptic Church', *Contemporary Coptic Nuns*, pp.733-750; 'Discovering New Roles: Coptic Nuns and Church Revival', *Between the Desert and the City: The Coptic Orthodox Church Today*, eds Nelly van Doorn-Harder and Kari Vogt, pp. 84-100.

The monastic establishment in 2001 numbered some 1,200, as reported by the official organ of the patriarchate, *Al-Kiraza*.[29]

For the first time in their long history, the desert monasteries are woven into the fabric of the parish churches of the cities, the towns and the villages. Many of the monastic clergy are no longer spending most of their active life in the desert, but have linked themselves into the spiritual life of the Coptic community as a whole. To join a monastery for many young Coptic men means the total identification of the person with the Church. This is an important witness in a situation where the Church represents the faith of a religious minority. Others embrace the monastic life as a sign of protest against the laxity and the worldliness of the 'Church' and society. Whilst difficult to assess it would seem that the ascetic disciplines practised today are considerably more severe than in recent generations. The monks have adopted quite a strict rule, that of St Pachomius, involving isolation within their cells outside the Office and manual works.[30] The higher ranks of the Coptic clergy are selected, from the ranks of the monks. Some may join the monastic life out of a desire for eventual leadership role within the community. Many of the young bishops in the Coptic Orthodox Church today are themselves products of this monastic revival.[31]

The spiritual character of the monasticism thus has a direct influence on the shape of the Coptic Church. In fact, different monasteries at various times have provided the Church with its patriarchs. Thus, for example, from the seventh to the thirteenth century 25 out of 36 patriarchs used to be monks of Dair Abu Maqer in the Wadi Natroun. From the seventeenth to the nineteenth century, ten of the twelve patriarchs came from Dair Anba Antonious monastery. In the middle of the twentieth century, sixteen bishops has served as monks in the Dair as-Surian. Under Shenouda, his home monastery Dair Anba Bishoi has provided numerous monks for appointment to the episcopate.

During the patriarchate of Shenouda III numerous new monasteries have been established: all these new monasteries, except

---

29 A O'Mahony, 'Tradition at the heart of Renewal: the Coptic Orthodox Church and monasticism in Modern Egypt', *International Journal for the Study of the Christian Church*, Vol. 7, no. 3 (2007), pp. 164-178.
30 See Armand Veilleux OCSO, *Pachomian Koinônia*, Cistercian Publications, 1981.
31 John H Watson, 'The Desert Fathers Today: Contemporary Coptic Monasticism', pp.112-139.

for those created for the Coptic community living in the diaspora and mission areas (Australia, North America, Europe for example in Italy, Germany and England and in Africa the Sudan, Kenya and Zimbabwe),[32] are re-occupied ancient monastic sites, abandoned over the centuries.

The renewal in the Coptic Church is a product of the wide range of forces, but has been identified above all with significant individuals who personified the monastic spirituality and leadership which is at the heart of this movement—Patriarch Cyril VI (1902-1971), Patriarch Shenouda III (1971 on) and the monk Matta el Meskeen. The two monks who became patriarchs gave institutional strength, structure and meaning to the monastic renewal. Edward Watkin observed in his appraisal of Cyril VI: 'Not only has a monk become a patriarch, but the Patriarch has remained a monk.'[33] The third, Matta el Meskeen, is not only a spiritual author, he is also the cornerstone of the extraordinary renewal of the monastery of Dair Abu Maqar in Wadi el-Natroun, in the Scete Desert; he is a major figure in the monastic renewal which the Coptic Orthodox Church has been undergoing since the 1950s.

Another major theme in the modern history of Coptic Christianity has been the establishment of new Coptic communities outside Egypt. Emigration of the Copts in sizable numbers started some three decades ago. Emigration from Egypt by Coptic Christians needs to be seen in the context of general Egyptian patterns. Nasser's nationalization policies in the economy also led to a number of well-to-do families leaving Egypt to settle in the West—amongst these were Coptic families. The presence abroad of economically resourceful individuals from this early phase of emigration has been important in the establishment of Coptic Churches in the West that followed at a later stage. The majority of the emigrants were professionals and intellectuals, thus forming part of the Egyptian 'brain-drain'. Today, the Coptic Church has several centres in Western Europe, the USA, Canada, and Australia, with approximately some 5-700,000 members abroad today. In response to this situation the Coptic Church has sent many of its best priests,

---

32 One observer has stated in 2001 that 450, 000, some twelve percent of Coptic Christians, now live abroad: Jacques Masson, 'Trente ans de régne de Shenouda III, Pape d'Alexandrie et de toute l'Afrique', *Proche-Orient Chrétien*, 51, pp. 317-332, p. 321.
33 Edward Watkin, *A Lonely Minority: The Modern Story of Egypt's Copts*, William Morrow & Co, New York, 1963, p. 118.

monks and scholars to serve the communities in the diaspora.[34] After the Second World War, and particularly since 1960, the Coptic Church has established itself in other parts of Africa outside Egypt, partially as a reaction to the independence movements which favoured according to Coptic ecclesiology, the implantation of the Coptic Church, seen as the most ancient African Christian Church.[35]

The Coptic Orthodox Church has been transformed under the leadership of Shenouda III. One significant change for the Coptic Church has been its transformation from a 'National Church' of Egypt to a Christian tradition which has been seeking to find a place in global Christianity.[36] The Coptic Church is also one of the largest autonomous religious institutions in the Mediterranean region; there are more Coptic Christians in Egypt than the Jewish population in Israel and nearly as many members of the Orthodox Church as there are in Greece today.[37]

The trend towards the study of 'world Christianity' with a focus on Asia, Africa, and Latin America has emerged in recent times; however, little attention has been given to the Eastern Christian Churches despite the fact that the Eastern Christians constitute one of largest Christian traditions in the world.[38] Eastern Christian Churches are mainly concentrated in Russia, Eastern Europe, the Middle East, East Africa and in diasporas in the West.[39] Eastern Christianity has between

---

34 Nora Stene, 'Into the Lands of Immigration' and Anitra Bingham-Kolenkow, 'The Copts in the United States of America', Nelly van Doorn-Harder and Kari Vogt, *Between the Desert and the City*, pp. 254-264 and pp. 265-272.

35 Christine Chaillot, 'Activitiés missionarires de l'Église copte en Afrique', *Le Monde copte*, no. 20, 1992, pp. 99-103; John W de Gruchy, 'From Cairo to the Cape: The Significance of Coptic Christianity for African Christianity', *Journal of Theology for Southern Africa*, no. 99, 1997, pp. 24-39.

36 Otto Meinardus, 'The Coptic Church towards the End of the 20th Century: From a National to an International Christian Community', *Ekklesia kai Theologia. Church and Theology* 12 (1993/94), pp. 431-472.

37 A O'Mahony 'The Politics of Religious Renewal: Coptic Christianity in Egypt', *Eastern Christianity: Studies in Modern History, Religion and Politics*, ed. A O'Mahony Melisende, London, 2004, pp. 66-111; 'Coptic Christianity in modern Egypt', *The Cambridge History of Christianity Eastern Christianity*, Vol. V, ed. Michael Angold, Cambridge University Press, Cambridge, 2006, pp. 488-510.

38 S M Kenworthy, 'Beyond Schism: restoring Eastern Orthodoxy to the History of Christianity', *Reviews in Religion and Theology*, 15/2 (2008), pp. 171-178.

39 See the Pew Foundation report on 'Global Christianity: A Report on the Size and Distribution of the World's Christian Population' in 2011 Online version of *Global Christianity: A Report on the Size and Distribution of the World's Christian Population*

250-300 million members worldwide—estimates can vary—which makes it the third largest-Christian denomination with approximately 12 per cent of the global Christian population.[40] Eastern Christianity in its various traditions is the overwhelming character of Christianity in the Middle East.[41]

The Coptic Orthodox Church is the largest Christian denomination in the Middle East. The Coptic Orthodox Church is part of the Oriental Orthodox ecclesial family. The Oriental Orthodox tradition (Coptic, Armenian and Syriac) are dominant in the Middle East.[42] The doctrinal position of these Churches is based on the teachings of the first three ecumenical councils: Nicaea (325), Constantinople (381) and Ephesus (431). They have traditionally rejected the Council of Chalcedon (451). In fact the Oriental Orthodox tradition consists of the following ecclesial communities: Coptic Orthodox Patriarchate of Egypt; Syrian Orthodox Patriarchate of Antioch and All the East, Damascus; Armenian Apostolic Church: See of Etchmiadzin, Armenia and Catholicossate of Antelias, Lebanon; Orthodox Church of Ethiopia; Orthodox Church of Eritrea; Syrian Orthodox Church of Malankar.[43] In the Middle East the Armenian Apostolic Church

---

(hereinafter *Report*) at http://pewforum.org/Christian/GlobalChristianity-worlds-christian-population.aspx. The *Report* estimated that there are some 2.18 billion Christians, representing nearly a third of the estimated 2010 global population of 6.9 billion. Christians are to be found across the globe which today means that no single region can indisputably claim to be the centre of global Christianity, which is not the case for other religious traditions. This is in contrast to the past when Europe held that position; for example in 1910 about two-thirds of the world's Christians lived within the continent. Today, however, approximately one quarter of all Christians live in Europe (26%); the Americas (37%); in sub-Saharan Africa (24%), in Asia and the Pacific (13%). The *Report* noted extraordinary changes in the global configuration of Christianity—in sub-Saharan Africa a 60-fold increase, from fewer than 9 million in 1910 to more than 516 million in 2010, and in the Asia-Pacific region, a 10-fold increase, from about 28 million in 1910 to more than 285 million in 2010.

40 http://www.pewforum.org/Christian/Global-Christianity-orthodox.aspx.
41 A O'Mahony, 'West Asia', in *Atlas of Global Christianity*, eds T M Johnson and K R Ross, Edinburgh, 2010.
42 S Brock, 'The Syrian Orthodox Church in the modern Middle East', A O'Mahony, 'The Coptic Orthodox Church in modern Egypt', and J Whooley, 'The Armenian Church in the contemporary Middle East', in *Eastern Christianity in the Modern Middle East*, eds O'Mahony and Loosley, Routledge, London, 2010, pp. 13-24; 56-77; 78-106.
43 Ch. Chaillot, *Vie et spiritualité des Eglises orthodoxes orientales des traditions syriaque, arménienne, copte et éthiopienne*, Éditions du Cerf, Paris, 2011.

governs a community of some five million people, scattered, like all the Armenians, across the globe. The Armenian Church is represented today by two Catholicossates: Etchmiadzin, which has primacy in the Caucasian and diaspora region, and Sis (Antelias) which has authority over most of the Orthodox Armenians of the Middle East; and two Patriarchates: Jerusalem and Constantinople. The Syrian Orthodox Church, whose Patriarch Ignatius Zakka II is based in Damascus, is today connected to the many millions of Syriac Christians in India through the Malankara Orthodox Syrian Church. The Coptic Orthodox Church is mainly based in Egypt.

The Oriental Orthodox churches have often been depicted in Western and Byzantine Church history as living in isolation from the rest of the Christian world and concerned with mere survival. This was, to a certain extent, true. A significant feature of Oriental Orthodoxy has been persecution and genocide suffered under Byzantine, Muslim and Ottoman powers. On the whole, relations between the Oriental Orthodox Churches and the Latin Crusaders states tended towards openness, which encouraged at times important ecclesial and theological dialogue. In the modern period the Oriental Orthodox Christian tradition has been marked by suffering, indeed martyrdom on a large scale, leaving a deep 'wound' on its life, witness, theology and spirituality.[44]

Fadel Sidarouss has reminded us that the roots of Christianity are decidedly Eastern: 'Consequently, when the West adopted Christianity, it in fact adopted an "other", something different; this Eastern alterity became constitutive of its Western identity, which enabled it to be more easily open to difference throughout its long history.' Knowledge of the Oriental Orthodox tradition in Western Church history has also been obscured for another reason—the Christological controversies of the fifth and sixth centuries produced a three-way split among the Christian Churches which still continues to this day, although it is only among the Churches of Syriac liturgical tradition that all three doctrinal positions are represented.[45] These controversies were originally over

---

[44] Otto F A Meinardus, 'The Coptic Church in Egypt'; Paul Verghese, 'The Ethiopian Orthodox Church and Syrian Orthodox Church'; K V Sarkissian, 'The Armenian Church', in *Religion in the Middle East: Three Religions in Concord and Conflict: Vol. 1 Judaism and Christianity*, ed. A J Arberry, Cambridge University Press, Cambridge, 1969, pp. 423-453; pp. 454-481; pp. 482-520.

[45] Sebastian Brock, 'The Syriac Orient: a third "lung" for the church?', *Orientalia*

how best to describe the relationship between the divinity and the humanity in the incarnate Christ—for the Orthodox and Catholic (and Protestant-reformed after the sixteenth century) traditions the Council of Chalcedon had settled the matter in 451. The Arab invasions and the rise of Islam in the seventh century effectively fossilized this division. However, as Sebastian Brock has pointed out, since the 1960s these Churches began a process of rapprochement with both the Catholic and Orthodox Churches which has significantly altered this situation. Pope John Paul II and the Syrian, Coptic and Armenian Orthodox Churches have signed 'Common Declarations of Faith' on the nature of the Incarnate Word. However, doctrinal divergence remains unresolved on numerous other matters.[46]

The modern ecumenical movement brought about a greater intensification of contacts between the Coptic Church, the Western Churches and Eastern Orthodox. In fact Shenouda, who was the first ever Coptic Patriarch to visit Rome in 1973, signed with Paul VI a significant and historic common declaration.[47] The importance of this dialogue was noted by Frans Bouwen, a Catholic theologian based at St Anne's in Jerusalem, a senior and one of the longest serving members of the Official Dialogue Commission between the Oriental Orthodox and Catholic Church: 'One of the most significant events in the history of the present-day ecumenical movement and one of the richest promises for the future is, beyond any doubt, the Christological consensus that has emerged, in the course of the last decades, between the churches that recognized the Council of Chalcedon and those that did not, since it was held in the year 451.'[48]

Despite their importance during Shenouda III's long reign relations between the Coptic Church and other Churches have not always

---

Christiana Periodica, Vol. 71, No. 1, 2005, pp. 5-20; 'The Syrian Orthodox Church in the twentieth century', *Christianity in the Middle East: Studies in Modern History, Theology and Politics*, ed. A O'Mahony, Melisende, London, 2008, pp. 17-28.

46 Sebastian Brock, 'The Syriac Churches in Ecumenical Dialogue on Christology', in ed. A O'Mahony, *Eastern Christianity. Studies in Modern History, Religion, and Politics*, pp. 44-65; 'The Syriac Churches and Dialogue with the Catholic Church', *The Heythrop Journal, A Quarterly Review of Philosophy and Theology*, Vol. XLV (2004), pp. 466-476.

47 Frans Bouwen, 'Le dialogue officiel entre l'Église catholique et l'Église copte orthodoxe', *Proche-Orient Chrétien*, Vol. 54, No. 3-4, 2004, pp. 320-346.

48 Frans Bouwen, 'Le consensus christologique entre l'Église catholique et les Églises orthodoxies orientales', *Proche-Orient Chrétien*, Vol. 43, No. 3-4, 1993, pp. 324-353.

been easy.⁴⁹ For the new leader of the Coptic Church, Tawadros II, re-establishing ecumenical relations will be of significance. Another challenge for the new patriarch will be the question of 'primacy' among the Oriental Orthodox family especially in the Middle East and for wider ecumenical engagement.⁵⁰ However, that said during Shenouda's long tenure, the Coptic Church has gone from being a local Middle Eastern Church to an increasingly global religious community.⁵¹ A measure of this is the fact that the new leader of the Coptic Church Tawadros II chose to meet with Pope Francis I in May 2013 in Rome on his first ecclesial journey outside Egypt. Francis I in his response, which echoed the earlier meeting between Paul VI and Shenouda III, confirmed in a significant way the importance of the ecumenical dialogue with the Coptic Orthodox Church:

> For me it is a great joy and a truly graced moment to be able to receive all of you here, at the tomb of Saint Peter, as we recall that historic meeting forty years ago between our predecessors, Pope Paul VI and the late Pope Shenouda III, in an embrace of peace and fraternity, after centuries in which there was a certain distance between us. So it is with deep affection that I welcome Your Holiness and the distinguished members of your delegation, and I thank you for your words. Through you, I extend my cordial greetings in the Lord to the bishops, the clergy, the monks and the whole Coptic Orthodox Church.
>
> Today's visit strengthens the bonds of friendship and brotherhood that already exist between the See of Peter and the See of Mark, heir to an inestimable heritage of martyrs, theologians, holy monks and faithful disciples of Christ, who have borne witness to the Gospel from generation to generation, often in situations of great adversity.

---

49 M Martin, C van Nispen and F Sidarouss, 'Les nouveaux courants dans la communauté copte orthodoxe', *Proche-Orient Chrétien*, Vol. 40, No. 3-4, 1990, pp. 245-257.

50 Fadel Sidarous, 'Le renouveau de l'église copte catholique aux prises avec son identité et son alterité', *Proche-Orient Chrétien*, Vol. 60, No. 3-4, 2010, pp. 298-313.

51 See my earlier contributions cited above.

> Forty years ago the Common Declaration of our predecessors represented a milestone on the ecumenical journey, and from it emerged a Commission for Theological Dialogue between our Churches, which has yielded good results and has prepared the ground for a broader dialogue between the Catholic Church and the entire family of Oriental Orthodox Churches, a dialogue that continues to bear fruit to this day. In that solemn Declaration, our Churches acknowledged that, in line with the apostolic traditions, they profess 'one faith in the One Triune God' and 'the divinity of the Only-begotten Son of God ... perfect God with respect to his divinity, perfect man with respect to his humanity.' They acknowledged that divine life is given to us and nourished through the seven sacraments and they recognized a mutual bond in their common devotion to the Mother of God.
>
> We are glad to be able to confirm today what our illustrious predecessors solemnly declared, we are glad to recognize that we are united by one Baptism, of which our common prayer is a special expression, and we long for the day when, in fulfilment of the Lord's desire, we will be able to communicate from the one chalice.[52]

To record and understand the significance of Shenouda III for the Coptic Orthodox Church will take some time; however, the Coptic Church today is today a strong and important religious institution for Egypt but also for the Christian tradition. Above all the relationship between the Coptic papacy and the Coptic Christian community has been substantial re-energized. To understand this I would like to end by citing the description of the events leading up to the funeral of Shenouda III by the Jesuit scholar and long-term observer of Coptic Christianity in Egypt, Jacques Masson:

> On Saturday 17 March 2012 at 19.00hrs, the death of Pope Shenouda III, patriarch of the Copts, was officially

---

[52] http://www.zenit.org/en/articles/pope-francis-address-to-coptic-pope-tawadros-ii.

announced. The news spread rapidly throughout the whole of Egypt. On Sunday morning, the faithful crowded in front of the patriarchate at Anba Roueis in Cairo, in order to pay final homage to their father. In accordance with tradition, the pope's remains were displayed, dressed in his priestly vestments and seated on his throne in the cathedral choir. The crowd was enormous, blocking the traffic all along Ramses Street. Such was the crush that three people died, suffocated against the barriers erected to control the crowd. On Monday, the patriarchate remained closed for fear of similar incidents. The funeral was held on March 20 at 11.00. The military police were deployed in five columns in order to direct and control the crowd in front of the patriarchate. The doors of the cathedral were closed behind those who had managed to gain entry, and the area around it filled with the faithful, who followed the ceremony on giant screens. Official representatives, who arrived late, ambassadors, delegates and the military, struggled to make their way to the seats reserved for them. The pope had been transferred from his throne to a coffin from Rome. The ceremony proceeded in a solemn manner, accompanied by the Coptic melodies of the choir. Anba Ermia, one of the pope's secretaries, remained standing, pensive, with one hand on the coffin, his gaze fixed on the pope's face. Here and there in the congregation silent tears ran down their faces. After the Epistle was read, the *Agios* was intoned by the whole crowd. With the whole of this immense cathedral singing to the glory of God, all-powerful and immortal, strong emotions were unleashed: the leader of the choir was unable to hold back his tears. After the Gospel, Anba Bafnotios, bishop of Samalout, read passages from the pope's letters to the faithful: short, simple phrases, counsels for Christian life. The crowd applauded. Then Anba Bakhomios, bishop of Beheirat and patriarchal administrator during the vacancy of the patriarchal see, gave the pope's panegyric. The ceremony ended 13.00. The coffin was taken by military helicopter to Wadi

Natrun and the pope's monastery of Anba Bishoi. The crowd awaiting the arrival of the pope at the monastery was as great as that at Cairo in front of the patriarchate. It blocked the car in which the coffin had been placed for more than half an hour. Everyone pressed forward in order to touch it, just as inside the monastery everyone endeavoured to touch the coffin with a handkerchief held in their hands, to become a relic to be piously taken home with them. The pope was finally buried at 19.00 in the vault prepared for him. After such funerals, it is difficult to give an assessment of the reign which does not turn into a panegyric.[53]

---

53 J Masson, 'Décès du pape Shenouda III: bilan d'un règne', *Proche-Orient Chrétien*, Vol. 62, No. 1-2, 2012, p. 63-64.

RUSSIAN ORTHODOXY AND ISLAM—
ETHICS AND SPIRITUALITY IN EDUCATION
Basil Cousins

There are strongly conflicting views about the role that belief and unbelief systems should play in contemporary national education. The fundamental issue lies in the concept of mission.

Mission is about propagating a set of beliefs values and ethics leading to sincere conversion and practice. Christian Mission and Islamic *da'wa* (the call to proselytize all non-believers) are examples applied globally. This equally applies to atheistic organisations[1] as well as to totalitarian political systems such as Communism and Fascism.

Belief systems and political systems inter-relate in a complex manner. National education is a key function in this relationship. Russian history provides leading examples. Until 1917, the Tsarist political model was based on the concept of an autocratic leader representing God on earth seeking to rule over a homogeneous 'Russified' population. This culture was forcefully replaced by Atheistic Communism from 1917 to the 1980s which strengthened its grip on autocratic power, with the Communist Party replacing the Russian Orthodox Church (ROC) as the vehicle of belief. After the fall of Communism, both the Tsarist and Communist systems were replaced by a more democratic constitution.

This essay examines the evolution of religious education and the profound changes in Russia over the past 200 years in the eyes of two leading nineteenth-century educationalists, one Orthodox—Nikolai Il'Minskii—and the other Muslim—Ismail Gasprinskii. Both developed important educational projects during a period of great social change and increasing secularity. The phrase 'Religious Education' covers religious, secular and ethical beliefs.

---

1 For example: Atheist Alliance International and many others.

Can lessons gleaned from the Russian experiences be applied elsewhere? In today's Russian Federation, we observe the interaction of two great religious belief systems seeking total conversion within the context of an all-encompassing secular system. A trend back to the involvement of religious beliefs in the Russian public arena is evident today. It is uncertain how significant this trend will evolve within today's secular environment.

Two case studies of the role of religion in national education are reviewed. The first covers the Russian Federation since 1993; the second the Autonomous Republic of Tatarstan.

The importance and nature of the role being played by the Russian state in Tatarstan cannot be overestimated. It is a development of the struggle by the Tsarist Empire with Islam and external influences over the past millennium. There has been continuous pressure to re-create a Sunni Muslim Khanate to replace the one destroyed by Ivan Grozni's conquest of Kazan in 1552.

The political management within the Russian Federation of the contest between the Christian, Muslim and secular missions could influence the future development of society globally. Religious education will be a fundamental instrument in this. The West and other world powers need understand and learn from the Russian experience. The issues facing Il'Minskii and Gasprinskii in nineteenth-century Tsarist Russia are as relevant today as they were then.

EDUCATIONALISTS

This essay compares current trends in religious education in the light of the abovementioned nineteenth-century educationalists.[2]

Nikolai Il'Minskii (1842-1891)

The son of a Russian Orthodox priest, Il'Minskii lived in Kazan, Tatarstan, after travelling extensively in the Middle East, where from

---

2 Their work is described in the author's M Phil: Cousins, William Basil: M Phil 'Russian Orthodox Church and Islam, The role of language and education in Mission. The contribution of Nikolai Il'Minskii in its historical context', Heythrop College, University of London, 2007.

1850-1854 he studied Arabic gaining an intimate knowledge of Islam and its sacred literature at the behest of the Holy Synod of the Russian Orthodox Church. He was sent 'to gain a better knowledge of Muslim attitudes ... to understand their weak points and study the possibility of a movement towards Christianity.'[3] On his return to Kazan, he founded the Il'Minskii System with the overriding aim of instilling the sincere conversion of the non-Russian tribal peoples to the Orthodox faith as the most effective barrier to the progressive spread of Islam. He created a system of primary education based on tuition in the students' native language, such as Tatar as the bridge to learning Russian language and culture. He helped create an ecosystem to support this initiative including an academy, a teaching seminary, a missionary society, a translation commission and a wealth of publications in various tribal languages. His ideas had significant impact on legislation, particularly the use of native languages in national and church primary schools, still reflected in the educational practices of the Russian Federation. The survival of a significant community of Kriashen (Baptised Tatars) after the fall of Communism was the result of his work.[4] Finally, it is considered that Lenin applied the Il'Minskii's concepts of employing local languages in education as a key means of gaining support for socialism in the 1920s and 1930s.[5]

Il'Minskii expressed views on the most beneficial approach to Muslim communities and the avoidance of 'fanaticism' within such groups. Fundamentally, his system aimed to create a body of well educated, highly motivated Christians whose example could influence their fellow Tatars to convert to Christianity.

He had little confidence in polemics and apologetics. Active measures to convert were counterproductive, creating resistance and awaking fanaticism. Instead he set out to influence the Muslims indirectly by educating the Baptised Tatars and by promoting the development of personal contacts between the baptised and the unbaptised.[6]

---

3   N I Il'Minskii, *About the System for the Education of non-Russians and about the Kazan Central Christian-Tatar School for the 50th Anniversary of the System and of the School as well as for the certificate of the Holy Synod of 29th May 1913 about the education of non-Russians*; footnotes and comments by A A Voskresenskii, published by P V Shchetinkin, Kazan, 1913, p. XI.
4   Filatov Sergei, *Religia i Obshchestvo*, Letnii Sad, Moscow, 2000, pp. 108-109.
5   Kreindler, I T, 'Lenin, Russian and Soviet Language Policy', *IJSL* 33, pp. 129-135.
6   Cousins, *op. cit.*, p. 102.

Il'Minskii's correspondence with Pobedonostev (Over-Procurator of Russian Orthodox Church, 1880-1905) on national education policies and missionary issues are considered to be very significant. These letters reveal his closeness to the conservative direction of Government policy (at the time), 'opposition to the Muslim clergy and ... hostility to the national movements .... Moreover, he was not actively in opposition to Islam. His principle work was above all of a missionary nature.'[7]

Il'Minskii foresaw that 'the great religious reformation within Islam would exert the same influence on the future evolution of Muslims as that exerted by the Lutheran Reformation on the traditional Catholic World.'[8]

His views are as relevant today in the Russian Federation and beyond as they were 150 years ago.

Ismail Gasprinskii (1851-1914)

Gasprinskii was a key advocate of Muslim modernisation in the pre-revolutionary Russian Empire. He was a pragmatist, accepting Russian domination as a political fact but resisting any form of assimilation which he foresaw as coercive, leading to the absorption of the other tribal groups by the Russians.

An advocate of a Western-style pluralistic-egalitarian social political model,[9] he was enthusiastic about the USA and other examples where the comprehensive equality of tribes constituting the state and their ethnic originality were respected and supported by mechanisms providing genuine ethnic-confessional pluralism.[10] A reformed Islam would not be an impediment—the main evil was ignorance. In his opinion, the main obstacle was the blind resistance of Russian clerical nationalism.

Gasprinskii was educated in a Russian school, later practising as a teacher. As mayor of Bahchesary in the Crimea, he played a role in the

---

7 Ishakova RR, *Teacher training in the Kazan Province from the mid 19th to early 20th Centuries*, Kazan, 2001.
8 Batunsky, Mark, 'Russian Clerical Islamic Studies in the late 19th and early 20th centuries', *CAS* 1994, pp. 213-235.
9 *Ibid.*, 218.
10 *Ibid.*, pp. 219-220, citing Miropiev.

modernisation of Muslim lifestyles, including helping to free women from their undignified status.

In 1884, he founded a model *cedid* school in Bahchesary with native language instruction and not Arabic, as traditionally used to teach the Qur'an. This aroused fierce opposition among the conservative mullahs. However, Gasprinskii was a clever politician, marshalling the progressives to support his concepts. Glazik records that by 1905/6, there were over 5,000 *cedid* schools in Russia alone. This model proliferated outside Russia as far as Mumbai.[11]

His great reforms included the newspaper called *Tercuman Perevodchik* ('The Translator'), the improved traditional Muslim schools, a Muslim Teacher Training Seminary in Kazan and the introduction of the 'New Method' into the *maktabs* with instruction in Tatar.

Finally, he introduced secular subjects such as arithmetic, geography and history into the curriculum. These supplemented the Qur'anic recitation and the teaching of the basic principles of Islam, previously the main subjects of *maktab* education.

Gasprinskii created a modern system for education. A massive growth in Muslim schools was observed at the close of nineteen century.

Education remains a critical issue for the Muslim community in Russia.

CASE STUDY—RUSSIAN FEDERATION
The nature of the state in Russia

The concept of the Russian state has developed from the autocratic model of Ivan IV Grozni in which the leader represented God on earth ruling a homogeneous 'Russified' population, expressed as 'One God, One Tsar, One Faith, One Culture, One Language'. Unlike western monarchies that were, at least in theory until the Protestant Reformation, subject to the Pope in religious matters, the Tsar of the Russian empire was the supreme authority on religious issues. This autocratic model aimed to impose 'Russified' homogeneity on the diverse cultures in the Tsarist Empire. It was re-interpreted and imposed by subsequent Tsars up to 1917. Both Peter I (the Great, 1682-1725)

---

11 Glazik, Joseph M S C, *Der Russisch-orthodoxe Heidenmission seit Peter der Grossen*, Aschendorffsche Verlagsbuchhandlung, Munster, Westfalen, 1954.

and Catherine II (the Great, 1762-1796) encouraged Western influences but retained a firm autocratic hold on power and wealth. Nevertheless, Catherine took significant steps to recognise and accommodate the pluralistic nature of the Russian Empire. Lenin (1917-1924) and Stalin (1924-1953) maintained the grip of autocratic power over the Soviet Union which overthrew the Russian Empire.

The fall of totalitarian Communism and the Party enabled a complete rethink about the fundamental nature of the Russian state. President Yeltsin (1991-1999) was instrumental in the development of the new political structures which replaced the Soviet Union. Yeltsin championed the Constitution of the Russian Federation as Russia's supreme law, passed through a national plebiscite in December 1993 proclaiming the sovereignty of Russian Federation over the heartland of the former Soviet Union. All have equal rights and obligations under the 1993 Constitution. The Russian Federation is made up of 176 national groups and almost as many languages.[12]

The 1993 Federal Constitution, at least on paper, is democratic and federal with striking similarities to the 1787 American Constitution.[13] It granted equalities of ideologies and religions, freedom of speech and equality before the law. It creates an environment in which the principles laid down by Il'Minskii could be implemented, namely respect for the tribal peoples and freedom of belief, the rejection of the use of force and administrative pressures in proselytisation, use of local languages in education but with a recognition of the importance of Russian as the state language.

There is an intense struggle between those maintaining the 'liberal' aspects of the 1993 Constitution and those seeking to circumscribe the freedoms granted. The ROC had succeeded in getting the Law on Freedom Conscience and Religious Associations signed by President Yeltsin in 1977, replacing the law defined by the Soviet Premier Michael Gorbachev in 1980. The new law severely restricted the rights of 'non-traditional' religions.[14] More recently, Medvedev's Legacy of Reform

---

12 Marc Lepetre, 'Language Policy in the Russian Federation: language diversity and national identity,' *Revista de Sociolinguistica*, Sociolinguistica Internacional Primevera, Noves SL, 2002.

13 Mannheimer, David, Comparing the American and Russian Constitutions, http://justice.uaa.alaska.edu/forum/24/4winter2008/a_constitution.html.

14 http://en.wikipedia.org/wiki/Law_on_Freedom_of_Conscience_and_Religious_Associations.

focused on political reform and diversity. Since returning to power, President Putin has initiated a series of counter-reforms. There is strong evidence that Putin is seeking to rule in an increasingly autocratic manner. He is 'modernising autocracy'.[15]

The concept of 'spiritual security' has been developed over the past ten years, strengthening the ROC position and reformulating the role of the FSB (Federal Security Bureau—successor to the KGB).[16]

Russian education—historic background

Education systems are intimately linked with the ethos of the state. The multi-ethnic populations of the Federation have experienced an extreme range of educational aims and practices.

The role of belief systems and ethics in schools in Russia has switched back from the traditional autocratic model of the Russian Tsarist Empire identified with the ROC via the totalitarian atheistic Communist model to the secularist 'democratic' federal model of the Russian Federation. There is a further transition towards encouraging religious belief to play a significant role in the functioning of the state at a political level as well as in the public education system.[17] Many leading thinkers in the nineteenth century promoted secular national education separate to the ROC: not least was Lenin.[18]

The term 'secular' describes the separation of the state and its institutions from religious institutions/clerics and freedom from governmental imposition of religion upon the people within a state that is neutral on matters of belief.[19] 'The term can also imply that human activities and decisions, especially political ones, should be unbiased by religious influence.'[20] The phrase 'religious education' in this context covers 'systems of belief or unbelief' which are central to the identity and functioning of the Russian State.

---

15 BBC, 'Putin's Russia: The Modern Autocrat', 22 December 2011.
16 Elkner, Julie, 'Spiritual Security in Putin's Russia', PhD essay, jce23@cam.ac.uk.
17 *Ibid.*
18 Lilge, Frederic, 'Lenin and the Politics of Education', *Slavic Review* Vol. 27, Jan. 1968.
19 Kosmin, Barry A, 'Contemporary Secularity and Secularism', *Secularism and Secularity: Contemporary International Perspectives*, eds Barry A Kosmin and Ariela Keysar, Institute for the Study of Secularism in Society and Culture (ISSSC), Hartford, CT, 2007.
20 en.wikipedia.org/wiki/Secularism, 21/09/13.

Ishakova[21] describes the struggle between the developing national school system and the Orthodox parish school system. A Europeanised style of education was needed to enable Russia to establish its position as a leading power.[22]

The 1860s saw the struggle between the ROC and the state come to a head over the issue of the role of Orthodox clergy in national education. The ROC leadership role in state education was progressively eroded throughout the nineteenth century but particularly after the 1905 Revolution and totally annulled after 1917. Prior to that, the national and parish school systems worked in parallel.

Communist Period (1917-1989)

The Church was denied any role in education or any form of public life throughout the Soviet period when education was a highly centralized government-run system. It provided total access for all citizens and post-education employment. The Soviet Union recognized that the foundation of their system depended upon complete dedication of the people to the state through education. The key drive was to raise literacy in the general population from under 30 percent recorded in the 1897 population census—the lowest in Europe. Lenin said 'It is impossible to build a Communist Society in a country where the people are illiterate.'[23] In 1919, Lenin signed the *likbez* decree (liquidation of illiteracy). By 1937, the total literacy rate was 75 percent. A key aspect of this had been the policy of indigenisation which promoted the development of native tribal languages such as Tatar as the quickest way of increasing education levels.[24]

The initial Soviet attitude to the encouragement of local languages echoes Il'Minskii's work. Lenin wrote '... the workers support the equality of nations and languages ... .' He spoke out vigorously

---

21 Ishakova R R, *Pegagogicheskoe obrazovanie v Kazanckoi gubernii v seredine XIX—nachale XX vekov* ('Teacher training in the Kazan Province from the mid-19th to early 20th Centuries'), Kazan, 2001.
22 The development of mass education in Russia is described in the author's M Phil, *op. cit.*
23 Dickens, Mark, *Soviet Language Policy in Central Asia*, Princeton University Press, Princeton, 1988, p. 2.
24 *Ibid.*, p. 8.

against "Great Russian chauvinism", criticising those who wished to make Russian the official language of the Soviet Union ... .'[25] This was very different from Tsarist times when Russian had been the official language. There was no *de iure* official language throughout the Soviet period although Russian was clearly the dominant language of government. In the early years, everyone had the right to be educated in his or her own language.

Dickens writes that Soviet language policy was inextricably linked with the Marxist-Leninist (later Stalinist) view of the evolution of nations 'from the clan to the nation, which is the ultimate outcome of the group.' Stalin defined a nation as a 'stable and historically constituted human community founded on its community of language, territory, economic life and spiritual make-up', the last contained in the idea of community of national culture.[26] 'Of these characteristics, language is the nation's most obvious and important attribute. There is no such thing as a nation without a common linguistic basis.'[27]

Russian Federation (1993-)

The 1993 Constitution of the Russian Federation guaranteed citizens freedom of belief and the right to free and accessible general education. As defined in the Law, the term education implies the purposeful process of educating and upbringing the citizen, implemented on the interest of a person, the society and the state.

In the opinion of Cristina Carpinelli,[28] the following aspects of the constitution are particularly relevant: the right to use mother tongue languages; freedom of thought and speech; bans on censorship; freedom of creativity, cultural access, rights to participate in cultural life and the protection of intellectual property; Russian as a state language overall but the Republics within Russia have the right to establish their own official languages to be used together with Russian.

The state guarantees the observance of the following general principles: the humanistic character of education coupled with the

---

25 *Ibid.*
26 *Ibid.*
27 *Ibid.*
28 Dr Cristina Carpinelli, 9/17/2007.*len.allexperts.com* › ... › Political Science › Russia (News & Politics).

overall priority of general human values, life, health and free personal development as well as fostering the students' civil spirit and love of the Motherland; unity of federal cultural and educational space is sought, preserving at the same time ethnic and regional cultural traditions and the secular character of education in state and municipal educational institutions.

It was to be expected that the ROC would press for a greater role in public education from the inception of the Russian Federation. The secularists resisted this over the past 20 years. The ROC has led the campaign since the early 1990s to get Orthodox Christianity onto the educational agenda. In 1997 it tried to introduce a course entitled 'The History of Russia's Orthodox Culture' into state elementary and middle schools. Opponents claimed that this violated the separation of Church and state. In 2002/03 the textbook titled *The Bases of Orthodox Culture* by A V Borodina was introduced with the support of Vladimir Filipov, the Federal Minister of Education (1998-2004). This was strongly opposed. Patriarch Kirill agreed to the inclusion of other religions. 'The eventual support of Muslim and Jewish communities enabled this initiative to move forward.'[29] Opposition continued from the scientific community and from other religious groups, particularly the Protestants.[30]

The introduction of religion in the state educational curriculum has implications for the relationship between the Russian state and the ROC in particular but also with other 'traditional' religions. Although minority faiths were excluded from the 1997 Law of Freedom and on Religious Associations,[31] the programme could help promote a pluralistic understanding of religion at state level.

The struggle for a larger role of religion in state education continues unabated. Vladimir Putin, prior to the recent presidential elections, decided to introduce religious education into Russian public schools.

He was supported by the Patriarch, the Chief Rabbi and leading Islamic authorities. Religious classes have been introduced experimentally in 20 Russian regions attended by some 300,000

---

29 Lonadier, Brett, 'Recapturing Russian Heritage: Religious Education on Public Schools', Web Exclusive, 18 October 2010, Center on Faith and International Affairs, Arlington, VA.
30 *Ibid.*
31 *Ibid.*

students.³² Parents can choose one of six models: four are religious—basics of Orthodox Christianity, Islam, Judaism, and Buddhism and the two remaining are Basics of World Religions and Secular Ethics. Religious communities can choose teachers for the first four modules.

According to data from the Russian Education Ministry, 42 percent are interested in secular ethics, 30 percent attend basics of Orthodox Christian Culture, 9 percent the basics of Islam and 1 percent Buddhism.³³

This move to introduce religion into the Russian public school curriculum has been welcomed by the leaders of the religions directly affected as well as by the Roman Catholics, even though they are not directly involved. The Jewish community was particularly supportive.

The clause laying down that the fundamentals of religion be taught in all schools was approved by the Federation Council on 26 December 2012 to go into effect on 1 Sept 2013. This does not specify which religions will be discussed in classrooms.³⁴

This initiative continues to be challenged. It has potential implications for church-state relations and religious freedom in Russia.³⁵ Professor Fedor Kozyrev, Centre for Religious Pedagogy, University of St Petersburg writes: 'In many respects, our future depends on our success in combining the idea of a pluralistic democratic state, as formulated in the Constitution [of the Russian Federation], with the spiritual ideals and traditional religious values forming the basis of the various cultures, peoples and creeds which is Russia.'³⁶

He argues that the effects of the long reign of state-supported atheism on the attitudes of society towards religion cannot be underestimated. The ROC has ceased to be an organic part of the way of life. Citizens are wary of any penetration of religion into public life, fearing that 'some kind of new ideological control may enter schools

---

32 Islam Today, 02.10.2012 , news report, *tvarsivi.com/?y=3&z=2012-12-18 percent2017...* .
33 Lonadier, *loc. cit.*
34 Zaimov, Styan, *Christian Science Reporter*, citing *The Moscow Times*, 3 January 2013.
35 Lonadier, *ibid.*
36 Kozyrev, Fedor, 'On the Place and Role of Religious Education in Russian Schools: Retrospection and Forecasts', The International Association for Religious Freedom, NGO in General Consultative Status with the Economic and Social Council of the United Nations; *East-West Church Ministry Report*, Vol. 10, No. 4, Fall 2002, covering the former Soviet Union and Central and Eastern Europe.

under the guise of religious education in schools.'[37] Long shadows are still cast by nineteenth-century liberalism and the experiences of the Soviet period.

He points out that there have never been theological departments in Russian universities. Peter the Great introduced the university concept as part of his drive to introduce Western concepts and practices into the Russian empire. St Petersburg University claims to be the successor of the university he established in 1724 by decree. As a result, seminary theology and academic science followed different tracks, leading to 'the isolation of the clergy from public life and the polarization of spiritual and secular principles in Russian culture.'

Professor Kozyrev describes secular society's distrust of the ROC. The enigma lies in the fact that polls consistently show that the majority of the ethnic Russian population claim adherence to the Russian Orthodox Church even if few practise their faith. Nevertheless, many intellectuals are joining the clergy. The current leadership of the Church, as exemplified by Patriarch Kirill, are highly educated and 'intellectual'.

Kozyrev clearly fears that ideology will 'enter schools under the guise of religious and spiritual education.' He cites the increasingly close collaboration between Ministry of Education and the Moscow Patriarchate. 'A new concept of moral and spiritual education has been developed, on the order of the Ministry of Education by the Orthodox-sponsored Pokrov Institute.'

The official position of the Church is set out in the 'Bases of the Social Concept of the Russian Orthodox Church'. Section XIV-3 sets out:

> From the Orthodox perspective, it is desirable that the entire educational system should be built on religious principles and based on Christian values. Nevertheless, the Church, following the age-old tradition, respects the secular school and is willing to build relations with it on the basis of human freedom. At the same time, the Church considers it inadmissible to impose on students anti-religious and anti-Christian ideas and to assert the monopoly of the materialistic world-view (see XIV. 1).

---

37 *Ibid.*

The situation typical of many countries in the twentieth century when state-run schools were made instruments of militant atheistic education should not be repeated. The Church calls to remove the consequences of atheistic control over the system of public education.[38]

This statement is seen by the secularists as an attack on 'free will'. They ask if 'the Church finds the forcing upon students of Christian ideas and views admissible.'[39] The aim of a report issued in November 2000 by the Pokrov Institute was 'to promote the spiritual consolidation of Russia and the instilling of patriotism in her students.'[40] Little mention is made of how traditional Christian values might be conveyed to atheists, Muslims and Jews. Kozyrev clearly fears that religious education may be a means of indoctrinating '… an outward semblance of values rather than becoming the means for students to develop their own abilities and to broaden their outlook.' He argues that neither the Church nor religious pedagogues show 'any will to analyse old mistakes and bring the principles of spiritual education in harmony with the realities of contemporary pluralistic society.' He generally considers that the system of religious education under the Tsarist regime failed to prevent 'a universal explosion of ungodliness, the desecration of churches and ill feeling towards the Church.'[41]

This is a simplistic judgement. The causes of the fall of the Tsarist regime, with which the ROC was intimately linked, were highly complex and deep seated. They relate to the struggle to impose an outdated concept of autocracy on a rapidly changing multi-ethnic empire in the throes of industrialisation and profound social change compounded by military failures and the abolition of serfdom in 1861 by Tsar Alexander II in 1861. This overall failure does not mean that pedagogical initiatives being developed in the nineteenth century were failures in themselves—far from it! An example of this can be witnessed through the creation of the national school system by the Tsarist Ministry of National Education. This was crucial to meet the urgent need for a workforce capable of supporting the demands of the industrial revolution and empire.

---

38 http://orthodoxeurope.org/page/3/14.aspx.
39 Kozyrev, *op. cit.*
40 *Ibid.*
41 *Ibid.*

Russian Orthodoxy and Islam—Ethics and Spirituality in Education

Kozyrov further argues that although 'many in our country find the current irreligious condition normal ... the impoverishment of the spiritual life of a child ... can never be the means of protecting the child's freedom of conscience thus violating the child's right to receive education.' He contrasts the path of indoctrination (of religion) to preserve national identity and consolidate society with an irreligious school education which while trying to preserve freedoms 'lose[es] all connection with our national spiritual tradition and, along with it, the ability to understand the spiritual identities, cultures and historic legacies of other peoples. ... the path lies somewhere in the middle.'[42]

A 'Spirituality without Indoctrination' movement of pedagogues and believers has been set up in St Petersburg. Their work includes 'promoting and introducing various programmes of religious education in schools that maximise the student's knowledge of the world of religion and their national spiritual tradition without infringing on their fundamental rights and freedoms.'[43]

'The alternative to indoctrination is not the absence of religious education in schools but, rather the consistent, well considered introduction to it.' They clearly understand that an attempt to pass religious education in school into the hands of the ROC will not cause any reconciliation. It may aggravate the differences between the secular and spiritual systems of education. This situation is likely to remain 'until the Church begins to realise that there is a difference between educational and missionary purposes'.[44]

Kozyrev then recommends the development of a domestic school of religious pedagogy, 'which, while coordinating its activities with the clergy, should be consistently secular.' He asks what ideas and values this education will be built on.

It is to be wondered how Il'Minskii and Gasprinskii would have viewed this approach. They would have favoured a more inward (conservative) approach, seeking cooperation with the secular power. 'The Russian Orthodox Church finds unlimited pluralism of religious institutions hard to accept—it is committed to cooperation and excellent relations with other recognised religions in Russia; it is clear, however, that Orthodoxy naturally views itself as the unique possessor of "the truth".'[45]

---

42 *Ibid.*
43 *Ibid.*
44 *Ibid.*
45 Walters, Philip, 'Turning Outwards or Turning Inwards? Russian Orthodoxy

Muslim religious education in Russia

The Muslim religious education system in the Russian Empire displayed enormous resilience throughout. During periods of persecution and suppression, it would go underground but never disappeared. Hakimov, a leader of EuroIslam, describes how his grandmother taught him the Qur'an during the Communist period.[46] When conditions improved, such education would vigorously reappear.

One of the strengths of the Muslim population in the Russian empire remains their willingness to make sacrifices to provide appropriate education for their children. Historically, Muslim schools received no state support. In practice, the teacher in the *maktab* (primary Islamic school) and the *madrassah* (secondary Islamic school) would be paid out of the mosque funds by the mullah. Despite this, virtually every village had its school in which the children were taught the Qur'an. Over a five-year period, they would acquire an adequate knowledge of both Arabic and Islamic Law *(Shari'a)* and Islamic tradition *(Hadith)*. In general, other secular subjects including Russian were not taught, even to future clerics. Unsurprisingly, such schools helped re-awaken nationalism among the indigenous populations. No sacrifice was too great. A young Muslim wishing to become a teacher would go abroad, if necessary, and return later, legally or illegally, to teach in Russia. This type of education was very narrow and did not enable young Muslims to play a role in the Russian state. Gasprinskii's successful educational reforms were specifically designed to broaden their education. By the 1890s, he achieved considerable support for his model *cedid* school system in European Russia. He took steps to expand it over the Russian Empire, targeting Turkistan. This initiative was resisted by certain Russian authorities. He did not give up and presented a petition to the Budlovich Commission set up by the Ministry of Education just prior to the 1905 Revolution on the question of schools for the *inorodtsi* (non Russians).[47] The Commission decided that the Il'Minskii System should be applied to all *inorodtsi*, whether baptised or not. It further permitted religious education in Muslim schools on the basis that the Il'Minskii

---

challenged by Fundamentalism', *Nationalities Papers* 35, no.5 (2007), p. 857, cited by Curanovic, *op. cit.*

46 Hakimov, Rafael, *Gde Nasha Mecca* ('Where is our Mecca?'), Manifesto for EuroIslam, booklet, 2004.

47 *Ibid.*

Russian Orthodoxy and Islam—Ethics and Spirituality in Education

System fully respected students' beliefs. Importantly the Cyrillic script was to be used to express the alphabets of the local languages acting as a bridge to Russian culture. The Commission recommended that the authorities should not intervene in the internal affairs of Muslim communities but imposed a number of requirements on the conduct of Muslim schools, including the need to get permission to open such schools and to include Russian and subjects such as mathematics in *maktab* curricula: 'Education should not encourage opposition to the state but should instil a feeling of 'patriotic solidarity.'[48]

The Russian authorities struggled to bring the Muslim education system under their control. Chicherina, a strong supporter of the Il'Minskii System, described the failure of imperial edicts issued in the 1870s which sought to bring the *madrassahs* and *maktabs* under the control of the Ministry of National Education and subject to inspection.[49] In the Kazan Education District in the early 1900s, there were at the very least 1500 *maktabs* and *madrassahs*.[50] Since 1993, there has been a strong resurgence of education in Tatarstan.

Case Study—Education in Tatarstan

Historically, Tatarstan has sought autonomous status since the conquest of Kazan in 1556 by Ivan Grozni. The post conquest Tatars were:

> An ethno-political formation consolidated on the basis of Islamic-Turkish tradition and memories of the Kazan Khanate. The Mid-Volga Basin was a battlefield of two traditions: Russian-Slavic and Tatar Islamic.[51]

Considerable nervousness about possible Tatar/Turkish domination of the Middle Volga Region was displayed throughout by the Tsarist

---

[48] Miropiev N, 'Russo Inorodcheskie shkoli sistemi' ('The Russian *inorodtsi* School System'), *ZMNP*, Feb 1908, New Series, ch. 13, pp. 183-210.
[49] Chicherina S V, 'About the Volga Basin Inorodtsi, the contemporary significance of the Il'minskii System', an essay read at the General Meeting of the Society of Oriental Studies, St Petersburg, 1906, p. 6.
[50] *Ibid.*
[51] Cited by Suleymanova Dilyara, 'Education, language and politics of identity in the post-Soviet Tatarstan', PhD Project, UFSP Asien und Europa, January 2011, p. 1.

and Communist authorities. They adopted a 'divide and rule' policy. Only a quarter of the Tatars in the RFSR were included in the borders of the Tatar Autonomous Socialist Soviet Republic (TASSR) despite the importance put on Federalism by Lenin. The ethno-federalism of the Soviet Union was largely a facade as all cultural and educational matters had to be approved by Moscow.

'After the fall of the Soviet Union, Tatarstan ... in 1990 declared itself a sovereign state.' The resulting political conflict with Moscow led to a compromise which gave it special status as a 'sovereign state associated with the Russian Federation'.[52] Since then Tatarstan (has been) carrying out '... a sovereignty project'.[53]

Language and education policy are regarded as key fields in which Tatarstan is implementing its nationhood project—a new post-Soviet identity. Dilyara Suleymanova writes: 'Schools are key agencies of socialisation in the modern world and serve as important of social reproduction.'[54] '... different types of school systems reproduce different social orders ... an integrated, centralised school system contributes to ... reproducing "the nation" as a single unified citizenry by propagating national culture, inculcating nationalists attitudes and promoting linguistic standardisation and assimilation. In contrast, religiously segmented school systems contribute to ... the production of a segmented plural society.'[55]

Tatarstan has a mixed school system with both types. The majority are regular schools which have Russian as the language of instruction with a typical secondary schools curriculum in which children of all ethnic backgrounds study but all pupils have to learn the Tatar language.. Alongside, there are a significant number of Tatar 'ethno-national schools (Tatar Gymnasiums) in which the language of instruction is mostly Tatar (mixed with Russian).

Education is taken seriously in the Russian Federation: 2010 was declared the 'Year of the Teacher'.[56] This was enthusiastically

---

52 According to the 1994 Federal Treaty between the Republic of Tatarstan and the Russian Federation.
53 Suleymanova, *op. cit.*, p. 2.
54 *Ibid.*, p. 3.
55 Brubaker, Rogers: Feischmidt Margit, Fox Jon, Grancea Liana: Nationalist Politics and Everyday Ethnicity in a Transylvanian Town, New Jersey, Princeton University Press, 2006, p. 270.
56 http://1997-2011.tartarstan.ru/DNSID=4a9c592699b4dd6f20da28a42e1abcf5&node_id=1396.

supported in Tatarstan as part of the national Education' project, approved by President of Tatarstan—Mintimer Shamiev. A particular feature of the education system in Tatarstan lies in the use of local languages in education. 'The Tatar language is taught in 1061 schools, Chuvash in 120 educational establishments, Udmurt - 41, Mari—21, Mordovian—5, Bashkir—1 and Jewish language in 1 school. There are as many as 30 Sunday Schools where 28 languages ... are taught.'[57]

This proliferation of tribal languages in education fulfils a key component of the Il'Minskii System—one whose breadth of application he was not able to achieve in his lifetime but one which builds on the pioneering work he did on recording and formalising the local languages. This work was carried on though the early Soviet period.

The aims of Gasprinskii to ensure that the Muslim population received a broad education which would enable its members to play a full role in Russian society is also largely fulfilled in the modern educational system in the Russian Federation but particularly in Tatarstan, an industrialised state. Over recent years, the Russian government has channelled funds into select Islamic schools to stem radicalism.[58] This type of activity mirrors the initiatives task by the Tsarist government in nineteenth century to influence and control education in their Muslim communities.

Given the context, the Russian government is to be praised for its initiatives in holistic education.

COUNTERING ISLAM AND SECULARISM IN RUSSIA TODAY

The Christian and Muslim RE programmes sought to create a degree of unity between and within their respective communities seeking a common identity but with no direct reference to secular issues.

The current situation of religious education in Federal Russian education is still tentative and experimental. Orthodox Christianity is one of six possible subjects that parents can select to be taught to fourth graders. There is currently no move to include other versions

---

57 Suleymanova, *op. cit.*, p. 3.
58 Russian beyond the headlines: Kremlin in Caucasus—pushing moderate Islam (in education), Anna Nemisova, *rbth.ru* › Multimedia Video, 25 August 2010.

of Christianity, in particular Catholicism and Protestantism. This limitation is, at least in part, influenced by the underlying claim of the Russian Orthodox Church to its right to claim exclusivity in its 'Canonical Territory'. This concept in is deeply embedded in the Russian psyche. It could severely restrict access to external influences. The recent anti-NGO legislation is a prime example of this.[59] Although this is viewed as anti-Western, such laws can be applied to Islamist and other external influences.

The Russian Orthodox Church will continue to push hard for a greater uptake of the exclusive Orthodox element and for further developments in the national curriculum including more in-depth teaching of Orthodox Christianity in the national education system. A key impulse to do this lies in the same need to resist the spread of Islam—as was the case in Il'Minskii's time. This drive now also targets countering the secularisation of society in the Russian Federation. There is potential common cause with Islam in this resistance to secularism but it is difficult to understand how common goals can be agreed between two such 'exclusive' belief systems.

The major difference lies in the psychological state of mind of the general population, very heavily influenced by the extreme anti-religious Communist persecutions, especially of the Russian Orthodox Church and Islam which resulted in the wide-spread 'de-churching' and 'de-mosqueing'. It remains surprising that such a high proportion of the ethnic Russian population claim adherence to the Russian Orthodoxy even few practice or have any real knowledge of the basic tenets of Christianity.

The need to counter religious extremism and the progress of Islam in the Russian Federation is clearly in the mind of the Russian authorities. The issues remain even more cogent than they were in the Tsarist Empire. Islam has gained enormous strength in the Federation since the 1980s. The influence of radical Sunnism, Wahhabism and Salafism has strengthened the resistance to Russian rule. This influence is currently less pronounced in states like Tatarstan which has a reasonably lengthy history of moderation. Tatarstan is a sophisticated, industrialised state whereas the Caucasus states are not. Over recent

---

59 BBC News Europe: 9 April 2013, 'Russia pursues election watchdog Golos under anti-NGO law'; 'Russia's Putin warns NGOs against meddling in Russia's affairs', Associated Press, 14 February, 2013.

years the Russian government has channelled funds into select Islamic schools to stem radicalism.[60] This type of activity mirrors the initiatives task by the Tsarist government in the nineteenth century to influence and control education in their Muslim communities. The situation has grown worse recently with the murder of Ildus Fayzov—the Mufti of Tatarstan and the most senior Islamic official in Russia's largely Muslim Tatarstan region along with his deputy. The motive was unclear, but Vladimir Markin, a spokesman for Russia's Investigative Committee, said both leaders were known for fighting extremism and their professional work was being investigated as one of the reasons for the attacks.[61] This attack is very concerning as Tatarstan has been largely peaceful and is held out as a showcase of religious tolerance in Russia,

The nineteenth-century Russian Missionaries appear to have most feared the Muslim reform movement that began to develop in the late eighteenth and early nineteenth centuries in Russia and elsewhere. They clearly sensed that a combination of European culture and Muslim dynamism would prove a threat to the integrity of the Russian state.[62] Il'Minskii expressed great concern about the weakening of the faith among the Orthodox Christians which he contrasted with the apparent strengthening of Islamic belief among the population. He had earlier formulated his concerns in a paper he wrote in 1849—'Reflections on the 1849 Tatar Mission'.

Il'Minskii foresaw that 'the great religious reformation within Islam would exert the same influence on the future evolution of the Muslims as was exerted by the Lutheran Reformation on the traditional Catholic World'.[63] In 1881, he made the statement:

> A dreadful storm is approaching—the Mohammedans,
> a new invasion, not Mongolian this time but Muslim,
> not by the barbarians of Asia but by civilised barbarians

---

60 Anna Nemtsova, 'Russian Government funds select Islamic schools to stem radicalism', 01/09/10. http://www.telegraph.co.uk/sponsored/rbth/society/7975826/Russian-government-funds-select-Islamic-schools-to-stem-radicalism.html (05/09/13)
61 *Ibid.*
62 Znamenskii P V, 'The role of Il'Minskii in Inorodtsi education in Turkestan', *Pr. Sob.* (1900) VII-VIII, p. 6.
63 Batunsky, Mark, 'Russian Clerical Islamic Studies in the late 19th and early 20th centuries', *CAS*, (1994), p. 218.

who have gone through universities, gymnasia and military schools.⁶⁴

In contrast, Islam has retained its missionary zeal, its *da'wa*, throughout the period even if it was on the defensive in the Russian empire since sixteenth century. Indeed, Islam significantly pre-dated the advent of Orthodoxy in the region. It successfully resisted the various forms of proselytisation undertaken by the Russian state and the Church. A high degree of resilience in belief and practice was demonstrated throughout, generally focused on the person of Muhammad and the Qur'an. The Russian Muslim community was able to expand during periods of political relaxation.

Statistics on the number of Muslims in the Russian Federation have varied considerably over the past two centuries, usually being set at around 10-15 percent of the total population. It is known that there are over 2 million Muslims in Moscow alone. There is concern that the high birth rate within Muslim communities contrasted with the low rate among ethnic Russians will enable the Muslim population to become dominant in the near future. Pew Research reports that Russia has the largest Muslim population in Europe. The number of Muslims in Russia is projected to increase from about 16.4 million in 2010 to about 18.6 million in 2030. The Muslim share of the country's population is expected to increase from 11.7 percent in 2010 to 14.4 percent in 2030.⁶⁵ The number of Muftiates, a political-ecclesiastical authority originally created by Catherine the Great, has grown to over 70 since 1991.⁶⁶ They are grouped into three major organisations which the Russian leaders play carefully.⁶⁷ There are over 5,000 registered religious Muslim organizations (divided into Sunni, Shi'a and Sufi groups), which is over one-sixth of the number of registered Russian Orthodox religious organizations of about 29,268.⁶⁸

---

64 *Ibid.*
65 Pew Research, 'The future of the global Muslim population- Region Europe, Spotlight on Russia', 27/02/1011. Survey, www.pewforum.org/2011/.../the-future-of-the-global-muslim-population, research study.
66 Yemelianova, Galina, 'Russian UMMA and its Muftis', *RSS*, Vol. 31, No. 2 (2003).
67 Utyabai R A and Azamativ, D D, The Central Spiritual Board of Muslims of Russia, CIS and The European Countries, *The Muslim Dictionary of the Bashkir State University*.
68 Russian Federal Administration Service; 'Сведения о религиозных организациях, зарегистрированных в Российской Федерации' (Data about

Russian Orthodoxy and Islam—Ethics and Spirituality in Education

The first ever sociological survey of religious adherents in Russian Federation was made in August 2102 disclosed that out of a population of 142,800, 41 percent claimed to be Russian Orthodox, 95 percent Muslim (with a majority unaffiliated either to Sunni or Shi'a Islam), 25 percent spiritual but not religious, 13 percent Atheist or non-religious and 7.9 percent undecided. The balance includes a very wide range of other belief systems.[69]

Given the diverstit of the population, a detailed study is needed of the issues involved, both in the Russian Federation but particularly in hinge states such as the Republic of Tatarstan with its large ethnic Russian and Tatar populations. The Russian Federation and Tatarstan education systems engage in the battle for establishing identities—one in the Russian state and the second in Tatar nationality. As ever, the Federal Ministry of Education in Moscow will continue to control religious education and other curricula in the national education system with a strong hand.

President Putin is clearly seeking to re-establish the Russian Federation as a leading global player. Russia approaches the challenges and opportunities in Syria and the Middle East in a sophisticated manner, carefully balancing Russian support for the various conflicting interest in the region and beyond. Putin, 'the first Russian leader to visit Israel (twice), could hardly have shown more enthusiasm for the Jewish State.'[70] This he combines with clear support for the ROC and seeking a rapprochement with Islam—internationally and within the Federation. He led Russia into the OIC (Organisation for Islamic Cooperation) where Russia is an observer, to ISESCO (Islamic Educational, Educational and Cultural Organisation). This is seen as one of the most significant achievements of the bi-religious co-operation in the international arena between the Muslim Spiritual Board of the Caucasus and the ROC.[71] He became the first Russian leader to officially recognise at the highest level that Russia is 'a Muslim country'.[72] He made a historic statement that:

---

religious organisations registered in the Eussian Federation). http://www.religare.ru/2_36302.html (02/09/13).
69 en.wikipedia.org/wiki/Religion_in_Russia, 20/09/13.
70 *Economist*, 16 March 2013.
71 Mukhametoc, Rinat, RIA Novosti and Russian International Affairs Council, 7 October *2012*. eng.globalaffairs.ru/number/Russian-Muslims-and-Foreign-Policy-15687.
72 *Ibid*.

Whichever way it goes the architecture of public religious education, belief systems including religion in its various guises and secularism/atheism, will continue to be taught in the home and in the various churches, mosques and secular institutions, whilst the public school system will seek to inculcate concepts of national identity, national unity, co-citizenship and collaboration so essential to the effective functioning of a successful, highly sophisticated, technology based modern state. It is to be hoped that these latter values are mirrored in at the domestic level as well. Education is an area in which the Christian Orthodox and Muslim communities can collaborate, if only to counter the impact of secularist ideologies.[73]

The commitment made by President Putin and Patriarch Kirill to protect Christian communities in Syria and beyond should have wider implications of the relations between Orthodox Christianity as a whole with Islam in a secular context. Any longer term solution must encompass a system of religious education which caters for the 'other' and encourages toleration between the various wings of a faith, such as the Sunni/Shi'a divide and as well as between different faiths and belief systems.

The Russian model and experience in this field could influence the future re-configuration of relationships between secular (i.e post-secular) and religious tradition across the world. More energy needs to be put into the political milieu—especially in the shared religious space.

CONCLUSIONS

Many of the features of the contemporary educational system in the Russian Federation fulfil the aspirations of the two reformers discussed as well as those of the secularists which they would have opposed. The national education system in the Russian Federation in the early twenty-first century is evolving towards a modified secular system in which parents have the right to select from six alternative religious/ethical modules for their children. A key driving

---

73 *Ibid.*

force lies in the need to establish a coherent national identity, able to embrace successfully multi-cultural currents as well as to counter extremist activity within the overall population. The campaign against totalitarian sects and the drive to achieve 'spiritual security' are key to understanding the role that the ROC is seeking to play in state education policies and wider contexts.[74]

The role of religious mission in this context could hardly be more challenging!

BIBLIOGRAPHY

Batunsky, Mark, 'Russian Clerical Islamic Studies in the late 19th and early 20th centuries', *CAS*, 1994, pp. 213-235.

BBC: 'Putin's Russia: The Modern Autocrat', 22 December 2011.

Brubaker, Rogers: Feischmidt Margit, Fox Jon, Grancea Liana: *Nationalist Politics and Everyday Ethnicity in a Transylvanian Town*, New Jersey, Princeton University Press, 2006.

Cardinal, Monique C, 'Religious education in Syria: unity and difference', *British Journal of Religious Education,* Vol. 31, No. 2, March 2009.

Carpinelli, Dr Christina 9/17/2007, allexperts.com/ep/354-76920/Russia-News-Politics/dr-Cristina-Carpinelli.htm, Political Science › Russia (News & Politics)

Chicherina SV: *O provolzhskikh inorodtsakh i sovremennom znachenii sistemi N I Il'minskago* ['About the Volga Basin Inorodtsi, the contemporary significance of the Il'minskii System'], an essay read at the General Meeting of the Society of Oriental Studies, St Petersburg, 1906.

Cousins, William Basil, 'Russian Orthodoxy, Contemporary Challenges in Society, Interreligious encounters and mission', *World Christianity—Politics, Theology, Dialogues*, eds Anthony O'Mahony and Michael Kirwan, Melisende, London, 2004.

Cousins, William Basil, 'The Russian Orthodox Church, Tatar Christians and Islam', *Eastern Christianity—Studies in Modern History, Religion and Politics*, ed. Anthony O'Mahony, Melisende, London, 2004.

Cousins, William Basil, M Phil thesis, 'Russian Orthodox Church and Islam, The role of language and education in Mission. The contribution of Nikolai Il'Minskii in its historical context', Heythrop College, University of London, 2007.

Curanovic, Alicja Cecylia, 'Relations between the Orthodox Church and

---

74 Elkner, Julie, Spiritual Security in Putin's Russia, PhD essay, jce23@cam.ac.uk.

Islam in the Russian Federation', *Journal of Church and State*, Vol. 52, No. 3.

Dickens, Mark, *Soviet Language policy in Central Asia*, Princeton University Press, Princeton, 1988, pp. 1-26.

Dowler, Wayne: *Classroom and Empire: The Politics of Schooling Russia's Eastern Nationalities, 1860-1917*, McGill Queen's University Press, Montreal, 2001.

Elkner, Julie, Spiritual Security in Putin's Russia, PhD essay, jce23@cam.ac.uk.

Encyclopedia Britannica, 'History of Education. The development of the universities'. www.britannica.com/EBchecked/topic/179408/education.

Filatov, S B, *Religia i obshectvo- ocherki religiosnoi zhizni sovremiennoi* ['Religion and Society—Religious Characteristics in Contemporary Russian Orthodox Church'], Letnii Sad, Moscow, 2002.

Glazik, Joseph M S C, *Die Islammissionen der Russisch Orthodox Kirche*, Aschendorffsche Verlagsbuchhandlung, Munster, Westfalen, 1959.

Glazik, Joseph M S C, *Der Russisch-orthodoxe Heidenmission seit Peter der Grossen*, Aschendorffsche Verlagsbuchhandlung, Munster, Westfalen, 1954.

Hosking G, *Russia and the Russians from the earliest times to 2001*, Allen Lane, Penguin, London, 2001.

Hughes, Lindsey, *Russia in the Age of Peter the Great*, Yale University Press, 2000, *www.goodreads.com/.../130367,*

Il'Minskii, N I, *About the System for the Education of non-Russians and about the Kazan Central Christian-Tatar School for the 50th Anniversary of the System and of the School as well as for the certificate of the Holy Synod of 29th May 1913 about the education of non-Russians*; footnotes and comments by A A Voskresenskii, published by P V Shchetinkin, Kazan, 1913.

Ishakova R R, *Pegagogicheskoe obrazovanie v Kazanckoi gubernii v seredine XIX—nachale XX vekov* ('Teacher training in the Kazan Province from the mid-19th to early 20th Centuries'), Kazan, 2001.

Kosmin, Barry A, 'Contemporary Secularity and Secularism', *Secularism and Secularity: Contemporary International Perspectives*, eds Barry A Kosmin and Ariela Keysar, Institute for the Study of Secularism in Society and Culture (ISSSC), Hartford, CT, 2007.

Kozyrev, Feodor, 'On the Place and Role of Religious Education in Russian Schools: Retrospection and Forecasts', International Association for Religious Freedom, Centre for Religious

Pedagogy, St Petersburg University, Research Report, www.theewc.
org/library/list/pagination/page/2/?&tag. I.
Kozyrev, Feodor: Religious Education in the Russian Federation: The
 Interpretative Approach to Spirirual Education in St Petersburg,
 Research Report, www2.warwick/ac/uk/fac/.../wergeland_
 russia_kozyrev_apr_2011.dcc.
Kreindler, I T, 'Lenin, Russian and Soviet Language Policy', IJS.
 Interpretitive Reply, www.degruyter.com/.../$002fj$002fijsl.1982.
 issue-33$002fijsl.1982.33...
Liting Leitvik, O, 'Religious education, communal identity and national
 politics in the Muslim World' , article, folk.uio.no/leirvik/
 OsloCoalition/Leirvik0904.htm.
Lonadier, Brett, 'Recapturing Russian Heritage: Religious Education on
 Public Schools', Web Exclusive, 18 October 2010, Center on Faith
 and International Affairs, Arlington, VA.
Marc Lepetre, *Language Policy in the Russian Federation: language diversity
 and national identity*,. Revista de Sociolinguistica, Sociolinguistica
 Internacional Primevera, Noves SL, 2002.
Lilge, Frederic, 'Lenin and the Politics of Education', *Slavic Review* Vol. 27,
 Jan. 1968.
Mannheimer, David, 'Comparing the American and Russian Constitutions',
 http://justice.uaa.alaska.edu/forum/24/4winter2008/a_
 constitution.html.
Miropiev N, 'Russko Inorodcheskie shkoli sistemi' ('The Russian *Inorodtsi*
 School System'), *ZMNP* Feb 1908, New Series, ch. 13.
Mukhametoc, Rinat, RIANovosti and Russian International Affairs
 Council, 7/10/ 2012.
Suleymanova, Dilyara, 'Education, language and politics of identity on post-
 Soviet Tatarstan', PhD Project, UFSP Asien und Europa.
Utyabai R A and Azamotov D D, 'The Central Spiritual Board of Muslims
 of Russia and the European Countries of CIS', *The Muslim
 Dictionary of the Bashkir State University*, <http://www.bdxc.tu/
 encikl/c/centr_du.htm>.
Yemelianova, Galina, 'Russia's *Umma* and its Muftis', *RSS*, Vol. 31, No 2
 (2003).
Walters, Philip, 'Turning Outwards or Turning Inwards? Russian
 Orthodoxy challenged by Fundamentalism', *Nationalities Papers*
 35, no. 5 (2007).
Zaimov, Styan, *Christian Science Reporter*, citing *The Moscow Times*, 3
 January 2013.
Znamenskii P V, 'Dva Prilozheniia k stat'e P V Znamenskago: Uchastie N I

Il'Minskago v Dele Inorodskago Obrazonovanii v Turkestankom Krae (Two additions to P V Znamenskii's article: The role of Il'minskii in *Inorodtsi* education in Turkestan)', *Pr. Sob.* (1900) VII-VIII.